Advance Praise for
From Scratch

"A tour de force. *From Scratch* takes readers along for an enthralling ride through exotic and not-so-exotic countries around the world to discover the source of what people eat and why they eat it, and to realize just how fragile our planet is. I was engaged, entertained, informed, and pulled along by David Moscow's boundless curiosity and his and his dad Jon's entertaining prose. Bravo!"

—**LynNell Hancock**, Professor Emerita, Columbia Graduate School of Journalism, and Director, Spencer Education Fellowship

"Because his mission is insane, it's insanely fascinating: David Moscow hunts the source of our tater tots, fish fingers, and highly haute cuisine. In these pages, the Moscows are able to dive deeper than in David's own stellar *From Scratch*, and it's a real treat. Here is a lightning-fast, teeth-first dive into that long production system that goes beyond the horizon to stuff our bellies. And the Moscows make it fun with a crafty combo of self-skewering humor and really cool characters (some even heroic), in stories larded with deep history that you're now happy to know. You don't need to be some kind of foodie to find this book tasty...and just brilliant."

—**Greg Palast**, *New York Times* Bestselling Author of *The Best Democracy Money Can Buy* and other books

"Perhaps because David is not a culinary insider—not a chef or a farmer or a hunter—the result is something as accessible as it is adventurous. As someone who has actually been in the field with David, I can say that this book wonderfully captures the feeling of being right beside him on his wild, educational, surprisingly humorous, and often shocking adventures."

—**Clay Jeter**, Director, Emmy-nominated Netflix series *Chef's Table*

"I'm still rocking in the wake of reading *From Scratch*, an all-out adventure of food exploration and education. With a food system that increasingly denies the existence of seasons, craft, and deliciousness, it's an urgent reminder of where our food comes from. David Moscow brings the ancient human art of feeding ourselves back into consciousness."

—**Chef Dan Barber**, Blue Hill at Stone Barns

"I was prepared not to like this. Oysters? Who gives a shit? But it's great— like reading an episode of a really good food show, and being taken behind the scenes and somewhere you have never been. The shit really pops. Great stuff."

—**Jeff Pearlman**, *New York Times* Bestselling Author of *Showtime: Magic, Kareem, Riley, and the Los Angeles Lakers Dynasty of the 1980s* and other books

from
scratch.

from scratch.

ADVENTURES IN HARVESTING, HUNTING, FISHING, AND FORAGING ON A FRAGILE PLANET

DAVID MOSCOW & JON MOSCOW

PERMUTED
PRESS

A PERMUTED PRESS BOOK

From Scratch:
Adventures in Harvesting, Hunting, Fishing, and Foraging on a Fragile Planet
© 2022 by David Moscow and Jon Moscow
All Rights Reserved

ISBN: 978-1-63758-402-6
ISBN (eBook): 978-1-63758-403-3

Cover art by Brian Morrison
Cover photos by Graeme Swanepoel and Marty Bleazard
Interior design and composition by Greg Johnson, Textbook Perfect

This is a work of nonfiction. All people, locations, events, and situation are portrayed to the best of the authors' memory and understanding.

PERMUTED PRESS

Permuted Press, LLC
New York • Nashville
permutedpress.com

Published in the United States of America
1 2 3 4 5 6 7 8 9 10

For Karen and Pat

Contents

Preface

I AM JUST AN ACTOR (*Big, Newsies, Honey*) playing a host posing as a journalist. I wouldn't say I am expert in much except eating. But that was enough to get me here, keyboard to paper, in the first paragraph of a book.

This book is a layperson's exploration of how food gets to our plate. That journey was filled with adventure and laughter and slips and falls and derring-do. It had near-death experiences like my almost drowning while spearfishing in the Sea of Sardinia and getting chased (and stung) by swarming, wild African bees in a sacred forest in Kenya. I traveled strange roads that led to once-in-a-lifetime moments like cheesemaking with a shepherd in his cave in the mountains of Barbàza and getting wasted on home-brewed tuber liquor with friends under a supermoon at the top of the Andes.

There are also meals in here. Some are unique. Some are gut-turning. Most are great, made by some of the world's best chefs. Some of my favorite recipes are jotted down from my four-year journey. There is some science (how oysters clean seawater), some economics (the forces that are rapidly changing Kenya), some history (pirates in the Mediterranean who brought spices to Europe), and a lot of global current events (overfishing and monoculture, but also marine protected areas (MPAs) and the reintroduction of tiny Four Corners potatoes into diets in the Navajo Nation and high-cuisine restaurants in Utah). Food production shows us how fragile our planet is and how food producers are on the front lines of coping with global climate change, threats to endangered species, and the environmental and economic crises created by hypercapitalism.

The book's genesis was in 2016. I was eating Korean BBQ at Sun Nong Dan in Los Angeles and Donald Trump was running for president. Sweating over the best short ribs I'd ever had (I should have never told the waiter, "yes, I do like spicy"), I glanced back into the kitchen. There, standing amongst the Asian cooks, was a Mexican man handling a pot. Nothing out of the ordinary—Central Americans and Mexicans are the backbone of the US food industry. At that moment, I had a sudden desire to make a documentary showing how immigrants (particularly Mexicans and Central Americans) are essential, hard-working pillars of American life. Americans, friends, neighbors, and family members were being attacked because of their skin colors and language; all the while they were making food, the most important element of sustenance. It seemed baffling to me that people whose families had been in California for generations, who created the taco (4.5 billion served every year) and the margarita (the most consumed cocktail in America), were being villainized. And people were falling for it! Suddenly I wanted to teach the world how to make a taco and a margarita. I would go work with subsistence corn farmers in Oaxaca to make the masa and with agave jimadors in Jalisco to make the tequila and record the labor and pride and hurdles these experts/workers face to bring food to our tables. And maybe, by doing so, help more people see the shared humanity that connects everyone.

Like most things in the film business, it didn't turn out like I planned. The documentary never got made and by 2020 it had morphed into a TV show, a show that wouldn't just speak about Mexican food producers, but about all food workers. We would put a spotlight on the people working behind the scenes in restaurants and fields, folks who aren't paid enough, aren't treated fairly, and are often looked down on. There are a few professions that most everyone agrees should be paid more—teachers, nurses, people who work for the common good—and food producers should fall into the same category.

By the time we made it onto TV in the winter of 2020, the premise had been given a structure and a name, *From Scratch*. I would travel to countries around the world, and each week I'd meet with a chef, famous or not, fancy or not, eat a meal they cooked, and then go out to harvest ingredients for that meal. I would sit down with experts to discuss the history of those ingredients, and be taught by the farmers, foragers, fishers, and hunters how to dive for scallops, avoid poisonous mushrooms, stalk an elk, cut wheat with a sickle or a thresher, blanch ground acorns, climb for coconuts, ferment a mezcal, or shoot a gun. This city guy would learn how to do all the things that he had forgotten or had never known. Then I would use the ingredients I collected each week to recreate the dish that I had eaten at the beginning of each episode.

In the course of shooting the show, from 2018–2021, I visited Mexico, the Philippines, South Africa, Kenya, Croatia, Malta, Peru, Costa Rica, Italy, Finland, Iceland, and states ranging from New York to Texas, Utah to Wyoming and Washington.

One of the things I'm most excited about is how this book allowed me to tell more stories, deeper stories than the show did. The medium of cable TV has lots of good things going for it, but discussing the profound isn't usually one of them. In a way, the book is "of" the show but is a completely different animal. TV is also a collaboration of lots of people—a shared vision. But, in company with my dad, this book gave me a chance to tell my unadulterated thoughts about what I saw and learned.

Work on this book opened my eyes to how interconnected our world is and how food production ties us all together. While Americans have a tendency to think of themselves on an island, or even as individuals standing alone, food teaches us that is not true. It takes sixty people to make one pizza slice! While I started out focused on communal ties of humanity and how we can all treat one another better, I came out of the journey realizing how interconnected we are to everything else on the planet, from mushrooms to round shad to lions to pine trees, and how much work we have ahead of us to save ourselves and our companions on this fragile planet.

Oysters:
New York / Istria

I USED TO DREAM OF OYSTERS. Huge purple and pink and red and rainbow oysters, nestled in the sand at the bottom of the sea, calling to me.

From age seven to ten, I dove for oysters while I slept, while in waking life I was still learning to swim underwater in my uncle's pool. In my dozing mind, I'd swim for hours, hunting for perfect shells to bring back to my parents, searching amongst the cans and bottles off the shore of Orchard Beach, the only beach in the Bronx, searching 'til I ran out of air and burst from sleep with a gasp.

I thought a pearl would be our ticket to a better life, out of our working-class apartment. If only I could find an oyster with a pearl, life would be different.

But I never dreamed of eating them.

* * *

Four a.m. on an early September day and already I was late. Mike told me the tide waits for no man, and it was looking like our wading for oysters was going to be more like swimming at that point.

1

Mike is Mike Osinski, the owner (with his wife, Isabel) of Widow's Hole Oysters in Greenport, NY. He's tall, at least 6'4", burly with the Southern charm of his Alabama childhood covered by the no-nonsense gruffness of a New Yorker. That's what twenty years on Wall Street does to someone. He offhandedly dominates a room and a dock, and looks and feels like Bill O'Reilly if O'Reilly had a beating heart inside his chest. But in spite of this, he is immediately likable with a wry smile making his bombast feel like an inside joke. Mike and I were going to harvest oysters during the single hour at low tide that his oyster cages emerge from the water—which is how I found myself neck deep in the Long Island Sound off the North Fork at four a.m. on an early September day, already late for work.

Mike came to oyster farming in a decidedly nontraditional way. He and Isabel were Wall Street programmers. They were authors of the Intex Structuring Tool, the world's largest-selling mortgage securitization software, which converted bundles of mortgages into bonds—and played a key role in the market crash of 2008. Mike and Isabel developed it in the late '90s and sold their share of their company in 2000. Mike told a reporter in 2009, "I didn't realize I was building a bomb at the time. I thought I was building something that was a valuable tool for the industry."

They bought waterfront property in Greenport as a second home because it was easily accessible to their Gramercy Park home and their partners in Boston. They learned that they owned five acres underwater when they were drilling pilings to replace an old dock and were hauled into court for lack of a permit. Their lawyer looked at the handwritten deed from 1875 and discovered that the tax map showed they owned "500 feet from mean high tide." Mike returned from court smiling and explained to Isabel that, at the cost of the $2,000 fine, they had doubled their property.

When their daughter Suzanna was ready for preschool, they checked out the swanky preschool near them in NYC. "Susan Sarandon's kids go there," the prospective parents were informed. And what was so great about the school? "It really prepares your kid for the kindergarten interview." Mike and Isabel decided they'd rather start growing oysters and raise their kids on an oyster farm.

The water around Mike's farm is perfect for oysters. Widow's Hole sits atop a bulge on the Peconic River, which is part of the greater Long Island Sound, an estuary where rivers drain into the sea. The water flow in these tidal estuaries brings calcium bicarbonate to build their shells and algae for oysters to eat.

I hung back for a moment, taking in the sunrise and the early boaters in Little Peconic Bay, squishing the silt and sand between my toes. Here was the first time I ever had a reason to take a swim that wasn't for amusement or health.

I was about to farm…in the water.

* * *

Swimming is one of my favorite things in life. And there was an excuse to wade around, even dive a bit. Now it's true this was a single moment, in the warm-water conditions of a New York fall. My feelings might have been different if we were doing this in February, or every day. But I couldn't help thinking that the eleven-year-old trapped underneath the thirty-five years of further wear and tear would have enjoyed that just as much.

Long Island holds a big place in my heart. Dad is an Islander. My first love lived out in Manhasset and I can't begin to count the hours on the LIRR spent going back and forth to her house or Jones Beach. I'd even braved the posh, crowded summers of the

East End towns once or twice, though I prefer the easy, car-free appeal of the more working-class Fire Island.

Widow's Hole and the other Atlantic oyster farms of Suffolk County, about ninety miles from New York City, are part of a fragile rebirth of a nutritious food that can be eaten in many different ways, of an emergent mollusk industry, and, critically, of an ecologically sustainable environment. Unlike most fish farming, oysters are a win-win for the environment.

Despite all this, I still didn't particularly like oysters.

My first memories of them as food were as my least favorite of the smoked tins that my dad would key-twist open for a snack. I preferred the sardines, but the slightly fishy, deep-smoke oyster nugget wasn't bad on a salty cracker. Palatable. It was the raw ones that threw me. The price, the texture, the taste. The few times friends forced me to try them at some fancy restaurants I was told if I covered them in Tabasco I wouldn't mind them too much. This reasoning made no sense to me. Why eat anything you have to mask with hot sauce? The hot sauce also didn't help at all with the texture. I couldn't get them down fast enough.

But then again, I came to oysters late—sixty years or so past their heyday.

* * *

Oysters have a very long history in New York and the mid-Atlantic coast from the Chesapeake Bay to Cape Cod, beginning with the Lenni-Lenape, who lived in the area for as many as 12,000 years before Europeans came (and forced the Indigenous people to resettle as far away as Oklahoma, Wisconsin, and Ontario).[1]

The Lenape harvested oysters, opening the shells by wrapping the entire oyster in seaweed and throwing it in the fire. Many millennia of oyster eating left behind huge shell middens.[2]

New York City's oldest street (not coincidentally named Pearl) was paved with tabby, a type of concrete made by burning oyster shells (many from Lenape middens) to create lime, then mixing it with water, sand, ash, and broken oyster shells. Tabby was much more common in the South but can still be found in the Colonial Dutch Abraham Manee House on Staten Island, built around 1670, and in Trinity Church down by Wall Street.

When Europeans came, they continued harvesting the oysters, drawing on the 220,000 acres of oyster beds in New York Harbor, totaling between a quarter and a half of the world's supply of oysters.[3] And the oysters they found were enormous! For example, oysters in the Gowanus Canal were "large and full, some of them not less than a foot long."[4]

America's first cookbook, published in Albany by Amelia Simmons in 1796, called repeatedly on stewed oysters as an ingredient, including in Simmons's recipe, "To smother a fowl in oysters": "Gill the bird with dry oysters and sew up and boil in water just sufficient to cover the bird, salt and season to your taste—when done tender, put in a deep dish and pour over it a pint of stewed oysters, well buttered and peppered, garnish a turkey with sprigs of parsley or leaves of celery; a fowl is best with a parsley sauce."[5]

During the nineteenth and early twentieth centuries, New York was the oyster capital of the world. Some said its oysters were the best, others that they just had the best marketing.

The Scottish writer and traveler Charles Mackay, writing in 1859, tells how a Liverpool hotelier envied his trip to America because "you will get such delicious oysters! New York beats all creation for oysters!" Mackay went on at lyrical length to add, "Mine host spoke the truth," and to elaborate that "if one may judge from appearances, the delicacy is highly regarded and esteemed by all classes from the millionaire in the Fifth Avenue to the 'Boy' in the Bowery, and the German and Irish emigrants in their own peculiar quarters of the city."[6] And the oysters were cheap—six cents a dozen.

Oyster saloons, cellars, and pushcarts proliferated. New Yorkers and other East Coasters ate more oysters than beef. In fact, the story goes that penniless immigrants could avoid starvation by helping themselves to free oysters at the shore. It's no exaggeration to say that throughout the nineteenth century, oysters were essential to every stratum of New York life, and literally kept people alive.

Many oyster bars were dimly lit and dangerous, but Joanne Hyppolite of the National Museum of African American History and Culture talks about an exception.[7] Thomas Downing's Oyster House on Broad Street, opened in the early- to mid-1820s and owned by a Black man and abolitionist, was one of the fanciest restaurants in the city. It served only upper-class whites and was a gathering place for the elite. It also served as a stop on the Underground Railroad.

Eventually, overharvesting, sewage, and landfill took their toll. By 1820, oyster beds around Staten Island became depleted. In 1921, the city health department closed the Jamaica Bay oyster beds; in 1924, a typhoid epidemic was blamed on oysters; and, in 1927, during another typhoid epidemic, erroneously attributed to oysters, the last NYC oyster beds were closed for toxicity. They remain closed today. Which is probably appreciated by the oysters in the Harbor.

So what was I doing in the Sound at four a.m.? I'm a big-city cosmopolitan—a New Yorker and an Angeleno. I grew up in the NW Bronx, but my life changed completely as I split my time between New York and Hollywood after becoming an actor and playing young Tom Hanks in the movie *Big*. A couple of years ago, I realized that, for all the great restaurants I went to and all the healthy meals I cooked, I had no connection to where the food I was eating came from beyond the plate it was served on or the store I bought it from.

But I knew from childhood summers in Maine, Utah, and Montana (where my mom was from) that there was more to where food comes from than that. My mom's grandparents homesteaded on the North Fork of the Flathead in Montana, and she stayed with them every summer, fishing, picking huckleberries, wild strawberries, and chokecherries, and snapping off and chewing on rhubarb stalks, sometimes adding salt. She canned berries and cherries and cleaned the fish, which got eaten for breakfast or smoked, along with venison.

My childhood had been the last time I had any connection with the source of my meals, and I wanted that connection back. So I created the cable series, *From Scratch*. The show takes me around the world, where I meet chefs—some in fancy restaurants and some in not-so-fancy ones—and then source all the ingredients in their signature dishes. In New York, I met Dan Kluger, the chef at Loring Place, named for the Bronx street where his father grew up, who's been using oysters as a chef since 1999. Chef Dan sent me in search of oysters for a dish of breaded fried oysters and salsa on an omelet, and a couple days later, I met Mike.

* * *

The water wasn't too cold, but my lateness meant the tide had returned, and that meant we were definitely going to get wet.

I'd had visions of picking up oyster cages from a boat, like you do with lobsters. And much oyster farming does rely on boats. But after thirteen years of hauling up 300-pound cages to the beach to air-dry the oysters, Mike adopted the Japanese Kusshi system in 2015 with the help of his son, Merc. In this system, cages are slung from a structure called a longline. Wooden posts driven into the seabed support horizontal cables the baskets hang from, submerged about a foot deep, and they get air-dried for an hour every day when the tide goes out. "We're growing a better oyster, with a 70-80 percent reduction in labor," Mike told me.

This daily tidal exposure destroys the biofilm that would allow barnacles and other organisms to attach. This is extremely important because, as Mike says, "Once a barnacle is on, it's on." The swaying of the baskets rattles the oysters and chips off new growth on the lip. This turbulence from tides, waves, and boats make the deeper cupped raw oyster that restaurants want.[8] The tides do the work, cleaning, and tumbling.

Instead of puttering out in a boat, to harvest from the longlines, you wade, pushing and pulling a pontoon alongside. For me, entering the water was as easy as walking off the beach. Mike splashed ahead, moving the pontoon next to one of the baskets that was half in the water. He was pointing out how the contraption worked, and how the flexibility of the cable allowed the oysters to roll and provided protection against storms.

The first task was to unclasp the baskets from the line and load them onto the pontoon. Each of the cages had a color-coded tag based on size and age. For example, the cage for oyster seed (nine-month-olds) from the Fishers Island hatchery was pink; the cage for the smallest twenty-one-month-olds was white; and there were a variety of colored cages, including blue, for the thirty-three-month-olds.

So we moved along, looking out for blue tags ready to harvest. The New York restaurants want a deep cup on an oyster—about the size of a palm, at least four inches across—though some chefs like Dan Barber of Blue Hill want a knife-and-fork, six-inch oyster.

The baskets were large and unwieldy, but the water helped with the lifting. We each took turns getting a basket over the edge of the raft and pushing it back to make room for the next. At some point, I realized I was no longer standing on the bottom. The rising tide meant I was floating, hanging onto the pontoon. Mike's height kept him slinging cages, but I pushed off the craft and ducked under the water, hat and all. I was now swimming for oysters.

Oysters are swimmers, too, as larvae—small beasts with hydrodynamic sensing responding to fast water or slow water by swimming up or down. The ones that manage to force themselves to the surface water are more likely to be swept towards shore and not become fish food.[9] One day they land and attach to a mineral mass, where they will stay for the rest of their lives. The rocky floor, broken shells, and docks accumulate oysters that build on one another, stringing along and piling high.

In order for an oyster to mate, it first eats floating phytoplankton as it filter-feeds. That valuable energy goes into making a gonad, either eggs or sperm. The rise in springtime water temperature increases the phytoplankton, and usually two months later the gonad arrives. The cycle starts again. Larvae floating, swimming, landing, growing, mating.

Mike towed the pontoon back to the dock. I climbed the ladder and he began handing the baskets up. The physicality of the work put me enough in a zone where I didn't notice the cold air. My mind was calmed by the procedure and the basic act of trying not to slip, which would send me and the oysters back into the bay. With the oysters parked on the dock, Mike pointed me towards

Sorting with Mike Osinski

an outdoor shower. I washed the seawater off and changed into dry clothes. And Mike waved me back to get to sorting.

We hoisted a basket of oysters up on a metal sorting table on the dock and opened it up to see the fruit of our (mostly Mike's) labor. From the outside they aren't much to look at. If you didn't know what was inside you'd think they were just dark, crusty little rocks. Mike grabbed one, laid it across his palm—"this one's good"—and tossed it into my bucket. I followed suit. Leaving the little ones where they were, putting the medium sized ones into a different basket, and keeping the large ones for eating.

We had a tarp overhead to block the morning sun, which was just starting to warm. I didn't notice Mike discard any oysters. If an oyster isn't big enough, or has a crazy shape, he'd put it back in the correct color-coded basket and back into the Sound to self-correct or grow.

Then it happened; the moment I knew was coming and that I dreaded. Mike took a shucking blade from out of the air like a magician. He targeted an oyster hinge and expertly popped it open, ran the blade under the nugget separating the adductor (the muscle holding onto the shell), and handed it to me. Expectantly.

I dodged his eyes but reflexively took the oyster. Now what?

Trapped, I glanced at the shellfish in my hand. Raw and glistening. And no Tabasco or lemon or mignonette sauce in sight. So there we were, me and the raw oyster on a dock in Greenport, LI. Both of us wishing we weren't in this situation.

* * *

While New York City oysters are unfit to eat—and will be for a long time because of the now-banned toxic PCBs that remain in the Harbor—Long Island oyster farming has a different story, one of prosperity, decline, and, now, rejuvenation.

The water in the Sound is pollution-free. Greenport was a huge oystering center in the early years of the twentieth century, with LIRR freight trains taking 20,000 tons a day to New York City and points west.[10] Instead of being banned in the 1920s, oyster farming thrived until the 1960s. Then it disappeared.

Mike gives three reasons for the disappearance. One was the dreaded oyster disease MSX, which spread from the experimental transfer of Pacific oysters into the Chesapeake Bay; they were immune but passed on the disease. A second was pollution from General Electric in Connecticut's river systems, which provided the seed oysters for the Long Island oyster farms.

But the biggest factor had nothing to do with the oysters themselves, and everything to do with the American diet. Mike points to the rise of McDonald's and the advent and competition of cheap, unhealthy, steroid-fed food. "How could an ounce of meat that took two years to grow compete with cheap beef and chicken? Your average chicken in the store took three months to grow." The short answer is, it couldn't. And the Long Island oyster farms nearly disappeared as a result.

MSX has not disappeared and is still deadly (to oysters, not people). Some oysters have developed resistance and creative cultivation strategies have reduced its mortality rate, but it lurks as an ever-present danger. Connecticut banned the export of seed oysters, and large hatcheries—including the five municipal and five commercial hatcheries on Long Island supported by Cornell University Extension—have resolved the issues caused by the GE pollution. One of these hatcheries alone can produce 20 million seed oysters a year. The problem of competition from factory farm food remains.

In the '80s and '90s, a new wave of oyster farmers like the Osinskis started reviving the oyster farming industry in eastern Long Island; there are now nearly a hundred farms. Most are small, and it's nowhere near the pre-'60s massive industry, but it's a start.

Needless to say, waterfront property on the Sound is not an option for lots of would-be oyster farmers, but a twenty-one-foot boat that can go out to a leased area of the Sound and back to a local ramp, with a culling machine on board, is. Most LI oyster farmers start small and do it as a hobby or a second career.

Mike and his kids talk about the pleasure of working outside, but are also unromantic. A farm is a farm whether on water or land. And oysters are farmed—even back in the day Long Island oysters were farmed, not gathered from the wild. As Mike says, "a farmer is an ultimate killing machine, killing barnacles, sponges, sycophants," anything that threatens the product. For Merc, the most enjoyable part is "just the fact of being on the water, being out in the waves, the rockiness, the deep blue of the water."

But growing up on a farm has its downsides. Mike's daughter, Suzanna, talks about being a kid on a family farm where you don't get to sleep in or take unplanned days off. Most of all, when she and Merc are asked about negatives, both respond with the smell of oysters permeating everything.

Two centuries ago, the massive NYC oyster was an entire meal. But since the '60s, Long Island oysters have been relegated to the role of appetizer. And they have largely disappeared from home cooking. Somewhere in the range of 95 to 99 percent of Long Island's oysters are sold to restaurants, largely for eating raw.

Mike says, "Oysters shouldn't be just an appetizer." Why not restore them as a main meal, the way New Yorkers ate them two centuries ago? He argues for them as a healthy source of animal protein and as an excellent source of zinc, which may help protect against COVID-19 and its ilk by boosting antiviral immunity and curbing inflammation. Oysters also provide iron, Vitamins A, B12, C, and D, calcium, selenium, copper, magnesium, and good fats. As we talked in the middle of the pandemic, Mike asked why New York State didn't buy large quantities for schools, hospitals, prisons, and other institutions, especially as the restaurant market had virtually disappeared for the time being, leaving the oyster farms with huge surpluses. A self-interested plug for his industry? Of course. But it's not such a crazy idea. Frankly, they are better for diet and for the environment, including reducing global warming, than factory farming.

Chef Dan Kluger of Loring Place agrees it's not crazy. He likes the versatility of oysters—that they can be eaten raw, fried, poached, grilled...and that they can go with neutral things like eggs and potatoes as well as balancing the richness of spicy and acidic things. He says larger, meatier oysters serve best in entrees.

There's hope that Long Island's industry rejuvenation will spread. Every minute, oysters are busy undoing the damage that people have done. An adult oyster filters up to fifty gallons of water a day, removing certain pollutants, including nitrogen. Too much nitrogen triggers algal blooms that deplete the water of oxygen, creating dead zones. The Long Island Oyster Growers Association—though not a disinterested observer—estimates that Long Island oysters collectively filter about 900 million gallons a day. The helicopter view sees this tiny mollusk as essential for planetary and economic health by purifying water.

And this is where the story returns to New York City. The Billion Oyster Project, founded in 2014, is an ambitious effort to put the restaurant shells, as well as live oysters, back into the Harbor and its associated waters to build the oyster stocks back up and help defend the city against storm damage, which will, of course, only increase with accelerated climate weirding.

The project has collected 1.6 million pounds of oyster shells, restored 45 million live oysters, and engaged over 6,000 New York City schoolchildren. Beyond contributing to reefs, the recycling of the shells is important because the shells provide the hard surface that other oysters need in order to grow. So as diners eat their oysters, raw or otherwise, they can feel they are contributing to the rebuilding of the Harbor if their restaurant is participating in the BOP.

When I asked Dan Kluger in fall 2020 about Loring Place participating in BOP, he said he was eager to get involved with it when the pandemic eased, as he was having to stay away from the more labor-intensive dishes, such as oysters, until it did. He recognizes the need to rebuild wild oyster reefs for environmental health. This is also one of the arguments for increasing consumption of farmed oysters, as wild oysters are functionally extinct in most parts of the world. The more oysters that are eaten, the more sustainable the oyster farms, and thus the more oysters that are grown, contributing to healthier seas and coasts.

Oyster farmers around the country reported deep declines in oyster sales to restaurants during the COVID-19 pandemic. In contrast, Dan Barber tweeted in July 2020 about the pandemic of a century ago: "During the 1918 influenza epidemic, oysters were the hoarder equivalent of today's toilet paper. Stockpiling was ubiquitous, prices skyrocketed, black markets developed. Poachers raided oyster beds."

* * *

As I stood on the Sound with the oyster in my hand, completely stuck, I realized that if there was ever a moment I'd like eating a raw oyster, it would be when it was a fresh-out-of-the-water oyster in the legendary home of oysters. So I put the shell to my lips, tilted my head back, and the oyster slipped in.

The first thing that hits your tongue is the liquor. People call it briny, but for me it was like seawater with a less salty, rounded flavor. Next came the plump oyster, which I usually would have immediately swallowed whole, but this time, I took a bite. The texture was springy, but when my teeth sliced through, it became creamy, in texture and taste, with a little bit of cucumber in it. Could this be? I glanced at Mike and nodded. *Yes, I can do this, it's not bad.* And then it was gone.

The experience was so unique that I didn't even know if I wanted to do it again. Harrowing, then interesting. *Next time*, I thought, *I'll be able to tell if I actually liked it—or whether it was the rush of experience that got the oyster down.*

* * *

The next time came sooner than I imagined. While in Croatia making a dish with Chef Marina Gaši of Restaurant Marina in Novigrad, Istria, I took a side trip to visit Emil Sosic. He made a name for himself ten years ago on an episode of *No Reservations*, harvesting black mussels for Anthony Bourdain. The young, cocky guy with a boat (whom Tony nicknamed "Tony") seemed right at home bantering with the world-famous star over steamed garlic shellfish. Turns out Emil/Tony, still cocky but a little heavier and now with two boats, also farms the European flat oyster. As its name suggests, this oyster doesn't have the deep cup I was used to. Its white, peach-flecked, flat shell holds a smaller muscle.

Meeting Emil on his barge at the mouth of the Limski Kanal in Istria, we puttered out to see his lines and cages. He farms the old way: No hatchery supplied his seed. He hangs a plastic, slatted "collector" next to a mama oyster in the spring and comes back in a year, hoping to see a batch of small, baby oysters clinging on for dear life. Felt to me like such a gamble to hinge the success of a farm on the randomness of floating larvae, but Emil says an economics background helps him crunch the numbers and that any oyster spawn shortfalls are already included in his slim margins.

Luckily, the year I visited Emil, the collector bore fruit, a new crop pulled up and ready to transfer to his mesh baskets for eighteen-month-olds. Emil wouldn't see those oysters again for another year. He mentioned that by keeping them underwater so long they wouldn't have muscle training, which I interpreted to mean they didn't learn to close their shells when exposed to the air. The European flat has notoriously weak abductors, so the beak doesn't close tightly. This means that after harvesting they won't last as long—a three-day shelf life in contrast to the East Coast oyster's week. But taking them out to "muscle train" ended up being too expensive.

Next we checked out his older oysters, no longer in baskets, instead strung down the length of a rope in sets of two—as done for generations. He pulled out his phone to show me a YouTube clip from '42, when the area was ruled by Mussolini. The Fascist propaganda piece showed the same canal, the same dock, and possibly the same ropes braided with oysters, though in fours, not pairs. Today, partner bivalves sit on opposite sides of the hemp with beaks faced away from one another so each gets its own access to a flow of food. The other difference I noticed from '42 was the sharp drop in oyster farmhands, from hundreds to only three today. Looking around, I felt a touch of kenopsia; the canal seemed much emptier.

When Emil pulled up the rope, there was a big problem. An enormous ball of algae that looked like orange grapefruit vesicles cocooned each oyster pair. And right next to the ropes, long white tubes, like small pinheads, covered the caged oysters.

With us on the barge were two marine biologists coming to investigate the algae and parasites attacking Emil's oysters. Taking samples, the scientists believed that the algae had arrived from Mexico that year on the underside of a boat and that the red worm

Photo by Marty Bleazard

Tony's barge at his oyster farm with Petra

that caused the white, crusty shafts was more abundant due to the warming seas. Seemed that in addition to invasive Pacific clams that had smuggled their way from farms in Italy to that protected canal, Emil was dealing with the effects of international trade and global warming. I mentioned the Japanese tidal desiccation technique Mike uses. But Emil was wrapped up in the disaster before him. "Petra, you will save me, Petra," he pleaded to the scientist.

Petra didn't look particularly optimistic.

Petra's pessimism was well-founded. Scientists have been documenting the major population declines of the European flat oyster due to overfishing, habitat loss, and parasite diseases,[11] while the competing Pacific oyster has established dense, reef-forming aggregations and achieved a self-sustaining presence off the Istrian coast. [12]

In fact, Emil made a stop on the way back, hopping off the barge and wading to some rocky outcroppings in his tall rubber boots. I realized those weren't rocks, but wild oyster reefs. He kicked a few Pacific oysters loose. "These taste terrible," he said, holding them out to me, "but they can't be stopped." He shucked one and motioned for me to take it. He likely was just being parochial, but it wasn't the most appetizing of presentations. I declined. The Pacific oyster has the honor of being introduced and invasive at the same time. Brought over to help after a blight and the collapse of the Portuguese oyster farms, it soon escaped and spread. Emil shrugged and tossed the oyster back into the canal.

The European flat oyster is not the only local seafood at risk. Noble pen shell clams are functionally extinct throughout the Adriatic and the larger Mediterranean.[13] Overfishing, including bottom dredging; climate change; pollution; and invasive algae have devastated the populations of shellfish and fish throughout the Mediterranean. The crisis has reached existential levels for many of the species. Without dramatic action by the Croatian government, we are looking at a collapse of the Adriatic ecosystem. There are solutions that have worked elsewhere: creation of marine protected areas, no-fishing zones, paying fishermen to alternate fishing seasons. But in a short-term, profit-driven, and politically volatile world, implementing solutions based on caring for the seas and understanding the long-term economic benefits of healthy oceans feels like a Sisyphean task.

After motoring back to shore, Emil/Tony popped champagne, started cracking open oysters (the European is shucked via the lips, not the hinge) and raw venus clams, and emerged from out of his momentary depression. He came alive on the boathouse deck with the red light of the camera and the chance to hold court to a captive audience. Shoving an open oyster my way (the "best oyster in the world," he said) and a cup of Istrian champagne, he told me how a large German man eating his oysters the previous week had proclaimed that the tour of the farm and the subsequent tasting was the best day of his life. Could have been. Even under gray sky with lead-colored water, the canal was stunning and Emil was a funny, sharp host.

And also, maybe the German liked oysters more than I. There I was again faced with a raw oyster, though this time armed with some lemon and tipsy with bubbly. I took the mouthful without hesitation and chewed.

The lemon was a nice touch and the oyster wasn't bad. Creamy with a slight metallic aftertaste that washed away in a sip of champagne. Maybe, again, it was just the experience, but dare I say I liked it.

This was the type of thing I could get used to: shucking and eating oysters on an estuary on the Adriatic.

With a bit more to drink, Emil came back around to the tight margins, the lack of oyster buyers (most Croatians don't eat them—only the tourists and the rich), and his extraordinary ability to keep afloat while other oyster farmers around him fell. Then he asked for six times the payment originally negotiated and I scrambled to locate an ATM.

* * *

I'd never thought about preparing oysters as a main meal at home, but I figured I'd take a stab. When I got back to the West Coast, I picked up some Pacific oysters from the Temecula Farmers' Market for my wife Karen, my son Harrison, and myself. Renato Silva from Dry Dock Fish Co. explained they were Willapa Bay oysters, which happen to make up 25 percent of American oysters. They're the "uglies"—they aren't usually used as restaurant-quality half shells, because they don't have the shape for it. Oyster snobbery is my gain—ugly food never bothered me and the taste is top-notch. Plus, Willapa Bay in Washington State is "the cleanest estuary in the country," Silva told me. And, finally, I was excited to try them because Dan Kluger mentioned he preferred the taste of Pacific oysters, "Even though I am on the East Coast and believe in eating local...I find Pacific more meaty and juicier."

Oyster aficionados will argue for their preferences as oenophiles argue about wines, but they'll agree that the oyster's *merroir*, like a wine's terroir, determines its flavor and texture and other significant characteristics. Add to that the fact that Atlantic (*Crassostrea virginica*), Pacific (*Crassostrea gigas*), and European flat oysters (*Ostrea edulis*), are actually different species—and none is the oyster species that produces pearls (despite the optimistic naming of Paerlstraat by Manhattan's Dutch colonists). That species, *Pinctada albina*, is in family *Pteriidae*, while *Crassostrea* and *Ostrea* are genera in family *Ostreidae*. *Pinctada albina*—and the pearls—are found off Japan, Polynesia, and Australia. There's a lot for an oyster lover to consider.

I'm not a vegan but I work with vegans, active and lapsed. It turns out there's a decades-long argument about whether vegans can/should eat oysters. Oysters are bivalve mollusks, but they don't have central nervous systems. PETA and the Vegan Society say they are definitely not kosher (pun intended). Other vegans (especially restaurant owners!) say that they are "less sentient than trees"[14] and don't feel pain so it's OK to eat them. Peter Singer wrote in *Animal Liberation*, "One cannot with any confidence say that these creatures do feel pain, so one can equally have little confidence in saying that they do not feel pain."[15] All of these viewpoints make sense.

The argument among the vegan community is a microcosm of the larger question of oyster cuisine. Can this tiny, slow-growing, hard-to-monetize food make it in the modern marketplace? It certainly has its work cut out for it. But there are a lot of things going for it as well. Maybe it is an environmentally, culturally important, ethical choice in contrast to industrial food. Or it could be—as eating habits change, as the food chain evolves with larger species becoming scarcer, more expensive, or less in demand—that it just makes more economic sense. However this plays out, hopefully, oysters will be grown and eaten in bigger and bigger quantities, and their shells will increasingly contribute to reef revitalization. For the time being, oysters may be mostly a fancy side dish, but at some point, with luck, they will make their way back to the center of the plate in homes as well as in restaurants.

Here's the meal I made at home. Put together a basic beer batter. Three-fourths cup of flour to crunch up the outside, three-fourths cup of IPA (India Pale Ale if you're not a beer drinker) to add lightness and break down the flour's gluten a bit, an egg to glue it together, lemon zest for some spark, and a pinch of garlic salt 'cause salt plus fat plus crispy breading is heaven.

Is it a cliche to mention how many times the kitchen shears and then the butter knife almost took off a finger while I tried to shuck a dozen oysters? Where was my oyster knife, where was my mesh glove? Later, I ordered them. Perusing online, I tried to avoid the world-eating megacorps and find a smaller company for my shucking kit. The prices ranged from $13.99 for a basic, pointed, flat metal knife with a mesh, cut-proof glove all the way up to a $595 steel oyster shucker akin to a tabletop bladed citrus press.

At the time, I finally found a rhythm with a small, tough butter knife. I slid it along the beak lips of the oysters, feeling for give without chipping the shell. Once the blade tip was secured, I pushed and twisted. The open shells revealed the off-white meat floating in the oyster liquor. I poured the liquor in a cup to add to the batter, then slid the knife underneath, severing it from its shell.

Keeping in mind Dan Kluger's advice to cook the oysters less than I'd expect to, I tossed the meat in the flour for a coat, then mixed the egg, lemon zest, garlic salt, IPA, and remaining flour into a bowl and dipped the oysters in. Peanut oil had been spitting on the stove for about ten minutes and it was nice and hot (I know because I burned myself when they went in).

It was delicious. Two-year-old Harrison and his mom agreed.

Dune Spinach, Avocado: Cape Town / Johannesburg

THE SAND DUNES OF CAPE TOWN are blowing away.

It isn't a new phenomenon. The European colonialists and the post-apartheid South African government have been trying officially to stop the erosion since at least 1845, when the English government disastrously imported Australian Acacia seeds to sow into the sand. When the Acacia plan came to naught, trash from the city was spread over the dunes in hopes of blocking the wind. Since then, Capetonians have constructed barriers, covered the dunes with branches, and, until 1974, continued to introduce alien plant species, all for dune stabilization. And their big plans failed. Instead, fires swept through and native plants collapsed and the aliens drained the freshwater resources. And the sand continued to leave.

But slowly, over time, an indigenous plant, *Tetragonia decumbens*, began to take hold again. This stocky succulent with yellow flowers and angular, thick, puffy leaves began to stabilize the dunes from the West Coast to Morgans Bay in the East. When I pulled up to the Kalk Bay dunes on a suburban Cape Town street, crossed from the sea side to the dune side, leapt over a ditch filled with plastic soda bottles and filth, scrambled up the sand, and looked out over the crest, a field of green lay before me. This was the plant I had come to find—at first glance, a common ground-cover plant with a salty/peppery flavor Abigail had sent me to forage. Though in looking at the small plants collectively holding the dunes from spilling into the sea, I thought that maybe this "dune spinach" could be a metaphor of sorts for the Cape Flats in which it grows—and perhaps for South Africa.

Abigail is Abigail Mbalo-Mokoena. She is the chef, owner, and creative director of 4Roomed eKasi Culture restaurant in Khayelitsha, the giant Cape Flats township that adjoins and is part of the city of Cape Town. She first gained public notice when she placed sixth in the 2014 Master Chef South Africa competition; in 2019, *Food & Wine* and *Travel + Leisure* magazines jointly named eKasi one of the thirty best restaurants in the world.[1] Graceful and self-possessed, she moves through the world creating ripples around her, no differently from famous movie stars I've met. It's an enchanting quality, composed of a mix of charm, a keen mind, and an incredible work ethic, that attracts people to her side.

The idea for eKasi began on a Friday night in the center of the township. Abigail's husband, Sam, started a food cart to serve at a recurring block party called Ace Groova Park, a basic *shisa nyama* stand (Zulu for "burnt meat"). A BBQ with some traditional food for a cheap price. But as Abigail got involved, the food became noteworthy. Rand after rand flowed in for *pap* and grilled chicken. The cart grew to a food truck, which was a hit. After Sam and Abigail raised enough money, the food truck was parked outside of their new brick-and-mortar restaurant.

So I traveled to Khayelitsha to meet Abigail, harvest food for a meal at eKasi, and cook alongside her. Abigail told me our meal was "based on a South African township life lived in a

Abigail at eKasi

four-roomed home in the heart of the Western Cape. Its inspiration drawn from fishes that used to be sold out of the back of a *bakkie* on the streets to our almost-forgotten, highly nutritious, indigenous foods and plants such as *pap*, dune spinach, and *spekboom* that used to grow abundantly in our backyards and on the fields."[2] As Abigail sent me to source a meal, I would not only explore the food of the township, but also the complicated history of the larger Cape.

The Cape Flats are a level expanse of sand southeast of Cape Town, subject to flooding in winter. Until the mid-twentieth century they were barely inhabited. Then the apartheid government began pushing Coloured (mixed race), Asian, and Black African populations out of Cape Town areas into the Flats in order to replace them with whites. In addition to forced relocations, many Black Africans, whose very presence was defined as illegal, settled informally into the Flats, as there was no place else for them to go. The townships were characterized by a lack of drinkable water and electricity, and by sewage-filled streets; houses were largely *ad hoc* "tin" shacks of corrugated iron, cardboard, and wood, along with some four-roomed houses built by the government to be occupied by multiple families.

Khayelitsha, a largely Xhosa-speaking Black township, was created in 1984. In one of the most publicized examples of brutal violence in the 1980s, thousands of Africans were forced from Cape Town into Khayelitsha by violent attacks and the burning of their homes. Khayelitsha grew quickly. Current estimates of its size vary wildly, and it is either the largest township in the country or second to Soweto, outside of Johannesburg, depending on your source.

Abigail's family was one of those that was forcibly removed into Khayelitsha. They lived with others in four rooms. Along with the hardship, the experience left her with a feeling that all the people in the space felt like family.

And after she left to become a chef, she decided she wanted to come back, saying she would use food "as a tool that will drive us back to the township."[3] She told me that, horrendous as the oppression of apartheid was, there had been a unity and sense of community that dissipated once apartheid was defeated. She opened the restaurant, architecturally modeled after the four-roomed home she grew up in, with three goals: to make a difference, to help develop Khayelitsha's economy, and to bring an influx of tourism to support the township's effort to shed its image as a dangerous place that tourists should avoid.

This has long been the image. When I said I was going to Cape Town, any number of people told me about its stunning beauty and the mansions clinging to sheer cliffs overlooking the "models and bottles" at beachside bars. They also told me to avoid Khayelitsha, calling it a bit "stabby," though, with a twist, they added that the violence there was mostly community-focused and that I was actually more likely to get hurt in parts of central Cape Town, where spark plugs get thrown through car windows for "smash-and-grabs."

A thick fog milked up the sunrise when I pulled in to meet Sam, diffusing the sun into a dim poached egg creeping up the sky. As I sat inside the locked touring van, human silhouettes raced to work at the edges of an open expanse of dirt and litter that seemed to be a little square. No grass, no hedges, no bronze statue with pigeons perched on its shoulders. Just dirt, covered in fog, so the dirt road and town square kinda blended. I was not to be let out, our South African producer declared.

We had been having a bit of a standoff 'til then. Driving into Khayelitsha, I had pressed my face to the windows, hoping to get out and shoot the early morning township waking up, but the cameras had never rolled. Tin-shack houses hemmed the road, some doorless with caved-in roofs. Every now and then there were painted concrete walls. But everything was smushed together with a sewer ditch running in front. Dirt roads, trash, rusted iron, barbed wire. Groups gathered on street corners waiting. Barefoot kids, some barefoot adults. My white local producer did not want this picture presented to the world. It had to remain a South African secret.

The township looked like people living at a tipping point. The climax of some terrible apocalyptic movie, except real. Here and now. The township was still reeling from apartheid and its aftermath.

* * *

Apartheid was a system of racial segregation and domination of the non-European population by the white minority, to assert full control over the land and to monopolize economic power. It built on centuries of previous white domination and was enforced through imprisonment, torture, banishment, and death.

But it was only the most explicit and merciless chapter in South Africa's history since Europeans arrived in 1588. Things didn't go well from the beginning: The Portuguese captain Bartolomeu Dias landed to fill his water barrels without permission from the Khoekhoen (also called Khoikhoi), the nomadic, pastoral inhabitants who had lived in South Africa since before recorded memory. A fight ensued in which Khoekhoen threw stones at the Portuguese and Dias shot and killed a Khoe-speaker with a crossbow. Nine years later, Portuguese under Vasco de Gama returned and again there was conflict over water, leading to the Portuguese firing the first cannon in South Africa; when the Portuguese departed, leaving a marker beacon and a cross, symbolizing Portuguese possession of the land, a group of Khoekhoen knocked both down.

The Portuguese never did settle, but the Dutch did, establishing their first permanent settlement at Cape Town in 1652, run by the United East India Company and serving as a resupply and layover for ships trading with Asia. Employees also could lease land and cultivate crops, which they had to sell to the Company. They quickly imported enslaved people from Madagascar, Mozambique, the Dutch East Indies, and Ceylon to work the land. The first Khoe-Dutch war, over land and livestock, was in 1659, the second in 1673, and the third in 1674-1677. The Dutch won; the Khoekhoen also died in great numbers from the measles and smallpox brought by the Dutch. The surviving Khoekhoen were squeezed off their lands.

The Dutch colony was eventually caught up in the European wars of the 1790s and the early 1800s between the British, French, and Dutch; the British consolidated their control in 1814, viewing Cape Town and the Cape of Good Hope as keys to maintaining the East India Company's rule in India.

The 1800s saw cooperation and competition across the entire African continent, including warfare, among the British, Boers (Dutch settlers), and African states. The overall trend was colonial European expansion—and consistently worsened conditions for Black Africans, who were subjected to forced labor and missionary efforts to supplant traditional worldviews with Christianity. By 1900, there were no autonomous African states left.

With the discovery of diamonds in 1868 and gold in 1886, South Africa suddenly became a much more valuable colonial asset as well as the site of an influx of European fortune hunters and settlers.

The Anglo-Boer war of 1899-1902 saw the British defeat of the Boers, using a scorched-earth policy and the first large-scale use of concentration camps. It consolidated British control of South Africa, leading to the creation of the Union of South Africa in 1910, which ultimately became the Republic of South Africa in 1961.

In 1913, the Natives Land Act allocated only 8 percent of the land for Blacks and 90 percent for whites. In South Africa, where there were relatively few, relatively prosperous Black peasants and skilled craftsmen, some Blacks were allowed to vote in Cape Town; but as large enough numbers of Blacks came under British rule that they could have had meaningful voting power, their right to vote was curtailed and eventually completely eliminated in 1936.

In WWI, some Blacks and Coloureds supported the war, hoping their support would subsequently lead to better conditions. It didn't. In 1948, the Afrikaner (Boer)-based National Party, with strong affinity to the Nazis, came to power and instituted apartheid (apartness), which lasted until 1991. The Homeland Citizens Act of 1970 built on the Natives Land Act, creating "homelands" or "reserves" where Blacks were supposed to live. This provided the excuse for forced evictions of thousands of Blacks, including those who were forced into Khayelitsha.

Resistance to apartheid took many forms, including nonviolent action. Following the Sharpeville massacre in 1960, resistance moved toward armed struggle, along with other forms of actions focused on creating "ungovernability."[4] In 1966, the United Nations declared apartheid a "crime against humanity." The Soweto uprising was in 1976. Major resistance groups included the multiracial African National Congress (ANC), the Africanist Pan-African Congress, and the nonviolent United Democratic Front and Mass Democratic Movement, which was aligned with the ANC.

Internal rebellion and international boycotts ultimately forced F.W. de Klerk, the last head of state under white minority rule, to abandon apartheid. In 1990, Nelson Mandela was released from prison after twenty-seven years, and in 1994, he was elected president in South Africa's first free elections.

* * *

Sam hopped quietly into the front passenger seat. My view of him from behind revealed a handsome man with a high forehead, behind his glasses a glint in his eye, and a short beard. He spoke softly to the driver, who spun the wheel, and we bumped forward. Sam glanced back with a smile and we got to chatting. It soon became clear he was going to be just the guide I was looking for. Aside from knowing local foraging spots, he hinted at showing me the sights, getting me out of the van and into the township. Little did I know how fortunate I would be to have Sam.

South Africa is fortunate to have Abigail. The car coasted to a stop in back of her original black-and-yellow-striped food truck (still available for parties!) which sat almost blocking the entrance of the restaurant. My film crew piled out with Sam to set up for Abigail's solo interview. I hung back, wanting our introductions to be "real" on camera, prepping for "the taste." Each episode starts with a chef interview and then me sitting down with them and a meal she or he has made. After handshakes, we chat about each dish as I taste it before I go off to collect the ingredients. I ask about why the chef has decided to make these particular dishes ("Your grandma made this every Saturday?") or the history behind the dish ("This came from sixteenth-century Maltese court records of a lawsuit between a butcher and a pirate?") but mostly what is in them ("So this little green piece that tastes like fire is *rocoto verde*?"). While I do focus on the mechanics of cooking, the real heroes are the ingredients. I'll sometimes know a few main ingredients ahead of time, but generally I like to be surprised.

After an hour, I figured her on-camera interview was coming to an end and I wouldn't interrupt anything important, so I headed in. I was met at the door by the local producer, Graeme, who was beaming. "She is amazing! So much good stuff. We asked about growing up with all the families in her house and she started crying." In the TV biz this is something producers die for.

My first impression was how unlike a restaurant it felt. There was an entryway that let in a ton of light and that seemed more like a sitting room. That opened to a large living room/dining room area with tables. In the far-left corner was a small, mostly open kitchen (so small that the food truck is also put to use in tandem for big groups).

Abigail met me in the center at a spare wooden table. Three plates and a clear glass of murky liquid—the color of the sky just after sunset—were laid out. We sat across from one another, introduced ourselves, and got into it.

Abigail's menu started with a foraged-vegetable crudité layered with dune spinach, *spekboom*, radish, turnip, and carrots, topped with nasturtium flowers and covered in an olive oil/lemon drizzle. The garden veggies I had some history with, some I'd even harvested before. But the native plants—the dune spinach, spekboom, nasturtium—were all new to me. I was definitely going to need a local guide to help me forage. The crudité was crisp, the veggies held their snap. The simple dressing allowed the natural flavors to emerge. Salty and sour—I was excited to figure out what came from where. Abigail explained that the dish would send me all over the Cape and introduce me to local farmers for produce and to the Khoisan for foraging.

Next up was the seafood velouté. I put the crudité plate to the side and slid the *pap* and seafood towards me. *Pap* is porridge, similar to polenta, and very likely the most famous, most consumed South African dish. Because it's inexpensive to make, the poor across southern Africa will sometimes eat it for all their meals (the breakfast version has a little butter or sour milk and sugar akin to a corn pudding). Usually made with corn, Abigail's version today was a sorghum base. Maize is a New World ingredient, so it's historically recent to SA. Abigail used the native cereal sorghum. Sorghum is a huge staple in Africa, with Nigeria being second in the world in production and consumption behind the US. The States's 8 million tons is mostly grown for animal feed and ethanol, but there is a small fan club of people who see it as an ancient heritage grain and a healthier, tastier ingredient in breads and pasta. In the *pap*, the sorghum was blended with potatoes, making the texture a bowl of buttery cream of wheat. This was to be eaten alongside the culinary star of the menu, her seafood velouté. In the center of an orange cream pond was what Abigail and other South Africans call a crayfish or kreef—to the rest of the world, a rock lobster. Around Cape Town these were once considered a pest and thrown back out. Later, I learned that although the government continues to issue permits to catch kreef, their numbers are now perilously low, at 2 percent of pre-exploitation levels.[5,6]

Next to the kreef in the soup there were what I call mussels and what South Africans also call mussels. They were in an orange glaze. There were some green sprigs floating alongside to flavor the broth, which I assumed were sage and parsley. The sage was right, but the parsley turned out to be *bukku*, a native medicinal plant which, out of all the ingredients, would end up causing me the most embarrassment trying to forage.

After the delicious main course, Abigail and I settled in to chat and to sip the *rooibos* punch. She paired the tea base with a little rhubarb, more orange, and some mint. The drink was refreshingly tart, and her company made for the last bit of enjoyable rest before my mission began. After I walked out of eKasi, I'd have seven days to track down and harvest this meal's ingredients all over South Africa.

Mama Christina runs the *Moyo We Khaya* (Spirit of Home) food garden in Khayelitsha that sells produce to eKasi. Christina Kaba ended her formal education at age ten when she went to work on her family farm. In 1986, she grudgingly followed her husband to Khayelitsha, his hometown, where she became an original member of the *Abalimi Bezekhaya*, a nonprofit urban agriculture organization that focuses on the greening of townships in public areas and schools. Abalimi ("the planters" in Xhosa) helps individuals, groups, and community-based organizations to develop permanent, organic food-growing and conservation projects as the basis for sustainable livelihoods, job creation, and poverty alleviation. Abalimi was formed in response to the urgent need to alleviate hunger and what is politely called "food insecurity" under apartheid. Even today about one in five households in South Africa faces inadequate or severe lack of food, and one in three children is stunted.[7,8] Mama Christina's involvement with Abalimi led to the creation of *Moyo We Khaya*. This was my first stop to pick up the various garden vegetables for the menu.

We turned from dirt road to dirt road, leaving the corrugated neighborhoods behind, passing by a brief collection of suburban houses with white picket fences and green lawns. A small group of middle-class Blacks, many of whom eat at eKasi (it's a thirty-to-seventy split, locals to tourists), have stayed in the township. We arrived across from a park, at what looked like a school and a chained, metal gate. The driver hopped out to deal with the imposing lock, and through the chain link I saw a squat, cherubic grandma in a headscarf, standing in the dirt while ordering around a much larger, twenty-something man with a wheelbarrow. As I got out of the van at the side of a stunning garden highlighted by rows of squash and cauliflower the size of basketballs and bushes of greens, Mama Christina was suddenly in front of me. "They told me you don't know what you are doing," she said.

Her competence (when I was with her, I felt like she was the most capable person I'd ever met) shone steel-like, but was softened by a rare, flashing, wide gap-toothed smile. This sharp tone was honed by the challenge of lack of money, rolling blackouts, uninterested youth, and local politics. When she finally won control of the initial one-hectare plot through battles with the city, Christina called over a loudspeaker, *"All those who would like to grow vegetables in the garden, please come! We've got the land, it's very exciting! All are welcome!"* She ended up having to ration space because so many people came, but to Christina's disappointment, it was primarily older people; relatively few young people responded. Christina's explanation, in an I-don't-suffer-fools-gladly tone, was "these younger people aren't used to working hard." With the land she was able to win a local subsidy of compost. She got each of the gardeners to spare change each month to share the electric bill. Collectively they opened bank accounts, collectively they built a market, collectively they found handymen to fix issues with the shed. The formation of the NGO taught all the farmers how to save—and handle—money, for the community to work together to be self-sufficient. There were issues—Mama Christina speaks about how men in general don't listen, don't want to be told what to do, and want to be in charge. But she found that women were the right people to work with.

Mama Christina didn't do it on her own—she was able to compel and cajole others to join her. Five women run the organization. Although I didn't meet "Mama Nancy," I heard that Mama Christina had brought in the principal of a school the garden was serving back in the early '90s. When Mama Nancy, the principal, retired, she joined the garden and became the chairperson. In the meantime, in 2016, Mama Christina was named the CEO of Abalimi as a whole and ran it until 2019. As Mama Christina's history with Abalimi shows, the organization has been a vehicle for local women's leadership; it has also been a powerful force for social cohesion under extremely difficult conditions. As Rob Small, another founder of Abalimi, has said, "Gardening and urban agricultural outputs could not and should not be measured by green spaces and vegetables alone—but also by a woman's ability to hold her family together. An urban market garden is not in itself a social-change catalyst, but a community garden is."[9]

Here, at *Moyo We Khaya*, I was picking up carrots and turnips for the crudité, potatoes for the *pap*, and rhubarb and mint for the punch. Mama Christina pointed to the wheelbarrow. The young man handed it over and walked off to locate ripe turnips for me to harvest. Mama motioned her chin at him: "He grows good broccoli." Definitely a point of pride as he had arrived at the genesis of the garden and, under her tutelage, with no prior training, was now successfully running a large plot in the garden and making money off the produce. She hustled off, dress swishing, and I pushed the wheelbarrow and struggled to keep up.

We came to rows of potatoes, the shoots topped by two-week-old purple and white flowers signaling that the tubers below were ready. I wedged a pitchfork under the raised row. Potatoes will turn green under direct sunlight, so soil is mounded over them until they are more than six inches below the surface. I knelt down, pulling on the stems and lifting with the fork tines. The plant, its roots, and its tubers burst out; the soil revealed to be a healthy, wet, dark brown. I rooted around with my hands for any remaining Mondials, a waxy type, the most common in South African food. Glancing over my shoulder I saw Mama Christina looking at me with appraising eyes. I never thought I'd say this, but I felt a rush of insecurity over potato picking.

From there we wandered through the now-two-hectare plot digging and cutting, tossing everything into the wheelbarrow as Mama Christina pointed out the successes and failures of the garden. Over there was a small, wasted plot of land, looking unkempt, with withered, broken plants, because a local man had gotten into alcohol and forgotten his duty. This contrasted with an amazing section of kale and cauliflower being weeded by two of Mama Christina's good friends and Mama's granddaughter, matriarchs in the community. Over there was a barrel of water filled with soaking *dagga* (marijuana leaves) to make tea. Mama Christina recalled a recent confrontation with police who wanted it gone; when she proposed that they arrest her, the young cops slunk away.[10] She described this with a big, knowing smile.

A picture emerged of the ups and downs. A picture of a group of local people fighting for the idea that the community could be self-sufficient. With my wheelbarrow filled—and me hot and sweaty and in desperate need of a bathroom—it was time to go. The gardeners had to walk back into town for their needs. Though she had won the funds for water from the government, Mama Christina told me she was fighting some local politicians who wanted the funds to make their way into their pockets. She explained that the reason the garden worked well was because of transparency and that "there isn't abuse of the money." She explained that there was government abuse of money because "they have forgotten where they came from." Later I caught an interview of hers on local TV speaking about the same issue. Nearly in tears, she said, "What do they think about God looking at [them]!?"

People everywhere in the world are always talking about corruption, whether it's presidential swimming pools paid for with government money and charged off to fire prevention; "campaign contributions" that buy legislators' votes; *baksheesh*; George Washington Plunkitt's "honest graft;" building inspectors who allow multibillion-dollar landlords to cut corners; COVID-relief bills that stuff billions in for the wealthiest; or cops on the take. It can be legal or illegal, carried out by men in sleek suits in law offices or by petty officials demanding a bribe before stamping some essential document. There are scholars who talk about corruption as rotting critical institutions so they no longer exist with integrity, just as rust corrupts a bridge.[11] There are even some who argue that corruption can sometimes be a feature rather than a bug, that it can be the grease that makes things work.[12]

In South Africa, people talk about corruption more than anywhere else I've been. It seems that whatever else is true, corruption's corrosive effects are exacerbated by huge disparities in wealth and power, whether in South Africa, Iceland, or the United States.

The politics of South Africa are tangled and are tangled up with corruption. With the ANC, which had such broad support at liberation, in power since apartheid, one would think the country would thrive. But as William Gumede wrote in 2019, "poor governance has squeezed the public finances, threatening social welfare programmes, [and] the appalling corruption, mismanagement and populist exploitation of black grievances to hold on to power"[13] has held back progress.

A few weeks after gardening with Mama Christina, I was working with David Higgs, the chef of Marble, a wood-fire fine dining restaurant in Johannesburg. My hotel was about three miles away in Sandton overlooking a mall. The square in the Sandton Mall in the wealthy business district of Johannesburg is modeled after St. Mark's Square in Venice. It's the centerpiece of the four-hundred-store shopping district self-proclaimed as "Africa's most iconic." In the middle stands a twenty-foot-tall bronze statue of Nelson Mandela. Definitely a strange juxtaposition, this statue of the leftist freedom fighter now perched in the most opulent real estate in the whole country.

The contrast gets even more discomfiting two escalator levels below. The ride down to the first floor opens to an atrium where a bulletproof Mercedes sits. A cardboard stand next to it promotes

Photo by Graeme Swanepoel

David Higgs and I cooking at Marble

the levels of protection. This SUV stands up against military-grade weapons like the AK-47 (7.62x39mm). The cardboard pointedly adds that it also offers protection against handguns, which are "likely to be encountered in general crime and hijacking scenarios. Handguns are commonly used due to the ease with which they can be concealed." The conjunction, just two floors apart, of the almost prop-like bronze Mandela statue and the bulletproof luxury car captures the contradictions of post-apartheid South Africa, the country with the greatest wealth inequality in the world.[14]

Joburg is the business and financial center of South Africa. The juxtapositions of wealth and poverty are stark. People living in huge houses behind walls, with big guard dogs and private security, right next to shantytowns and townships lacking basic services. This is an important part of the jarring reality of both Cape Town and Joburg. In these heterogeneous, twenty-first-century cities with wealth generated by a vibrant financial economy, not much of the wealth is shared and thus the pot's not melting.

South Africa was the site of some of the earliest known examples of controlled fires being used for cooking, even before the emergence of *homo sapiens*. For example, ashes discovered in Wonderwerk Cave indicate that *homo erectus* may have cooked animals and plants a million years ago.[15] A recent discovery in another South African cave shows that modern humans may have roasted vegetables 170,000 years ago.[16] Thus David Higgs and I were symbolically making a meal with wild game and mostly traditional plants over fire at Marble. The centerpiece was to be blesbok (a commonly found antelope) steak. I failed to get a blesbok on the hunt, though I ended up with a warthog (also common). This lean, tough swine doesn't cook as well on the grill, so we had to tweak the recipe a bit. The steak was to be paired with a native leaf salad and popped sorghum bread which used a traditional *Umqombothi* maize/sorghum beer for the yeast. Finally, I needed avocados and macadamia nuts to crust them with and then roast in David's wood oven. This gave me an opportunity to see the north of the country. We headed out of Joburg to agricultural land around Kruger National Park.

I met Dian Pretorius, owner of Heidel Spits farm in Nelspruit. The son of a farmer, he owned and managed a large farm of five kinds of avocados. We were walking through his groves looking for large fruits—counts of twelve, meaning it only takes twelve to fill a box. I still couldn't get it out of my mind how international trade had taken this precolonial, domesticated American fruit from Mexico, Guatemala, and the West Indies to the farms of South Africa. I was looking for Hass avocados, which were bred in

California in the1920s by mailman Rudolf Hass. The most widely grown avocado in the world, it largely superseded the then-standard Fuerte. It's bright green when young but becomes a darker blue-black, as well as rougher-skinned, as it ripens. The fruits don't ripen on the tree, meaning they are hard when picked. I was using a picking pole—a long shaft with shears and a bag at the end. After I put the bag under an avocado, I pulled a string and the blades cut the stem; if I'd done it right, it plopped nicely into the bag. I was still working on this technique, unable to cut and bag correctly in the same motion. Dian was my spotter and I trailed behind, looking up into the trees, mining his avo knowledge. He said Fuertes, which are super creamy with a little Worcestershire sauce, are the way to go for the best guacamole, while the firmer Haas are best for sushi.

Notably, we also ended up talking about land reform. When I asked if this was his family's farm, he said no, that while he had grown up in the area, he had been living in Australia for a few years and had only recently returned. Offhand, I asked why he had left. With a glance to the rolling camera, he said that his father had been murdered at the last farm they had worked on in South Africa. Farm murders had been in the news while we were filming, and most of the white South Africans I spoke with said that they feared South Africa was headed towards becoming another Zimbabwe, where wealthy white farmers who had dominated Southern Rhodesian land ownership under British colonial rule had been forced from their land or had left voluntarily, fearing disappropriation. They claimed that Zimbabwe's agriculture industry collapsed because "there was no one left who knew how to farm." Land redistribution and its implementation in Zimbabwe has been intensely controversial since the end of colonial rule with independence in 1980.

In South Africa after the fall of apartheid, as in independent Zimbabwe, the central economic question was what to do about the fact that the overwhelming amount of arable land had been seized by colonizing Europeans, while native Africans had been largely forbidden to own or lease agricultural land or to learn the business skills to manage it. Thus, under apartheid, 90 percent of the land had been owned by the white minority, which made up 9 percent of the population. Even in 2017, Blacks owned 4 percent of land owned by individuals, while Indians owned 5 percent, Coloureds 14 percent, and whites 72 percent.[17]

Dian and his father had been hired to manage the farm of a wealthy white South African. The farm had been sitting unused and they were charged with getting it up and running. I should say, the land had been unused *as a farm*. But it had been used for living. Local Black families had moved onto the land and built homes. Dian and his father's job was to get them off. Backed by a court order and with a nod from the sheriff, Dian's father had been breaking down the shacks to run off the "squatters." In response, Dian said, the Black families had invited him to a meeting, where he was killed.

Dian fled to Australia in grief but came to realize that he didn't want to lose his country as well as his father. And, surprisingly, he also realized that the distribution of land needed to change. He argued there was a way to do land reform that had already been set in motion in South Africa but was then put on pause. He said that former president Jacob Zuma had started to buy up large farms owned by white farmers to give back to the local communities. The idea was that the community would give some land to local people to live on and farm but would also hire the white farmers back to run the larger parcels and teach the new Black farmers what to do. This would keep the money local, teach Black farmers how to run farms, and create alliances between the white and Black farmers, all while maintaining the economy. Dian said that the current president, Cyril Ramaphosa, had put it on hold.

A less enthusiastic view of Zuma's program had been given by another farmer, Gerrit Roos, back in 2014, when it was in operation: "The government gives land to Blacks and gets a white farmer to teach them to farm, and sometimes it works and sometimes it doesn't. The new owner is often unprepared for the capital and equipment needed to farm the land; within a year or two the land ends up back in government hands and the original farmer buys it at a discount."[18] Professor Ben Cousins of the University of the Western Cape wrote recently of land reform during Zuma's time in office, that "corruption was rife and elites were favoured."[19]

The initial land reform strategy was to match "willing sellers" with "willing buyers." When this did not lead to significant change, the government tried a number of strategies. Landless people occupied land in large numbers without waiting for anyone's approval. And corruption and favoritism have been ever-present.

In October 2020, President Ramaphosa's government announced a new plan: to release about 900 state-owned farms for public purchase or long-term lease, under conditions that strongly favored Black farmers and made the land nontransferable so it wouldn't end up in more powerful, white farmers' hands. Prospective land recipients must show evidence of farming experience or willingness to learn. The government promised inexperienced farmers technical assistance in the agricultural, financial, and record-keeping elements of landholding, and it acknowledged what everyone knew, that corruption had been a problem.

But Dr. Cousins argued that this plan was still bound to fail because it focused on promoting Black "emerging" commercial farmers. He said that relatively few people would benefit; they would be marginal to the large-scale, commercial farms; and they would face high probabilities of failure due to debt and inadequate support systems. He argued that the better focus would be small-scale farms producing fresh vegetables and other produce and small stock such as sheep and goats. That could create a substantial number of jobs, because small-scale farming is more labor intensive.

The economics of South Africa's impoverished, landless majority has also led to poaching by large cartels, which can hire local people to do the actual poaching. We've heard about the rhinos, but not about the macadamias, avocados, oranges, etc. There is a huge security industry of cameras and fencing set up to catch bands of burglars who pull up with trucks in the middle of the night and clean out a harvest.

In the face of this, farmers have come up with varied responses. The farmer in Limpopo with whom I harvested macadamias uses camera traps designed to track wildlife to monitor movement on his farm. The couple who produces the delicious, spicy olive oil at Portion 36 Olive Orchards that I collected for Abigail's crudité have opted, against their adult children's advice, not to build walls or barbed-wire fences. Arend and Birgitta Hofmeyr told me that they refuse to live that way and believe that that kind of security only exacerbates the problem.

I saw firsthand another alternative, at the Goede Hoop Citrus and Carmién Teas operations in Citrusdal, where I visited for Abigail's velouté and punch. There employees are given ownership stakes in the farms.

Walking through the orange groves, Goede Hoop's director explained that the company subscribes to employment equity. He said they are "actively in process to address the imbalances" and have given 10 percent of the company's shares to Black employees, including both permanent and some seasonal workers. He emphasized that this was done without a government mandate. The founder of Carmién, Mientjie Mouton, told me while we were out harvesting "tea" leaves, that its partnership means that "six hundred and twenty-six workers and dependents have a shareholding in any Carmién Tea product." The Carmién Tea website states that the company "actively supports community development on shareholders' farms." They are betting that this is a more sustainable response to the problem of poaching.

An interesting side note—Goede Hoop sells oranges around the world. China buys the most, and thus makes the market. For example, the occasional little orange carpels (sections) that I found and loved in oranges as a kid have been bred out of all the oranges because they aren't wanted in Beijing (so that's where they disappeared to!). China ends up getting the roundest, brightest oranges, with the US and then Europe in descending order of quality. I grabbed some from a box marked for shipping to China to give to Abigail.

After hitting the coast for lobstering and pulling thick black mussels from tidepools, I only had a few ingredients left. I'd already harvested sorghum up by Joburg for David Higgs of Marble, and I was down to the remaining native forage items and the milk, cream, and butter.

Visiting Camphill Village West Coast's dairy farm to make butter with CEO James Sleigh was another bright spot. It was as if Abigail picked the places to give me a lift on my journey around South Africa. Seeing the brutal Black poverty, being terrified at every stoplight in the city, keeping bags away from the windows, getting yelled at by my producers for taking a two-block walk from my hotel after a producer was robbed at knifepoint on day one, overwhelmed me pretty quickly. But Abigail's list of food producers felt like an oasis from the simmering warfare based on race and class that surrounded me.

The dairy has been hiring special needs workers since it began. Camphill Village was founded in 1939 by Karl Konig, a follower of the Waldorf teaching method. Konig built a school for children outside of Cape Town on land donated by the mother of a disabled child. In 1964, the farm was created to help those children once they became adults. Until the end of apartheid it was for whites only, but now it is assertively multiracial. James Sleigh, Konig's grandson and CEO of a Cape Town advertising firm, got "fed up with the rat race" one day and left to take over Camphill and make milk. His friends started out thinking he was crazy, though now, he says with a smile, "they are a bit envious."[20]

Not only does Sleigh now make milk, but Camphill is also well-known for delicious, organic, hormone-free full-cream yogurts, cheeses, crème fraiche, quark, labneh, feta, cream, and butter. I milked a cow, watched the pasteurization, and, à la John Henry, got to race a machine through the butter-making process. James gave me a bit of a head start on the butter turner and handed over ten rands (90 cents US) when I beat the machine. With what felt like a broken wrist and armed with some hand-turned butter, I headed off to meet the Khoisan.

Khoisan is a term used to describe two of the original groups of inhabitants of South Africa, San and Khoekhoen, who have lived in the land continuously longer than any other people on the globe. Genetic traces go back as far as 60,000 years.[21] There are an estimated 100,000 San today in southern Africa, very few of whom have been able to maintain their traditional hunter-gatherer way of life. They were pastoralists, raising sheep and cattle as well as gathering herbs and engaging in trade. Social anthropologists explore the overlaps and boundaries between the San and Khoek-hoen in the days before the Europeans came.

As so often happens, groups of people are named by their enemies, and the names start out and sometimes end up as insults. The San, or Bushmen, were hunter-gatherers. There are many San groups and they used no single name for themselves; instead, the Khoekhoen, who were not their friends, labeled them San—"those without cattle." The Dutch called them Bushmen, from the word for "bandit" or "outlaw." According to one account, "the San interpreted this as a proud and respected reference to their brave fight for freedom from domination and colonization."[22]

"Bushmen" is now often regarded as derogatory, with the South African government and academic sources now generally using "San." The people known as San generally prefer names referring to their own individual groups, while some choose "San" and others "Bushmen," if they have to be referred to by names others have chosen for them.[23]

On what was once an 850-hectare wheat farm in Yzerfontein sits !Khwa ttu, an award-winning San heritage center. Here I would be hiking out with guides to forage some of the final ingredients—spekboom, wild sage, and bukku—in what looked to me like a barren desert wasteland....

Spekboom, a sour-tasting succulent, was first up. Unknown to me at the time, it was on people's lips as an environmental super-plant, able to take in huge amounts of CO_2 and act as a carbon sink.[24] After locating this ancient food source along the path, the !Khwa ttu guide, Kerson, explained that, "Twelve thousand years ago everyone lived by hunting and foraging. With the recent change in [humankind's] subsistence strategy we all risk... the end of our planet." We walked further across the dry plains and Kerson pointed out edible plants left and right.

My initial incredulity turned to realization. Of course the "desert" was filled with life; our ancestors had been living and surviving here for millennia. The glory of it had almost been wasted on me. The San lived in small groups of 20-200 people and moved over wide areas of southern Africa where I was standing now. Women gathered *veldkos*—food found on the open grasslands (veld); men hunted antelope such as eland and gemsbok. Even more amazingly, an example of San rock art has been dated at 73,000 years old, 30,000 years older than previously discovered art in Europe.[25]

We came upon some wild sage for Abigail, sage that San and Khoekhoen fishermen soak in buckets of water and use to wash the smell off after the day's catch. I pocketed this for the velouté.

Then came the bukku, also known as bookooo and buchu—which I could never pronounce correctly, much to the hilarity of Kerson and his fellow guides. Over and over, Kerson would pronounce it, this Khoekhoe word describing the oily, evergreen shrub from the genus *Agathosma*, and over and over I'd butcher it. The intonation didn't even have a click consonant signaling differences in meaning between words (or at least I couldn't hear it, which might have been the problem). It's an amazingly powerful plant. Christopher Low writes, "the smell of buchu has been conceived by the Khoisan as a potent force with a role in healing, in perfume use and certain rituals."[26] According to Cape Kingdom Nutraceuticals, a Cape Town-based company that acquires and processes the buchu plant, "the plant's natural anti-inflammatory properties help with pain relief and chronic illness without the side effects of other anti-inflammatories."[27] With bukku safely stored in my shirt pocket, as the smell kept reminding me, I said goodbye to Kerson and hopped in the van headed back to the township to meet Sam for some roadside nasturtium and dune spinach.

With one day left (my final cook with Abigail was the next morning), it was Friday night and time to party. Conversations with Sam had continued to circle back to how I needed to break free from my locked van and get out and experience the township culture beyond foraging. With his help, we convinced my producers that a taste of smiley, a beer, and a stroll on Spine Road would be "good for TV" and would round out the picture of the township.

Spine Road is the location of the block party that started it all, where Sam's cart was stationed way back when, where the township comes together to share a drink, blast music from cars, set up little wood fired grills, and crowd around open-air bars. Smileys are something else entirely, and I ought to have asked before agreeing to try one.

Sam woke me from a nap on the headrest in the van to tell me we were on our way and, guessing by his grin, I knew he was up to no good. Intloko (Xhosa for "head"), otherwise known as a smiley, is a boiled and blowtorch-seared sheep's head. While Cape Town-central butchers got the prime cuts, historically the township got the leftovers. The searing tightens the skin around the mouth, giving it a ghastly grin. Axed in half and laid out on some newspaper, it's a pugnacious sight. This is where we kicked off our Friday-night tour—though, frankly, I could have used a beer first. I will say Sam did it right, starting me off on a piece of the cheek. When cooked long and slow, cheeks are my favorite cut of meat. When it's prepared and served in a restaurant, whether it's guanciale in Lupa's pasta in New York or the beef cheek taco at Austin's Leroy and Lewis, the cheek's soft, gelatinous texture and dense, rich flavor blows my mind. But cutting it out of the face of an animal is a different story. So slicing open the skin, then digging into the sheep's grinning head and eating it was tough.

But I had wrapped my head around it. I knew this jowl and it was good. In my mind we were done, I had cut out the cheek from the face, tried it, and we could move on. But Sam had other ideas. He leaned over and started sawing out an eye.

"You wanna try the eye?"

Hell no! "Sam, do you eat it!?"

"Sure."[28]

Why me?!!

So Sam cut himself a piece to show me, then popped it in his mouth.

And handed the other half to me. I looked away. Maybe if I didn't look at it I could do it.

And so I took it, but as I brought it to my mouth, I glanced down. Big mistake, as half an eye looked right back at me. And once it was in my mouth my teeth couldn't cut it. It was tasteless but gummy—and somehow tough at the same time. Sam couldn't keep the smile off his face watching my horror. Through laughs, he said I would thank him for the experience and, in the end, he was correct; we bonded over my repulsion, and this tale is a mainstay at cocktail parties.

I definitely needed some beer at that point. Which meant onto Spine Road. We heard it before we saw it. Music bumping from car stereos a couple blocks away. The traffic slowed as people cruised, waving to friends, showing off their rides, and looking for parking. There was a bit of hesitation on my part, remnants of the cautionary narrative I'd been fed. But before I knew it, Sam and I had beers in hand and were making our way down the sidewalk next to the smoking grills and mobs of people waiting in bar lines. Kids ran after one another through milling adults, old men leaned against walls with cups in their hands, women staffed the braais. A group of young adults saw the cameras and offered to co-host the

Sam Mokoena and a smiley on a Friday afternoon in the township

episode with me. Ordering a *boerewor* and *skilpadjies* (a sausage and lamb-liver dumplings), blinking away the smoke, and trying to figure out the rand-to-dollar conversion (the whole shebang cost me a buck and quarter), I realized that my fears had melted away and, for the first time, I felt comfortable in this country. For whatever major problems existed (and major problems definitely exist), there was a big, glorious life here. Sam and I cut up the sausage on a paper plate with a plastic knife and ate it, still way too hot, with our fingers, standing by the side of the road in the dirt as the sun exited the scene.

So, perched on the dune, harvesting dune spinach with seagulls screeching overhead, I thought about the history of those sandy Cape Flats. How the British government of the nineteenth century tried to control the shifting sands to open up travel to the interior by heavy, ox-drawn wagons, no doubt to expand its control over the Boers and the Indigenous African peoples. And how the acacia didn't work, and the trash piles started sweeping fires, but this tiny, edible succulent, a native plant, was holding the sand dunes together.

Without romanticizing, or looking for easy answers, I wondered if people like Abigail and Sam, Mama Christina, James Sleigh, and the Hofmeyrs, along with the dairy cooperative and companies like Goede Hoop and Carmién, could be the dune spinach that holds South Africa together. South Africa faces enormous problems of vast inequalities, inherited from centuries of deliberate divisions. It would be a miracle if it could resolve them in the first twenty-eight years of majority rule—especially when, in fact, millions of people *did* expect miracles from their new government and are desperately facing the reality that their daily life hasn't changed all that much. But strangely, hope was the word that came to mind; hope that Abigail and friends represented the change that South Africa needs. That the work of committed individuals could transform the society in ways that even the long struggle against apartheid was not able to. I also recognized that I was witnessing joy, the joy of creation even against overwhelming odds—the recognition that one doesn't have to accept oppressive realities. Another world *is* possible. Can small-group, localized projects based on excellence and collaboration that respect land and build community be part of something transformational? Can they make a difference, as income disparities intensify across the world, corruption and repression go hand in hand, and we hurtle toward vast species eliminations, climate weirding, and planet catastrophe?

Beer, Octopus, Snails:
Malta / Sardinia

Malta is a sun-dappled archipelago of prickly pear, pome-granate, and carob, with orange, sandy-soil gardens carved into cliff faces, handed down through generations with a handshake and patrolled by stray cats that have nicknames. It's *futbal* in the street, in the park, and on the beach; it's packs of cliff-jumping kids. Maltese with Arabic names and British stiff upper lips eating French rabbit stew or Italian pizza, in towns that look like movie sets (and most likely have been movie sets). But as the local saying, "*M'hemmx warda bla xewk*" translates, "*there is no rose without thorns.*" This stark, stunning land has its thorns.

For much of its history, Malta was near center stage in the wars between Catholic Europe and Muslim North Africa and West Asia. Sitting between Sicily and Tripoli, Tunis and Athens, it was the home of Christian military orders turned pirates, who launched themselves from here to attack the Ottoman Empire in search of slaves, spices, and gold. This history is still reflected in the island's people and cuisine. And all of this history is based on Malta's relationship with water, both fresh and salt. The deep blue sea—as well as the just 15.9 inches of annual rainfall making their forty-year journey through the 382 feet of limestone to the water table—means life or death here.

I came to use the water for a beer.

I was there to make a meal with Corinthia Palace's Chef Stefan Hogan, a Maltese who, as a kid, waded for urchin to eat straight out of the sea with some hand-torn bread. He began catering at sixteen with Maltese Catering School and then took a thirty-year journey cooking around the world (St. Petersburg, London, Tripoli), only to find himself back home. Our initial menu ideas focused on the international culinary mélange that is Malta. But as we needed to find ingredients on the ground, the meal gradually became whatever I could harvest locally on this dry cluster of rocky islands.

He ended up making something terrific from what I found underfoot: prickly pear, fish, snails, carob, wild vegetables, and sheep's milk. But it was touch and go, a real test, considering Malta doesn't really feed itself. Local agriculture supplies only 20 percent of its food; the rest is imported. While I tasted Stefan's meal that I

Tasting a meal with Chef Stefan Hogan of Corinthia Palace

was to recreate, he mentioned something that was a hint of what was to come. In describing Maltese farming, Stefan offhandedly said it hadn't rained in ninety days. It was then I grasped that Malta walks a very thin water line. In a country with no lakes or rivers, fresh water comes at a premium. Prior to arriving, water wasn't even on my mind, but it turned out water was going to be my most valuable ingredient.

Our first foray for food was out to sea. Of course, after ninety days straight of sun, there was a storm the day I went out on a boat. Rain battered our van as we grabbed a ride from Malta across to the smaller Gozo to meet an octopus fisherman. Once on the boat, clouds sat on the horizon like a threat as we bobbed, waiting for Luke Cassar to show. Luke is a native. Like Chef, he left to explore the world, living as "a vagabond monk" in monasteries throughout Asia. He believes that everyone in Malta should leave the country at least once to "see what they are made of and learn who they are." We nodded as he walked up, handed me his spear, and hopped on our boat with long dreads pouring out from under his bandana. I couldn't help but think that he looked the part of a legendary Maltese pirate, though when he opened his mouth, his character was closer to westside Angeleno, very mellow and reflective—he said it's his meditation practice and his relationship with the ocean. "The sea here is our wilderness. We don't have mountains and forests and lakes. If you want a sense of wilderness, you find it in the [water]."

As our boat made its way around the island to Fungus Rock (Grand Master Pinto of the Knights decreed it off-limits for centuries because of a medicinal herb grown there), Luke discussed how diving for food is incorporated into his meditation these days. When he first returned to Malta, he and his brother started a bar. But soon the sea called. It was in his blood; his father had started him spearfishing when he was five. But today no one was doing it. It was a lost art and he saw a niche for himself. "I decided to [spearfish] in a sustainable way and educate people about it. I run a free diving business, a spearfishing business, and I teach meditation." Luke's expertise and solidity was a godsend. The last time I went out for octopus, a year before in Sardinia, I'd almost drowned.

* * *

For centuries, Sardinia had been maligned by the rest of Europe as backwards and lazy—a "delinquent zone;" but now tourists from Milan and London were flocking there for the sleepy lifestyle. Turns out the Sardinian way of life created a Blue Zone, where many of the people live to be over a hundred. I had gone to see if and how this was related to their food culture. That disastrous day in Sardinia had started innocently enough. Giuseppe Pirosu, a champion free diver and spearfisherman who was to be my guide, met me in the Bosa Marina. I was there to find octopus for Christano Andreini's *fregola*. Laden with capers, sweet peppers, and fennel, topped with grilled octopus, it's a gem at his Michelin-starred *Al Refettorio* in Alghero. Strangely, although Sardinia is an island, over the long arc of history Sardinians mostly lived inland in the rugged mountains because the coasts were more susceptible to raids and invasions; thus, Sardinian diets have been less seafood- and more meat-based. I probably should have gone for sheep.

As we spun the boat up and out of the marina, Giuseppe mentioned that the waves were rough that day and I should stick close. He was right; the water was choppy and murky, the spearfishing unsuccessful. We did find one baby octopus in a hole in the reef which crawled out of my hand, turned a couple different colors, and squirted the cutest little puff of ink at me. I didn't have the heart to go after it, so Giuseppe mentioned harvesting sea tomatoes instead. They are the sea anemone *actinia mediterranea* and are red and round like a little cherry tomato, and, when rolled in flour and fried up, they are a dish called *orziadas* and can be used instead of octopus on a pasta.

The sea tomatoes sat on the waterline of a deep cove. The rough water made Giuseppe nervous, but I had the delusional confidence of a TV host. To quell Giuseppe's nerves, we agreed we wouldn't bring a camera operator with us and would be filmed by an overhead drone so Giuseppe would only have to keep an eye on me. The water was strangely calm as we swam into the cove and found the anemones and went to work prying them from the rocks—which was tough, because they were back in these holes and I was treading water. All of a sudden, the water in the cove dropped. Giuseppe and I looked at one another and knew what was coming: big waves. I started swimming for dear life. But I wasn't quick enough and the sea came in.

Boom! Boom! Boom! I was tossed up against the reef. The first wave filled my snorkel, which wasn't good. Now struggling to breathe—every attempt brought more water into my snorkel and lungs—I also stupidly kept on my weight belt (from the spearfishing), which dragged me into the deep. Another wave crashed, crushing me against the rocks. But I had Giuseppe. Seeing the terror in my eyes as I went under, he swam to me, released my belt, took a deep breath, and bulldozed me through the waves and out of the cove.

When we got back to the boat, my crew, who had been watching via the drone, clapped and hollered, "Great job, that looked amazing on camera!" But Giuseppe knew how close I had come to drowning and the boat ride back was real quiet. However, there was one sea tomato for the chef in my still-clenched fist.

* * *

Now Luke in Malta had to deal with my PTSD about getting back into the water. But Luke began talking to me about the inner peace that diving can bring. He sees free diving as an intuitive way into meditation. "There's something called the dive reflex; it's our body's natural reflex." When a person (or other mammal) dives under the water, physiologic checks and balances are modified. During submersion, we hold our breath, the heart rate slows down, and our peripheral vascular system constricts, forcing us to relax.[1] Luke describes this moment as beautiful and "awaken[ing] a part of you that is normally dormant. At times, free diving feels like you are flying. You are gliding through the water weightless." I couldn't imagine a better escort into the depths to quell my fears than a free-diving, spearfishing monk.

The sea was rough; we bounced across the waves, the wind growled as those clouds opened up off the coast and blasted us. Strangely, over our shoulder, the island sat in the sun. Trying to keep my mind off the whitecaps and tempest, I asked how good the fishing was. Luke responded that the fish there were very used to people. "They are smart. They are cautious. I would call them 'street smart' if they were in the street. I guess they are 'sea smart!' You have to really study their habits and the temperatures, and know your equipment. It takes a lot of passion and persistence because you will fail *a lot*."

The Mediterranean has been fished hard for a long time. Twenty-two countries have been hammering this sea for 10,000 years, and the tragedy of the commons is turning parts of it barren. I wondered whether Malta was experiencing some of the problems other countries were, and I asked if Luke saw an impact under the water. Luke said that it was an issue and was why he chose spearfishing. "I started studying fish, their habits, and their habitats. When you do this, you know which fish are plentiful and which are not. You can choose only sustainable fish. You can choose not to catch a pregnant fish. When you are spearfishing, you select your fish and just what you need; it's very different than fishing with nets or even rods. I also work with a group in Malta called Fish for Tomorrow and they keep track of which fish are sustainable."

Luke motioned to the captain, and we pulled into a cove between Fungus Rock and Gozo to anchor. Tense, but suited up with a spear gun in hand, I summoned the confidence and went overboard. My game plan was to stay as close to Luke as I could.

Octopi are nocturnal, so we would be looking for a den. Luke mentioned some telltale signs, like black fish that hang around the entrance, keeping an eye on the octopus, almost like little onyx arrowheads pointing it out. Or if you were to come across a pile of crab shells, look above it, and you may find a den that an octopus is keeping clean. A den can be any crack or crevice or car tire or

Luke Cassar back from a dive at Fungus Rock

bottle. Octopi like tight quarters, so it might mean diving down to the bottom and sticking your hand into a dark hole, something that made every cell in my body scream each time. I will say that meditation via diving must come through experience. My time down there was all burning lungs and desperate surges to the surface.

At one point I gripped the back of the boat, half in, half out, the futility overwhelming—while Luke frolicked below like a seal. I never even reached a point of comfort, much less a place of grace. Also, with the rough water and rain, the cove was a bit murky (the rain brought the soil runoff from Fungus). Plus, it had no octopi in it (or we couldn't find any)—whether due to overfishing or just that kinda day, I'll never know. Luke did happen upon an unsuspecting amberjack which he neatly speared, and it was going back to Chef as the main course. And I didn't drown, so I chalked the day up as a win. On the way back, we discussed the future (he also had a toddler). I told him I wanted to bring Harrison to see this incredible island and maybe our sons could play. Luke's response startled me. "It is a beautiful country. But we are spoiling it now. The last ten years, we've really grown, really fast…. There are a lot of people moving here and we seem to be building mindlessly. So if you want to come visit, you should come back soon."

By flying into Malta I had done myself a disservice. This tiny nation begs for arrival into the aptly named Grand Harbour (more humbly known as the Port of Valletta). This passage, used since prehistory, allows a gradual reveal of the 3,000 years of modifications to this inlet. When our boat returned from the fishing trip and hooked around a breakwater southwest into the natural harbor, the shore came into hi-def relief. In front of me and to starboard loomed the main city of Valletta, with star-shaped, 500-year-old Fort Saint Elmo at the head of the Sciberras peninsula. Sailing down the length of this skinny, elephant-shaped anchorage, I saw its legs off to the left (marinas pocketing the four smaller quays) and the trunk disappearing into the distance. To the right, the baroque city that's grown up around the harbor and eaten most of the neighboring villages is the second-densest area in Europe. The ancient buildings sat like a bright limestone frieze on top of the dark sea. But I could also see the future Luke mentioned…in the distance, the fiercely growing economy's building cranes poked up all over the horizon. They were scrambling to erect homes for a population of 514,000 and rising, the population expecting to jump 34 percent in the next thirty years—to 668,000 by 2050.[2]

Malta's populated history goes back to the Stone Age, but with some major interruptions. The earliest known inhabitants lived there about 5,900 BCE.[3] They came from various parts of the Mediterranean world, including Europe and Africa.

There was enough water for the first inhabitants when they arrived. They came by sea and probably started settling close to the shore and gradually moved inland, drawing water from natural springs.[4]

But according to archeologist Caroline Malone of Queen's University in Belfast, climate changes ultimately made Malta uninhabitable for a long period of prehistory. "There was a substantial break of around 1,000 years between the first settlers and the next group who settled permanently on the Maltese islands." As Professor Malone said: "While the first inhabitants were able to survive for a long period of time, they ultimately had to downscale radically when the conditions became too difficult. Their destructive farming methods had a catastrophic impact on the soil and, combined with drought, meant that eventually it all came crashing down, as the islands became much too dry to sustain dense agricultural practices."[5]

Snails here are also looking for water. And in Malta, the lure of the morning dew is the bait. They emerge briefly and then retire before the condensation evaporates in the heat. So I found myself up in the dark, heading out to meet a protege of Stefan's, Konrad Grixti, at his in-laws' garden in the town of Dingli. Konrad pep-talked me with, "It's not that hard, you just need to move a few stones." Konrad, in his forties, also explained, "[Dingli] was much smaller [when I was growing up] than it is today. I would dare say it was half the size. Growing up there gave you that feeling of being carefree. Running out into the sea, riding your bicycle all over town was normal. We played ball a lot outside. Today, Dingli is much larger."

When we pulled up to the edge of town, I was expecting a bustling metropolis. But it still felt quaint with two-story buildings and a huge sky and not a soul in sight. There, unstable short stone walls divided neighborhood plots ("Please don't lean on that!"). Families planted olive trees and wine grapes, collected wild asparagus and wild capers, harvested tomatoes and eggplant for Nanna's *kapunata*. Permission granted generations ago to someone's ancestor meant hunters still stalked those fields, eyes scanning the sky for birds. In Malta, if it flies, it dies—the season I visited, 200,000 birds had been killed. But the hunters shook their heads in frustration when asked about their luck. No more birds could come out to play, 'cause they were all stuck inside on someone's wall. As we left the hunters behind, they remained eyes up, ever vigilant (and a political force in the face of EU restrictions).

However, we were winding our way with our eyes glued to the ground—I was expecting to find the large, extravagant, French escargot—only to be amused by their littler brothers, Għakrux raġel. These quarter-sized snails are the only edible snails on the island and survive here because they can live for months without water. Truth be told, we didn't even need to move rocks. While it took a moment to spy the first one perched on a low leaf, once we were shown what to look for—tan, tiger-striped marbles— they were everywhere. They studded the stones and peppered the plants. It was like the lights had been flipped on. We strolled, meditating (if only Luke coulda seen me), with no thoughts but snails, on a lovely morning walk. Snails can keep for weeks when caught. You collect them, put them in a net, hang them some- where cool, and leave them to fast and clean themselves out (the grass they eat would give a bitter taste to the dish). They have been on the Malta menu forever. Liam Gauci, the dynamic curator of the Maltese Maritime Museum in Birgu, tells a story found in a 300-year-old watchtower log. Soldiers arrived at the tower thinking it abandoned only to find snails cooking on a fire. Then the watchman showed up to explain he had just left briefly to get a fish to eat with his snails.

We collected ours 'til the dew dried up and the mollusks vanished into the air.

* * *

The second group of settlers, who came in about 3,850 BCE, estab- lished a civilization that lasted for an extraordinary 1,500 years before climate conditions and drought became too extreme. Malta was repopulated after the collapse of this civilization, and a number of settlements and villages were established. This group of inhabi- tants probably came from Sicily. In the eighth century BCE, the island was colonized by the Phoenicians, and successively by the Carthaginians, Romans, Vandals (who may have generally been given an excessively bad rap by the non-Vandal historians who wrote about them), and Byzantines. The island was invaded and left largely uninhabited by the Arab Muslim Aghliabids in 870, until it was reinhabited by Muslim settlers from Sicily in the early- to mid-eleventh century. The ying of collapse is also faced by its yang of resilience and survival. The Arabs, coming from Sicily's similarly arid climate, understood how to manage the water resources.[6]

They introduced dry-stone wall construction and field terracing, trees and crops with low water requirements (e.g., carob, olive, citrus, figs, and cotton), and the water wheel. The population of the islands at the time was probably around 20,000 people, mainly living in scattered villages near natural water sources. Although rainfall was not evenly divided between winter and summer and had to be conserved across seasons, the water supply itself was not strained by the population.[7]

The Normans conquered the island in 1091 and Malta subsequently remained under the control of a variety of Christian rulers. In 1530, the Holy Roman Emperor Charles the V leased Malta and Gozo to the Knights Hospitaller in perpetuity, "with power of life and death over males and females residing within their limits," for the payment of one Maltese falcon every year.[8] This is when the story becomes especially dramatic.

The Knights Hospitaller, also known as the Order of the Knights of St. John or the Order of the Knights of Saint John of Jerusalem or, later, the Knights of Malta, were founded in the late eleventh century. They cared for sick pilgrims and wounded Crusaders in Jerusalem but were also responsible for their defense, and gradually became a powerful military force. When the Crusaders' Second Kingdom of Jerusalem fell to the Mamluks in 1291, the Knights initially relocated to Cyprus, and then to Rhodes, where they were based from 1310 to 1522. Defeated by the Ottomans (who had recently conquered the Mamluks) after a six-month siege, they escaped to Sicily before being designated to settle in Malta. The traditional account is that they were reluctant settlers in Malta with few alternative choices, and only gradually came to appreciate their new home. However, Liam Gauci calls this "an urban myth" and says they appreciated the importance of Malta's magnificent harbor before settling and were pleased to become Malta's rulers.

They certainly knew what they were getting into as far as the availability of fresh water. They had sent a delegation to scout out the islands before they accepted Charles's offer. The delegation described the very limited availability of fresh water, describing Malta as barren, lacking greenery, and afflicted by contagious diseases. We have a vivid description written by a Knight a few years later: "…The water is salty and putrid, but there are good springs which are probably due to rain fallen in winter time. The origin of these springs is not very deep, they often disappear in summer but they always diminish in volume. One generally drinks rain water collected in tanks or in ditches…"[9]

So the attraction of the islands for the Knights was definitely the amazing harbor. They did not become the rulers of Malta to become farmers.

* * *

While driving back from foraging snails in Dingli, we stopped at farms for other ingredients in the meal. Farms here are small, farming mostly solitary work, and, given a new pair of ears to listen, the farmers like to chat. I heard about pleasures of Maltese olives ("The best in the world!") and growing organic ("We have been doing it for years, before they had a name for it") but also the grumblings about the encroaching city, the illegal boreholes, the explosion of automobiles which speed around the horse carts, and, finally, the swimming pools. The swimming pools that the farmers do battle with, that suck up all the water because there is little regulation. Boreholes for non-agricultural purposes are being used to extract, on average, three times as much water as those used for agricultural purposes.

Initially I thought the complaints were traditional fears of change, of progress. A desire for the "good 'ol days" lives in all of us. But the more I listened, I found it wasn't only sentimental longing. Over some famous pork sausage (strangely I never saw a pig in Malta), the salty, tart, *Ġbejna tan-nagħaġ* sheep cheese, and a glass of Ta'betta, a local wine, I realized the grumbling was the early wail of an alarm. The farmers and other food producers were on the front lines of a possible environmental apocalypse due to overpopulation. Gloria Camilleri told me about how when she bought Vincent's Eco Estate (and farm), it was surrounded by other farms; now hers was all alone, and she pointed to tall apartment towers seen from the drive. The intimidating buildings arrived at the same time that the rains had dried up and, in her mind, the events were tied together. Trying to race ahead of the drought, her farm manager was twisting his farming practices this way and that to avert disaster. Gloria's spark of idealism and love for her land led our conversations down a morose path. "Nothing will be the same unless people do something about it."

Renny Desira, of Renny's Herbs and Salads, who was already transforming his plot of farmed land into a tented hydroponics garden to save water, felt a different but related dread. He and his wife, Nina, smiled at the success of their children (both off of the farm now and working in offices) but mourned as well—neither child would be taking over the farm. All of us, their children included, sitting around an outdoor table in the twilight of a cloudless sky, were joined by Chef. Stefan, with his hawk nose and determined eyes, and Renny, the farmer, softer and gentle, spoke around and around trying to put their finger on what was gnawing at them. In the car heading back to Valetta, what lingered was their worry over the death of Maltese culture, particularly through the end of its food. Will their lives and long history be overwhelmed by the needs of the new tech workers and British tourists? Who will eat the cheese? The famous sourdough bread *tal-malti*? Or will everything become imported pizza and chips? And how does Malta hold on to itself yet not turn into a Disneyland of its pirate history. Chef seemed haunted by current injustices against the culture, and Renny feared more for the future.

Their struggle wasn't about reviving the past. They argued that the only way to endure was to form a new identity while still maintaining the country's uniqueness. While they fretted over losing their Malta, the heart of the matter could also be history repeating itself—new immigrants arriving *en masse*, and the country growing beyond its means. As the Maltese have put population pressure on these small islands and pushed the boundaries of their lot, Malta has sometimes buckled under the weight. This tenth smallest country on the planet by land mass was once covered in rivers and forest and scrub, but the trees have been replaced with people, the rivers with rocks; the islands now overwhelmingly rely on trade and tourism.

With each population spurt Malta flies too close to the sun. As recently as 2016, Maltese farmers had such limited water that the Bishop of Gozo led prayers for rain to help. It was apropos that we drank wine during this conversation on this summer night—the wine that people historically drank when the wells went dry.

* * *

The Knights' arrival was a coming together of like-minded pirates, making their living from the sea. Malta had long been a home base for corsairs. Maltese historian Paul Cassar comments that by the tenth century, "the Maltese shared with the Greeks, the Sardinians, and the Genoese, the reputation of being 'the worst members of the fraternity of rovers.'"[10] But the Knights brought the piracy to a whole new level.

They turned the harbor into a base for raiders. Prospective corsairs would buy and arm a ship, recruit captain and crew, and set off after Ottoman (and sometimes Christian) shipping. The Maltese Maritime Museum comments, "The Order instituted a whole economy based upon the principles of Holy War, yet it boiled down to simple economics. Protect the private ships with stupendous fortifications in Malta, encourage their raids by providing weapons and dockyards, and ask for a fifteen percent tax. Ten percent went to the Grandmaster, and another five percent went to the cloistered nuns of St. Ursula as thanks for their continual prayer for the success of the raids."[11]

But while the Knights' eyes were on the sea for wealth, they were conscious of the need for a reliable supply of fresh water, especially in their new capital of Valletta, not least to be able to secure it against siege. They built a sixteen-kilometer aqueduct, reservoirs, and cisterns and created one of the most advanced drainage systems of the time to prevent contamination of the water supply.[12]

I went to visit Liam Gauci to learn more about the history of Maltese food and its relationship with the sea (Liam's under-graduate thesis focused on food found on Maltese ships in 1727). Because the corsairs had to apply for their government license to operate, to pirate, they had to keep detailed records. "These records are like tax returns—logging everything they took, how much, the value, what the crew was eating!" Everywhere in the files Liam saw food. Through old government documents Liam discovered how

Liam Gauci at the Malta Maritime Museum

sugar and coffee made their way to Malta. He found court records in which a captain didn't pay for his salami and the butcher sued him. They contained the salami recipe. When Liam came across this type of information he started playing around, recreating the dishes. "For years, my friends had to endure these conversations and experiments as I imposed these ancient recipes on them."

We wandered the halls of the museum, under construction (as the exhibits were being moved). But the limestone columns and high ceilings of the old naval bakery felt like art in themselves. Liam brought me into his small office, which was stuffed with odds and ends. Picture books stood in piles and paintings leaned against walls. Liam put on thin gloves and handled old pistols and bottles, pointed out ancient anchors and maps. The hours flew by. After we examined treasure brought up out of one of the numerous shipwrecks off the shore, Liam brought me up a circular staircase to the exit where bread was delivered to sailors for hundreds of years.

We walked out to a terrace to get one last shot, and suddenly we were done shooting for the day. But Liam had other plans; he invited the crew and me to join him for dinner. And not a regular old dinner but a museum experience he created called "Taste History," which explores the flavors and foods of Malta in the 1700s and 1800s. The meal took three hours and 200 years.

With Liam's research as the guide, two chefs and a scientist brought historical recipes to life. Liam held court as we dined on ancient recipes for bread, seafood, meats, and pasta. Liam says pasta isn't Italian. "It's Mediterranean. It was eaten in Malta, Lebanon, Italy, and North Africa." We had ours with a rich, salted tuna roe. We tried the famous sausage recipe from the seventeenth-century lawsuit. The wine settled us comfortably in our seats and made some of the dishes a little hazy. Was that rooster or rabbit? Did we move on to barley risotto or rice cooked in pig fat? Marty, our director, remembers "there were a lot of things stuffed in things"—and then stuffed in us. Everyone was rapt, all of us recognizing how special this experience was—a dinner curated by a curator. Liam was like a jazz musician at the top of his craft, riffing. Regarding the corsairs: "They were humans like me and you, with the same aspirations—they wanted to be successful, make money, find love, and provide for their children…. They were sailing out of Malta, stealing anything that belonged to the Ottoman Empire, and bringing it back to make money. They were stealing from an empire that was filled with spices. What makes good food? Spices. So the story of the corsairs and the story of our cuisine is intertwined."

After sausage, it was dessert. A bitter orange sherbet. Ice the Knights had transported to the island on an ice boat. The eighteen-hour round-trip journey was a show of the Hospitallers' power as they brought the ice from the top of Sicily's Mt. Etna, 200 miles and a far-off country away.

Liam moved forward through the decades. "My grandmother has a great snail recipe and when I asked her for it, she told me that the secret ingredient was Coca-Cola! I went to my grandmother for this traditional recipe and learned her secret ingredient was soda! Clearly, no one from the eighteenth century was cooking with soda. That's the evolution of the kitchen!"

We all stepped out onto the terrace of the old naval bakery to look onto the most beautiful harbor I've ever seen, at sunset, wine cups in hand. Someone brought around Maltese *anisetta*. The cigarettes came out (sorry, Mom), and we all cupped our hands to light them in the wind.

* * *

The Knights were hardly alone in their piracy. Their Muslim counterparts, based in North Africa, were the Ottoman Empire's Barbary pirates. The corsairs on both sides were players in the complicated dance of trade and war between and within the Christian and Muslim worlds bordering the Mediterranean. Gradually, as the major powers found trade with their traditional enemies to be more profitable than continued conflict, the pirates, both Christian and Muslim, lost their relevance and their power.

The Knights, many of whom were French aristocrats, suffered a major blow to their power when the French Revolution deprived the wealthy knights of their French base. In 1798, Napoleon seized Malta and ended the Knights' rule on his way to Egypt. Ironically, the excuse for the attack, which had been long planned, was that the Knights denied Napoleon watering access for more than four warships at a time, the limit set by treaty.

Although many of the Maltese had welcomed the overthrow of the Knights, the Church and aristocracy continued to exercise tremendous power, which led to a rejection of many of the revolutionary changes brought by the French, and to their overthrow, with the assistance of the British, in 1800. The British ruled until independence in 1964; the last British military bases were closed in 1979 and Malta joined the European Union in 2004. During WWII, Malta's location made it a major strategic base for the Allies, enabling them to interrupt the Axis's supply lines to Libya and to supply British armies in Egypt. It subsequently became a launching pad for the amphibious attacks on North Africa, Sicily, and the Italian mainland. Churchill called it an "unsinkable aircraft carrier." [13] Because of its critical location, it was subjected to an intense Axis siege and, in 1942, Malta became "the most bombed place on earth." This horrendous experience became an indelible part of Maltese identity and is reflected in Malta's flag, which includes a representation of the George Cross, awarded to Malta by George VI in 1942.

Today Malta finds itself at the peak of a hard-charging economy bolstered by "advantageous tax schemes," making it a country people want to move to and do business with. According to *Forbes*, Malta "weathered the euro-zone crisis better than most due to a low debt-to-GDP ratio and financially sound banking sector."[14] The government is pushing the country to become a hub for international web gaming, IT services, and tourism. It maintains one of the lowest unemployment rates in Europe. Between 2014 and 2016, Malta led the euro zone in growth, expanding more than 4.5 percent per year.[15]

* * *

With such a premium on water, how do the food producers manage? I was about to find out, because snails are usually braised in spices, local herbs, and a stout beer. So, for the snail dish, I had to make a bottle of Lord Chambray Fungus Rock (their stout). First stop was collecting water from one of the ninety-five boreholes in Malta or forty-three boreholes in Gozo. Off I went to the Ta' Bakkja Pumping Station. From the outside, the large, cinderblock shed looked like an auto shop in the desert somewhere on the way to Vegas; iron pointy gate entrance, lots of parking in the courtyard, big blue metal doors, men in overalls and boots milling about. But inside there were no cars, no oil stains…just a rusty cage hanging from a chain on a crank above a square hole in the floor.

David Sacco (chief production & treatment officer of Water Services Corporation) handed me waders, a hairnet, an orange helmet, and a N95 mask, and my cameraman/director Marty, David, and I climbed aboard. David, balding with a tanned head, a starched, button-up shirt, and a serious love for engineering, explained that "there are perched aquifers in the western part of Malta that are shallower and sometimes emerge in springs," but that the water was in small supply and mostly used by locals via wells. He was taking us to the harder-to-get-to "larger reserves where the fresh water drains down through the limestone and floats like a lens on the ocean" (because it is lighter than salt water). The aquifer beneath Malta lies in direct contact with sea water! David Sacco nodded to the tattooed, aging punk manning the gears and, with a groan from the gear box and me, we started the twenty-five-minute descent down the shaft into the wellspring of the island.

In 1854, Dr. Nicola Zammit proposed drilling deep wells to exploit untapped water reserves which, according to him, were recharged from the neighboring continents, i.e., Africa and Europe. As wild as his reasoning was, the powers that be accepted the idea and a deep shaft was sunk at Torri ta' l-Armier. This was the first development of the Mean Sea Level Aquifer and was followed up in 1900 when the Wied il-Kbir and Wied is-Sewda pumping stations were connected by a gallery.[16] This underground web grew and grew.

Climbing out of the cage, I was handed a walking stick; David Sacco, his words echoing in the first chamber, said "the walkway we are using is underwater with steep drop-offs into the ocean below." This scared all us crew but none more than Jared, the supremely talented director of photography/editor, who decided to sit this one out for the sake of his expensive cameras (he remained, arms crossed grumpily, by the elevator shaft with his toys). Even Marty, usually insanely fearless, used a GoPro instead of a film camera to have one hand free and maintain surer footing. With these drop-offs in mind, I carefully made my way down a short ladder into the channels. Entombed arched passageways, half-submerged in the aquifer, were carved through the sepia lime-stone. Sloshing through the hip-high reservoir, we zigged our way from narrow corridors to galleries and way stations marked by village names. Arrows, painted on the rock, lit by our flashlights, pointed deeper into the dark, kilometer after kilometer under the island. Stepping into a gallery's larger, subterranean chamber felt like something out of Tolkien; I was waiting for Gandalf, waving his own walking stick, to loom from around a corner threatening, "You shall not pass!" There, in this hollow beneath the earth, I knelt down and filled a bottle.

But it turns out Lord Chambray doesn't use groundwater. By the 1960s, the groundwater was being used 50 percent more than was sustainable. Malta opted not to charge for water use, restrict boreholes into the aquifer, or create water catchment systems. Instead, it turned to the sea—desalination of it, to be exact. Desalination removes salt and other chemicals from sea water, to make fresh water available for human consumption or irrigation. Today, between 35 and 66 percent (depending on the source) of Maltese fresh water is coming out of a number of desalination plants.[17] This is what supplies Lord Chambray its clean, fresh water. So it was time to visit Ghar Lapsi.

In the '70s, desalination technology had made great leaps, and the Maltese invested in reverse osmosis on the southwest part of the island. With the right machinery, water and salt could be pried apart. This would guarantee water to the central and southern part of Malta, where rapid industrialization and urbanization were creating the greatest pressure. In 1982, the Ghar Lapsi plant was the largest desalination plant in the world.[18] The holes for the collector pipes were driven down into the limestone below sea level and the sea water was sucked with great force. David Sacco explained, "if you are lucky, like we are in Malta, and have porous rocks, you can drill beach wells. So that you have natural filtration as the first line of defense." The first filter for larger debris being the limestone itself. Pumps bring the water up to a reservoir above the plant where it flows down into the thousands of semiperme-able filters stacked in rows in the main station, where the water is forced through. Reverse osmosis works by applying pressure to the salty water on one side of a membrane. The minerals stay there while the water passes through to the center of the tube to drain out. DuPont, which makes the filters at Ghar Lapsi, says that their membranes filter salt as well as organic materials, endo-toxins/pyrogens, insecticides/pesticides, herbicides, antibiotics, nitrates, and metal ions. After walking through the process from start to finish, cliffside to filter room, I ended up faced with a spigot that lives at the end of one of the filtration tubes. I opened it to fill a small cup. Hesitantly taking a sip, afraid of the nasty gag of seawater, I was hit with a thunderbolt of delicious, crisp, fresh water.

"Water is life," David Sacco said as we were wrapping up, "and we don't have any natural resources, so we have to rely on the sea." This far-reaching, almost evolutionary step of turning sea water into fresh is as epochal as the biblical water into wine, though the science is fragile and the platform for a country like Malta is rickety. Desalination plants are susceptible to major problems. A July 2021 article in *Climate Change Post* explains: "The Maltese islands lie amidst one of the busiest shipping lanes in the world, and any accidental oil spill could cripple some, or most, of the national facilities for a relatively long time with very serious consequences on potable water production. Should Malta's current water-pro-duction sources fail, Malta has only two days' water supply to contend with."[19] Now, this two-day supply would mean the aquifer has also failed. But this isn't so farfetched, either. The rising sea level due to global warming is an impending disaster. As the sea rises, it will put pressure on the fresh water—a rise of a meter will make 40 percent of the aquifer brackish and non-potable.

Malta has also seen an increase in extreme storms at shorter intervals as a result of climate change, resulting in less rain, less infiltration, and more runoff. With lower infiltration amounts, there is less groundwater recharge. The urbanization of Malta contributes to the problems. There is as much as 80 percent runoff in urban areas, compared to 2-5 percent in rural areas.[20] Roughly two-thirds of the land in Malta is considered urban.

Water quality is also a problem. Groundwater over extraction has raised salinity rates. Salt crystals in fields were noticed as early as the 1960s, and some fields had to be abandoned. If the groundwater continues to be used as it is currently, it will also need to be treated by reverse osmosis. Petroleum and fertilizer are showing up in increasing amounts in the groundwater. "*Kull ilma jaqta' l'ghatx*" is a famous Maltese proverb which translates to, "any type of water will quench thirst." But in this case, its advice is dead wrong.

So what happens now? Both the government and its sharp critics agree in principle that reduction in water use and maintenance of water quality are now essential to Malta's ability to survive, much less prosper, in an era of climate change.

There are lots of proposals of steps that can be taken. For example, groundwater management and pricing could top the list, including restricting and charging for its use. Harvesting of rainwater runoff, reuse of treated wastewater, and growing fewer water-intensive crops would conserve water. Further adoption of solar and wave energy could reduce dependence on oil, thus reducing the cost of desalination.[21]

All of these proposals face technical challenges, but the main challenge that seems to come up is complacency. Raphael Vassalo, the columnist for *Malta Today*, expressed this fear in 2017: "Why is the usage of water not the most tightly regulated aspect of our everyday lives [...] as it so manifestly should be, on an island which doesn't actually have a permanent supply of its own?"[22]

Three years later, Lindsey Hartfiel and colleagues wrote, "Part of the concerns for water quality and quantity center around the lack of awareness about the issue. A national policy to address the problems does not exist yet, and the public is generally poorly educated on the water issues presently being experienced."[23] They suggested that the creation of the desalination program has created a false sense of security, compounded by the continued currency of such myths as the replenishment of the water supply by African or European rivers.

In 2021, Professor Simone Borg, Malta's climate action ambassador, responded urgently to the Intergovernmental Panel on Climate Change report: "If the climate continues on the current course, Malta will become a desert...." While the global causes of climate change require urgent international action, Borg emphasized those that Malta can affect, and the importance of a united national effort. "We owe it to our children and grandchildren to make a change..." she said.[24]

Malta's physical and cultural survival will require huge civic engagement and an end to the complacency in the face of crisis. I can only hope that the complacency is ending in time to make a difference and this lovely island's resilience will win out yet again. This riddle brings to mind a moment in the middle of harvesting for Chef, when I was looking out over the cliffs into the sea outside the desalination plant. I had climbed around a fence obviously meant to stop people from getting too close to the edge (rightly so—the porous rock crumbled easily under my feet), but I really wanted to see the sluice where the excess water, now concentrated with three times the salt, flowed out down a channel and back into the ocean. With water spouting in a rush from a corrugated-metal drainpipe onto a wide slope, it reminded me of the spot where dead Hollis Mulwray was fished out of the

LA River in *Chinatown*. Once back on solid ground, I asked someone from the plant if the fragile limestone ever gave out, and he said that erosion was a looming problem. The limestone had been coming down, bringing the cliff's edge closer and closer to the main building. He said there were about thirty years left, but that he wasn't too worried about it. When I asked why, with a wry smile he said, "Because I'm retiring soon."

Wild Game:
Texas / Wyoming

HUNTING FERAL PIGS AFTER DARK is legal in Texas, so time wasn't an issue. But having no sunlight was definitely gonna be a problem and at 7:55 p.m. the light was fading fast. The feeder, which slings corn, was forty yards away and was already dim; the woods at the far side of the meadow 140 yards away were totally black. The release of the murderous heat, the settling of the earth, the breeze after sunset was in full swing. On top of the dusking, Jesse, my hunting guide, said the spring abundance meant the hogs might ignore the lure of the corn, having so much food in the woods. His words lay heavy—we had been sitting in the hunting blind for a couple of hours now, the feeder timed for 7:00 p.m. long gone off with nothing to show for it, except for a wild turkey, which I briefly contemplated trying to bring back to Chef Garcia in lieu of a boar.

But during the desperate, whispered conversation in which Jesse asked if I had a turkey stamp (hunting permit), and whether the bird was male (legal) or female (illegal), and I, trying to keep it in my telescopic scope, asked how to tell the difference, it ran off into the brush. I'd lost my chance.

My hopes had been high for a boar. After having almost run into a bunch of wild pigs in the pickup while bumping my way down the dirt road onto the property the night before, I hadn't seen one since. Not in the wallows, nor stalking the mesquite-covered hills, nor in a snare we'd left along a trail.

I was leaving the next day, so this was the last chance to bring home the pork belly to make a dish for Chef Ray Garcia. A whole team of people had schlepped to south Texas to shoot the pilot episode of what we hoped would be a TV show about food cultures around the world, and it was looking like it was gonna be the quickest cancellation ever. I was deep in thought, mulling this disaster, when my director of photography whispered, "I see one." Looking out at the feeder, there was nothing. He pointed, "Not there." I followed his finger to a swirl of moving grass out past the feeder about 110 yards away at the edge of the wood. "There!"

I blanched. We all got quiet. Jesse put his head in his hands. That was really, really far for me; I had only practiced on a fifty-yard target and I had never shot anything in my life. Well, except for the pigeon.

I have eaten around 30,000 animals in my lifetime. A crazy-sounding number, but not particularly high for an American in this era. That's two meat dishes a day from the ages four through forty-six. This doesn't include all the Italian subs piled high with a bunch of different cold cuts or the Vegas all-you-can-eat brunches. I don't remember any of these animals, because I didn't pull the trigger, use the knife or the lever. I just remember that pigeon, flopping in death throes—a pigeon I didn't eat, but which sits as a flash-frame in my mind these thirty-five years later.

My mother's side, the Sterners/Holcombs/Mathisons, mostly reside in Utah with a smattering in Oregon and Alaska—and a few in Montana, where the older generation was raised. They are a hardy group. Big, solid folks, working class, rural-tough, cops and veterans, ranch cooks, railroad firemen and engineers, truckers, construction workers, and nurses. My mom's childhood stories describe a home full of love but not much money. One pair of shoes for school and one for play, both bought a half-size bigger on layaway. Local kids banding together to find bottles and cans in the trash to turn in with sticky fingers for change to buy soda pop. Food-wise, her father drove a couple hours away to a farm for the Thanksgiving turkey. Turkeys are notoriously nervous, and some have heart attacks while getting loaded onto the trucks headed to the slaughterhouse. Those were the ones he was interested in, for a tenth of the price.

And my mom remembers the hunting and fishing during the summer at her grandparents' homestead on the North Fork of the Flathead. Venison, kept in the icebox submerged in the glacial "crick" next to the house. I remember the bear rug in the Holcombs' cabin from a bear that chased the family dog into the house, the rug now covering its own blood stain. This hunting wasn't for trophies but for food and protection. It's what a working-class family did to make ends meet. Even today, cousins of mine will go out with the .30-30s they got as some childhood birthday present, sit in a tree blind for a couple of days, and come back with meat for the winter to send around to their brothers' and sisters' families.

My dad's side of the family is Jewish, and, he jokes, was more likely to hunt for a parking space in New York City than for wild game. He ate lots of meat growing up in the 1950s but didn't know anyone who was a hunter (while his father had scored top of his army class as a sharpshooter during WWII, he never owned guns). His family didn't keep kosher, but my father stopped eating pork after a friend gave him a copy of *Esther, the Wonder Pig* and in honor of Wilbur from *Charlotte's Web*.

It turns out my dad's not alone among Jews in his upbringing. Jews have the lowest rate of gun ownership among all religious groups, with 13 percent of households owning firearms, compared to 41 percent for non-Jews.[1] Most Jewish religious authorities say hunting for sport is not allowable because it's wasteful, cruel to animals, and risky for the hunter. "Hunting for food is, in principle, not objectionable. However, [in kosher law] land animals must be ritually slaughtered by hand to render them kosher, which would make hunting them for food with a firearm ritually impermissible."[2]

I grew up in the Bronx, and my introduction to "hunting" was a bit different from my mom's side. Across the street from my apartment was a little park. On Google Maps it's called Classic Playground. It sits at the south edge of Van Cortlandt Park, the largest park in the Bronx. But Classic Playground itself is only about a block long and half as deep, surrounded by a chain-link fence and filled with three full-court basketball courts, swings, a jungle gym, and a handball court. During my elementary and junior high school years, I'd spend my afternoons hanging out there, playing and sneaking into the golf course through a hole in the fence. My best friend and I grew up in that park. Nonstop games and chatting about girls. And all the while I spent my time avoiding the older tough kids. Moving to a new neighborhood as a child is rough. Especially in the Bronx. Having arrived in this neighborhood as a nine-year-old, I was always going to be an outsider. Which meant ducking any attention from the local drug dealers, hoods, and burgeoning sociopaths.

But one afternoon as I walked head-down past a group of older kids huddled around something on the ground, I heard my name.

Not David, or Rafe (my childhood nickname), but "Moscow!" They motioned for me to come, and stepped aside for me to join their circle. When I did, I saw a pigeon flopping around on the ground, a smear of blood on the concrete, and a kid clutching a BB gun, which told the story. One of them—*Michael? Joey?*— shoved the gun at me, looming large. "Here. You kill it." The first time I shot at an animal. The only time until now.

So when I started thinking about *From Scratch*, I came with a decidedly split personality about hunting. But I also kept thinking that if I were going to keep eating meat, I had to deal with the fact that at the core of every meal was the death of an animal. I wanted to confront my distance from what I was eating. I couldn't continue to think of dinner as arriving from the supermarket wrapped in plastic or on a plate from the restaurant kitchen. It was uncomfortable to think of killing the animal, but hypocritical to be comfortable letting someone else do it for me. And it was also a chance to learn about another set of cultures, in which hunting is deeply embedded.

For our first episode, I was working with *Esquire* magazine's 2015 Chef of the Year Ray Garcia of Los Angeles's Broken Spanish, a restaurant that Ray described as an "authentically inauthentic Mexican restaurant," on an organic pork *chicharron* dish (akin to *porchetta*) with a side of tortillas. To make this amazing dish, he takes one large pork belly, trims the gristle and some fat. Lays it fat-side down and slathers the meat side with two cups pureed garlic confit. Adds a fist of salt, a sprinkle of pink salt to tenderize, a cup of *chile de arbol* and layers ten heads of sliced elephant garlic; rolls it and ties it up into a bundle and *sous vides* it overnight. Then, he slices the bundle two inches thick and dunks the slices in boiling oil to fry the outside to a crisp and tops it all with some microgreens and a squeeze of lemon, its juices flooding the plate. There is no better meal in LA.[3]

A week before sitting down with Ray to discuss the dish, I had been in Hennessey + Ingalls, an arts and lifestyle bookstore in DTLA. I'd stumbled upon *A Field Chef's Guide to Preparing and Cooking Wild Game* by Chef Jesse Griffiths of Austin's Dai Due. Flipping through this big, gorgeous coffee-table book, I realized it was basically our show in print. Jesse was writing about hunting for your own meals, and about the importance and pleasures of cooking wild game and fish, touching on the environment, sustainability, the local food movement, and why knowing where your food comes from is a human and humane philosophy. That's when I decided that rather than harvest a farm-raised pig, I should go on a hunt for wild (feral) pigs. If I were going to be making a show about eating seasonally, preparing sustainable and ostensibly organic meals but also discussing food history, I needed to delve into the food production that's part of our origin story—I needed to tap into the hunting that humans have done since our beginnings.

It felt like hunting was the elephant in the room in my exploration of food cultures. And if there were going to be anybody who would help me suss this out, Jesse (who also runs a hunting butchery school), with his local sustainability philosophy and his Winchester .270 bolt-action, would be the guy.

* * *

Hunting in general has been on the wane; only 50 percent as many people hunt now as fifty years ago. Only something like 4 percent of Americans hunt these days, while birdwatching, hiking, photography, and other wildlife-related activities have increased, and it's not clear that hunting will ever regain its numbers.[4] But hunting has long had an outsized place in the American imagination.

Some 70 percent of Americans express support for it. It's also deeply embedded in multiple mini-cultures, ranging from killing game for food to separate working-class and upper-class sports patterns, each with their own ethos and codes of ethics, some of which get enacted into myriad state laws and regulations, and, not incidentally, hunting season and permit rules. And Native Americans have fought long battles to enforce their traditional hunting rights under often-violated treaties.

In 1623, Plymouth Colony specified that "fowling, fishing and hunting be free,"[5] a sharp contrast to the pattern in England, in which it was the province of the monarch and nobility; English forest law, often strictly enforced, limited who could hunt, where, and when.[6] In the 1700s and 1800s, Daniel Boone, Davy Crockett, Jim Bridger, Buffalo Bill, Annie Oakley, and Calamity Jane were celebrated and romanticized, and American hunting was intimately associated with the westward push of the United States—the "opening of the frontier," (and the displacement and subjugation of Native Americans).

As Philip Dray describes in *The Fair Chase: The Epic Story of Hunting in America*, the nineteenth and twentieth centuries saw the rise among middle- and upper-class sports hunters of an ethic focused on the "fair chase": "the good hunter's appreciation of wild places, his respect for the game he hunted, for the rules of fair play and observed hunting seasons,"[7] which reached its peak in the period up to the 1950s. It was during the late 1800s and early 1900s that Teddy Roosevelt—and the Boone and Crockett Club he helped found—saw hunting as an expression of manly sport (and good preparation for potential soldiers). Many women in the West in the late 1800s also became hunters, from choice or necessity.

Roosevelt and the Boone and Crockett Club also advocated for conservation to maintain and protect wildlife, especially big game. From the beginning, theirs was a complicated legacy of animal protection coupled with class bias, ethnocentrism, and racism. Roosevelt's leadership led to the founding of Yellowstone, the first national park, and to the national park system—but also to efforts to suppress Native American hunting within Yellowstone: Roosevelt called it "a serious evil."[8] Charles Hornaday, a passionate hunter and Roosevelt collaborator, and the first director of the Bronx Zoo, reintroduced buffalo/bison to the West after their near-extinction, pushed strongly for wildlife protection, and came to oppose hunting because of the danger of species extermination. He was also an avowed racist who attacked racial and ethnic minority hunters in particular, essentially for not being elite, white gentlemen.[9]

A major outcome of Roosevelt and his colleagues' efforts was the inextricable linkage of hunting and conservation by establishing user fees as a primary funding source for conservation, a relationship that has continued to the present. Thus, hunters are now major funders of fish and wildlife sustainability efforts, through permits and licenses. The decline in hunting threatens this funding.[10]

Hunting exacerbated class and race tensions in the post-Civil War South, as rice-growing died out and rice fields became wetland habitats, attracting large flocks of migrating waterfowl. Landowners leased their land out to hunting clubs, and the South became a hunting destination for wealthy Northerners. At the same time, subsistence hunters competed for the same wild game. Black hunters, who had previously been forbidden to hunt or been limited to small animals, were among these subsistence hunters, not only competing for game but challenging the assumptions of Black subordination.[11]

From the early- to mid-twentieth century, the "fair chase" ethic of hunting was applied by Aldo Leopold to a broader vision of conservation and wildlife preservation. Leopold, whose writing, especially *A Sand Country Almanac*, would posthumously strongly influence the environmental movement that emerged in the 1960s and '70s, argued that humans should not seek to dominate the environment but rather should see themselves as part of the overall ecology of the environment. He believed that wilderness and animals other than humans have to be valued for themselves, not only in relation to human needs and desires. Leopold opposed hunting abuses but also thought it was unrealistic to think that hunting would go away.[12]

Hunting hit a peak in 1982 with nearly 17 million hunters. It has steadily declined since then as rural populations have decreased while urban populations have increased. Hunters are more than 90 percent white and more than 70 percent male. About 30 percent are baby boomers, who are aging out (people tend to stop hunting in their late '60s and early '70s).[13]

While hunting has remained primarily a male-dominated activity, in the 1980s, gun manufacturers started targeting women hunters as a growth area for sales, especially as women had increased discretionary income. I've found the demographic information inconsistent and contradictory, but according to one source, the number of women hunters doubled to about 2 million during the 1990s, and the percentage of women hunters rose from 3 percent to over 10 percent.[14]

* * *

Jesse hoped that a new group of people were turning to hunting, something that Americans from both red and blue states could be interested in. Texas sells the most licenses at over 1,160,000, but Pennsylvania comes close at 967,000, and New York sells a surprising 564,000.[15] Just like canning and gardening, getting back to the land was in the air. When I was speaking with him later, Jesse said he could sense "that people were feeling removed from their food, and that hunting creates the most fundamental, upfront connection to your food." It comes with all this baggage, both negative and positive. People have definitive feelings about it—big feelings about it. This complex mix would make hunting a dynamic first episode.

When I called Jesse up, he said that Texas had no shortage of wild pigs (the most in the nation), so we should come down there to shoot and shoot. Boar are active in the chilly spring days before the furnace of a central Texas summer. Then, as the weather warms, pig activity settles into patterns easily read.[16] So that was going to work well for a TV shoot schedule. Little did we know how complicated it would get! Turns out wild boar care nothing for call times.

Wild boar (or boars—take your pick on the plural), wild pigs, feral pigs, and wild hogs are more-or-less synonymous. There are about 2.6 million of them in Texas, about half the total in the US. They are considered an invasive species, so there are no limitations on hunting or otherwise killing them. They reproduce rapidly—about nine piglets per sow per year, and estimates of the damage they cause to the environment, other species, agriculture, and urban and suburban areas vary wildly. A species is considered invasive if it is non-native to an area and causes harm to the environment, the economy, or human health, especially if it reproduces rapidly and spreads aggressively.[17] Sounds a bit like humans.

Both the very presence of wild pigs in Texas and the huge spike in their numbers in the last forty years are fully traceable to human actions. And few people say there is a realistic way to significantly reduce their numbers, even if desired.

Wild pigs have been around for about 40 million years and pigs have been domesticated for about 9,000 years. They originated in Asia and spread to Europe. Domesticated pigs were introduced to what is now the continental United States by the Spanish conquistadors in the sixteenth century as a food source. Early European and then American settlers let pigs roam free; some escaped to the wild. In times of crisis, many settlers abandoned their land and the pigs wandered off. In the 1930s, Eurasian wild boar were brought to Texas and released for sport hunting. They bred with domestic pigs and with domestic pigs that had become wild.[18] The numbers of wild pigs skyrocketed starting in the 1980s, for a variety of reasons. Catering to the demands of hunters, ranchers nurtured wild hogs and sold hunting leases across the state.[19] Omnivorous wild pigs thrived and multiplied.[20]

Jesse is a big dude with a large, red beard which only just masks high, plump cheeks and a stubborn chin. At some point in the distant future, he could probably get gigs as Santa. Jesse came to hunting relatively late at the age of thirty. But growing up, his family fished a lot, he loved being outside, and hunting always fascinated him. A very closed-mouth kind of guy– definitely not a talker, or at least not with me. In this Texan way, he was cagey about a New Yorker who didn't really know what he was doing. As I met him at Dai Due, which *Bon Appetit* calls "trailblazing" and "uniquely Texan,"[21] Jesse was leaning back and looking at me the whole time, always seeming to be wondering about my New York motives, though a dry wit would peek out every now and then when he was most comfortable.

Jesse told me that there's a heritage pig farm down around Corpus Christi that he gets his restaurant's pork from. The farmer raises incredible Berkshires and Red Wattles and Old Spots—only Old-World breeds—running basically wild, foraging acorns across a ton of fenced-in acreage. But the farmer also has a lot of land that isn't fenced and there are deer and wild boars roaming around, so he lets hunters come down and bunk in some of his cabins.

These cabins are on untouched, primal shrubland right on Lake Mathis (officially Lake Corpus Christi) which is fed from the Nueces River—the one-time Texas/Mexico boundary. Jesse told us that it would be hot, brutally hot, during the day—Mathis has a humid, subtropical climate—so we needed to pack a hat and light clothes. And that I better get some snake boots for the rattlers.

So after hitting up a Dick's in Austin for knee-high boots for the crew (I'd have bought snake waders if they made 'em—Western rattlesnakes grow up to seven feet long), my team jumped into a white passenger van and headed south with a brief stop in Lockhart for BBQ. Four hours later we pulled up to a crossroads in Sandia, TX, population 370. The meeting spot was Grunt's Texas Cantina, a one room clapboard drinking hole sitting alone in the middle of a dirt patch with Old Glory twisting on a flagpole out front. We walked into the icehouse and I was like, "Oh, my goodness, I've seen this place in movies." Two blacked-out windows and the crack under the door seemed like the only sources of light. It was dim and small. There was a pool table. A flickering neon, generic beer sign.

We got there early, around three p.m., and people were drinking—about six of them at the bar. We took some seats at a table, a bunch of city slickers, ordered a round, and waited. The owner of the pig farm, Loncito Cartwright, showed up; tall, gangly, and rugged, in beat-up boots, Loncito rang very cowboy, but at the same time, hippie. His cowboy hat sitting atop long, gray hair tied in a ponytail. Right off the bat, he felt iconoclastic, especially here in Texas, the guy who raised pigs but cared about heritage organic and named his company Peaceful Pork. With large tracts to wallow and snort around in, his pigs live the life until the day that they're put on a truck. He's an example of the raising of animals for consumption done in a humane and ethical way. At the same time, his hippie hair belied one of these guys with a "don't tread on me" Texas attitude. He spoke in broad, looping circles about how, for different reasons than his "low-taxes, anti-immigrant" neighbors, he wanted space to grow and raise his own food and drink his mezcal. That mezcal that would give him an edgy glint in his eye around eleven p.m. As we walked out to his pickup truck, I mentioned the mezcal I brought as payment for the weekend. He had insisted on "no cash," just five great bottles (I called Ray for advice)—that we would end up sharing.

By the time we turned off the road onto his property, the sun was hitting the horizon. We wove our way down farm roads and through post-oak and wire fences, dust behind us like a comet's tail. With every gate we had a laugh as my producer Todd tiptoed out of the safety of the truck, clumsy and inexpert, to open and close them—the snake boots were deep in our luggage. Then we passed a farm dog coming up the road. Blind and walking with this horrible limp, he looked like a mutant from a nuclear meltdown.

We were like, "What happened?" Loncito was like, "Oh yeah, the dog got bit by a rattler, disappeared for a couple of weeks, came back. This is what it looks like now." No more laughing at gates after that.

And then, suddenly, like a little meteor shower shooting across the sky, we saw ten boar flit over the road, first one, then another, and then a sow and *whoosh whoosh whoosh*, her seven babies. The farmer pointed an eyebrow, "This time of year all sows are either pregnant or have piglets with them." As quick as they were there, they were gone into the brush. But seeing them got my heart racing. There were wild pigs here. For me to hunt.

* * *

People have been hunting in south Texas for at least 11,000 years. How they've hunted has changed dramatically over that time. Most of the time, deer have been the most important game species. Bison were also important but largely disappeared about 9,000 years ago. Small game have always been hunted as a regular food source, but haven't had the cultural and economic cachet of deer.[22] Now, deer are still the primary target of hunters—Texas Parks and Wildlife estimates that hunters killed 838,000 whitetails (the most in the US) during the 2017-2018 season, in addition to 44,000 mule deer and 51,000 javelina.[23] But killing boar is big business with very modern technology; helicopter companies charge thousands of dollars to customers to take them airborne to shoot boar with machine guns.[24]

In 2017, Texas Agriculture Commissioner Sid Miller put forward a bill to poison all the wild boar on the grounds they did so much economic and ecological damage.[25] The bill made strange bedfellows of the NRA and environmentalists, who joined together in killing it for a host of reasons, ranging from the danger of people eating poisoned pork, to the risk to other animals, to the economic damage to the hunting and eradication industries, to the particularly painful aspects of death from warfarin.

What stands out to me is how very Anthropocene and very American this situation is. People brought boar from Europe and Asia, first for food and then for sport, without thinking about long-term consequences. Boar, a very intelligent and sentient species, multiplied and became both a "nuisance" and a source of BBQ and profit. Now, the economy and politics are fitting themselves around boar's enlarging and seemingly permanent presence. People have been the driving force at each stage of the boar's story, and now boar's fate again depends on humans' decisions.

At the same time, a wild pig (or deer or elk) has lived its whole life in freedom, with its worst moment coming suddenly at the end. Most of our food comes from factory-farmed animals who live their whole lives in horror, with death ending the misery. Advocacy groups such as Factory Farming Awareness Coalition have documented their conditions. Talking to food writer Mark Bittman, podcaster Ezra Klein said that "capitalism and philosophy [have converged] to create a food system that…is poisoning us and poisoning the earth and inflicting cruelty to other creatures on a scale that breaks your mind if you try to contemplate it."[26] Nicholas Kristoff, then a *New York Times* columnist, wrote of the torture undergone by Costco rotisserie chickens.[27] And one of the most concise and horrifying descriptions came recently from a mainstream TV station in Wichita, Kansas, in the heart of factory-farming country. Andrew Lisa of ABC's KAKE-TV graphically summarized current factory farming:

> "Designed to maximize production and profits while minimizing expenses without regard to animal welfare, factory farms breed, raise, kill, and process hundreds of thousands of animals in enclosed, unclean, dark, poorly ventilated, and horribly overcrowded indoor industrial settings without fresh air, grass, or sunlight. Not only are disease and infections rampant, but animals—often from birth—undergo tortuously cruel procedures like tail docking, beak-burning,

and castration without any pain mitigation, all of which is performed by poorly paid, overworked, mostly-immigrant employees who are frequently subject both to physical injury and psychological trauma."[28]

So, in contrast to how the bulk of our meat arrives on our plates, can hunting be seen as a more humane alternative?

* * *

The caravan pulled up to a stunning, newly renovated farmhouse. It was so nice it brought to mind legendary farmer Joel Saladin's quote: "Frankly, any city person who doesn't think I deserve a white-collar salary as a farmer doesn't deserve my special food."[29] We all piled out to find Jesse and his staff in the kitchen with awesome wild boar tacos from Dai Due waiting for us. We unsealed the first bottle of mezcal—smokey, scotch-like Fidencio Sin Humo (which I have since used as a whiskey replacement in Old Fashions). With the taco's warmth in my belly and the light buzz in my head, I found an angle of repose against a counter and grinned—surveying the scene, listening to our director Clay Jeter (the supremely talented director of multiple *Chef's Tables*) and Jesse play six degrees of separation in the food world. The night's sounds eventually crept in from the windows.

Up at dawn, I looked out over Lake Mathis, which had been hidden in the dark. Flat and layered with mist, tons of water-birds were taking off and coming in like it was Heathrow. We got a shot of the fog lifting for opening-credits atmosphere and headed to meet Jesse and do some target practice (killing some paper from a picnic table with a sandbag tripod). His hunting safety lesson contained one of the most important and powerful pieces of advice that I would hear, and it was repeated in different ways again and again from the ethical hunters I have worked with since: "The last thing you want is to wound [the animal] so that it runs off" in pain.[30] The most important thing about hunting an animal is to make sure you know what you are doing so you can get a clean, killing shot. The distance to the target, the type of weapon, the angle, the roughness of the terrain, the weather, and my own skill level would all play into whether or not I should try for the kill (or whether I should even be out there hunting). So we spent the morning shooting at a target at fifty yards until I could hit the circle at the center over and over and Jesse felt comfortable.

Jesse explained we were going to try and get the boar three different ways. First we would lay some snares. The snare worked like a loop slip wire (similar to a garrote), which we would tie to a fence. We would walk the fence until we found a pig trail running beneath it (or, as Jesse calls it, a "Hog Highway"). If a boar tried to nose under, he or she would find themselves noosed; any movement would only cinch the snare tighter. Once the snare was set, you would leave and come back to check it every few hours. This was the laziest of the three techniques and wouldn't test my skill with a rifle—all you do, once the pig is captured, is put a bullet in its brain up close with a handgun. A unique issue was the possibility of catching another animal like a deer or coyote by mistake, because you can't cut them loose, so—note to self—you don't want to catch other animals, and you want to put the pigs out of their misery quickly.

Between visits to the snare we would go after pigs on foot, which we felt was gonna be the most cinematic, but unreliable. Boar stay in the shade or the mud all day, surrounded by mesquite grassland, when they're wallowing; with a wing and prayer you might be able to get in there and sneak up on them through one of the few stands of live oak or, more dangerously, through the long thorns of a blackbrush acacia. Thus, very unlikely.

If those failed, we were gonna get in a blind, which was a wooden, ten foot-by-five foot structure out in one of the meadows fronted by a corn feeder that had been running nightly for two weeks in preparation. Blinds are usually built like sheds, with rectangular portholes for shooting; but some are even tiny perches up a ladder in a tree with no walls, and they can also be tents. We would have two, one shed and one tent. A tent (which you have to leave there a couple of weeks ahead of time so that the boar get used to it) for the crew to film and record sound out of, catty-corner to a wooden shed about five feet off the ground which Jesse, my DP, and I would be in. The feeder is a battery-powered, 400-pound, "varmint-proof" metal box that projects corn "thirty to fifty feet in a wedge-shaped pattern"[31] on auto every evening at seven to create a consistent feeding time.

Truthfully, the corn feeder threw me. Luring the boar felt like cheating in a way, and I definitely didn't feel like it fit in my idea of the "heroic hunter." Walking the wallows in big boots holding a rifle felt close to what I imagined, but the snares were more like trapping (is that hunting?), and sitting in a blind felt a little like a gray area. But while setting up the snare, Jesse reminded me this was hunting for food, not sport. It's not a macho thing, it's a necessary part of catching and cooking wild game. Jesse is very much a food hunter. Later he told me, "I stop hunting when I have enough food, and I hunt only for the animals I really enjoy eating, like deer, pigs, turkey, and dove. I don't mind if I don't get an animal at all."

Jesse also mentioned a couple of issues. We had one fewer day in the field than we thought. We couldn't hunt tomorrow because we needed to freeze the pig overnight to butcher it the next day before our flights back to LA. Additionally, the boar had just gone through a winter, so they were gonna be skinny—which meant my chef was likely not going to be happy, because he needed a fatty belly for the dish. In my mind I told myself that I was gonna get lucky and find the fattest pig in the woods.

But by around five o'clock, I was just hoping for even the scrawniest pig. I had gotten nothing but a sunburn. And Jesse, well, Jesse was kind of bugging out. He knew the TV show was riding on us getting a boar, and his phone call promising tons of Lone Star swine now felt like fantasy. We'd checked the snares... nothing...checked again and again...still nothing. I could feel the tension vibrating off of him. We did a couple cursory walks into the wallows following tracks, but the brush was dry and crunchy and the boar heard us coming and we heard them take off. So, at six o'clock, we drove out to the blind. We had to get in there and settle before the seven o'clock feeding. And, in the dark interior, we all realized this was it, now or never—it all rested on this blind, this feeder, and this hunter. Our eyes were glued to the field in front of us, willing for pigs. Seven o'clock came and went, the corn spat, the turkey split, the sun dropped like a leaky balloon, and then Matt noticed some grass moving in the distance.

In the tall turkeyfoot grass, you could barely see the hog. I don't even know how Matt did, but, after he pointed, I could just make out a brown hump, the top section of the ridge of its shoulders, as it leaned down to eat. Not the largest target—*fuck me*. When I found it through the scope, the profile of a pig's back leapt close, right up against my eye, and I relaxed. Trying to keep the gun aimed slightly lower, at the area broadside into the shoulder (for pigs, hunters say you try to "pin the shoulders together" 'cause the skull is too dense) it suddenly felt like a video game—almost made me forget it was an animal. It became about the process.

There was something I wanted to accomplish through this scope. I was trying to stop the image in the scope from jiggling all over the place, and Jessie was in my ear, saying, "Breathe. Like I told you, breathe, like I told you."[32] Had he told me how to breathe? Oh yeah. I had to breathe in, then breathe out so that I was steady, pull the trigger at the conclusion of the breath. Any shifting with these breaths would create exponential repercussions 120 yards away. So I breathed, like he told me, and I pulled on that trigger, which felt like a hundred pounds, and *CRACK!* I saw the legs go up and the pig go down as the scope recoiled out of my sight.

And then it all came out. The whole day of worry, the late-day frustration, in a *whoop!* Jessie and I gave each other a big hug. And we were pounding on Matt, the DP's, back. All bouncing off each other and hollering inside the blind, "Did ya catch that?!", into the walkie to Clay. I mean, we were alive. We were alive, in that moment, filled by this intensely singular experience. Totally separated from the fact that I just killed an animal, that wasn't even on my mind. I had done what I set out to do.

The remove, caused by the physical distance and the scope—that video game feel—ended when we started down the steps of the blind. As we moved across the field, it was dark, and we came upon her twitching, black shape…. It was a sow with no piglets. She wasn't dead; I had spined her. She was on her side, sort of spinning in a circle, and you could see that was where the grass had been flattened and crushed. And she was snorting blood. Her upturned eye was looking at me like a furious "WHY?!" beaming like God's flashlight. And what I had done hit me all at once, a wave of terrible sadness.

Domesticated pigs and wild boar are smart. Pigs are smarter than any other domesticated animals and they are easier to train than dogs and cats. They are very social and are among the cleanest of animals—they won't pee or poop near their living areas if given a choice. They wallow in mud to cool off because they can't sweat. They are naturally lean unless overfed by humans.[33] They also feel pain and squeal when they sense pain.

Jesse said, "We have to put her down quickly." He handed me a pistol. I walked over about six feet away; she squealed and huffed a mist of red, and he yelled, "Closer!" I moved within a foot and *bang*, "Closer!", *bang*, in the head. She slumped and some birds took off out of a tree like in the movies.

It was horrible. Me standing in the night holding a pistol, the limp animal with a dark hole in its side and two in its face, the circle of matted, bloody grass. Her shriek echoing in my mind. Right there I got why Americans have moved away from hunting and generally removed themselves from the slaughter of the animals they eat: this moment of death, combined with the Disneyfication of animals and our deeper understanding of animals other than human. The knowledge that these creatures we once believed were only there to serve our needs have sentience and language and customs and names like Porky, Babe, Wilbur, and Piglet. Right there, I wanted this experience to be over, to shirk my responsibility of field dressing and butchering. To create a wide berth between this act and me. Right there, I had a revulsion rise up with flickering thoughts—to get away from the filthy, wild-piggy smell, not wanting to touch the caked mud in the bristly hair or the congealing blood, or the ticks, the ticks that pig must have. And finally, I thought…this was why I had come to hunt—to confront the reality of where my food comes from.

Now, Jesse went into autopilot while I was still processing what had just occurred, stuck in the liminality. He motioned for me to grab the back legs, which I don't remember doing, and he got the front. We shuffled across the field towards the pickup truck. I was watching her loose body jiggling and swaying, thinking about her death and how the jiggling related to a lack of consciousness. And then my eyes caught on her belly. "Wait a minute.... This pig has a very fat belly! Maybe Ray isn't gonna be so disappointed." Jesse saw me staring, just said, "It isn't fat...."

And that's when I noticed the large teats.

* * *

Three years after the visit to Lake Mathis, thickened calluses repping a few years working on a show about food production (no longer do I have "actor hands"), I found myself on a bow hunt for elk in Sheridan, Wyoming, for Harley-riding Native American Chef Antonia Armenta-Miller of Bonafide Food Truck, named by Food Network as Wyoming's top food truck.[34] Antonia served me a meal of grilled and skewered elk her brother had taken the previous year. She accented it with horseradish cream and a buffalo berry/wild plum sauce, all found within twenty minutes of Sheridan. My mission was to replicate this dish from scratch.

Photo by Marty Bleazard

Chef Antonia Armenta Miller in front of her food truck in Sheridan

Sheridan is a little town right at the base of the Bighorn Mountains, about twenty-five minutes from the Montana border. It's named for Philip Sheridan, who commanded post–Civil War US army forces on the Great Plains and celebrated the extermination of the buffalo by sportsmen and, especially, by "market hunters" who killed buffalo for their skins because it would lead to the "settle[ment] of the vexed Indian question" by eliminating Indians' food supply.[35]

Folks around Sheridan are very afraid of Californians moving there and changing their way of life—most everyone I met brought it up. They should be, because it's gorgeous there (and citizens have 3.6 times the voting power of Californians), though I heard that February rolls around and smacks everyone and all the Angelenos scurry back to their corner of the country. We were there in the middle of the coronavirus pandemic, and nobody was masked, and nobody believed that it was even real.

Hunting-wise, times had changed a bit. Hunting was on the rise due to an unexpected turn: COVID. In 2020, hunting numbers across the country shot up, likely because it was an outdoors activity. People were "staying away from folks by looking for turkey."[36] States' resident hunting permits jumped 13 percent in Michigan, 30 percent in Nevada, and 28 percent in Idaho from 2019. Michigan saw a 67 percent increase in permits for people who had never hunted before, and a 141 percent increase in youth permits.[37] Economics also played a role. Food pantries usually reap the benefits of deer season, but wild game drop-offs in 2020 went down, even with the jump in permits. Makes sense with the collapse of the economy, and as hunting provided pounds of fresh, free-range, wild meat at between $1.50 to four dollars per pound while meat bought at a grocery store could reach as high as twenty dollars per pound. And also being self-reliant, in this frightening time, hunters could take care of themselves. There was this fear in the air of the unexpected, of supermarket runs and gas shortages; that a civil war was brewing and how was anybody going to survive? I'm sure lots of hunters said "I told you so" when COVID hit. With hunting, you know, at the very least, you can go and feed yourself.

Bowhunting is just one of a number of ways to hunt; there's also rifle, spear, traps, spotlighting in the dark, even muzzleloaders with lead shot—though in Wyoming, you are not allowed to fly over in helicopters with machine guns. My Wyoming outfitter, Gene Leath, had started me with a compound bow and soon realized it was going to take a lot more practice for me to bowhunt ethically. The right-handed bow he borrowed from a friend had such a heavy draw weight—a measurement of the force needed to draw a bow—that I could barely pull it open to aim at my pretend elk. Bowhunters need to be able to smoothly draw without having to lean back, but at the same time try to use the heaviest weight they can for more ethical (lethal) shots. In the back of my mind, I had a feeling Gene wanted this New Yorker to realize how hard bowhunting was—someone can't just show up and think they can bag an elk.

Even when we switched to a fifty-pound weight (the minimum when hunting elk or moose in Wyoming), left-handed bow (I'm ambidextrous), which I could draw, I wasn't able to cleanly hit the target at forty yards. It's standard to practice at twice the distance you intend to hunt—in this case, twenty yards. Gene realized I was a bit over my skis here and, echoing Jesse in Texas with regards to not hurting the animal without killing it, he switched me to a crossbow. He mentioned that was sometimes used as a gateway from rifle hunting to bow. The hunter needs to sneak up closer with a crossbow than with a rifle, so there is more of a level

Struggling with a bow as Gene Leath looks on

playing field, but a crossbow is less technically complicated than a compound bow.

Without the extra distance a rifle would give me and without the blind, the hunt was much harder. We needed to get close, and that meant walking for hours to and through a riparian area in a zone for which I was permitted, but which Gene said didn't have many elk. I had gotten my tag late in the season, so it was a zone no one else really wanted. That said, Gene had scouted a couple elk there the weekend before and knew where they hung out. This was much closer to the "fair chase" sporting type of hunting mythos I was familiar with. We hiked, smelled fresh scat (a trick he plays on all the New Yorkers and Californians?), spooked antelope, and finally sat, crossbow ready, watching until the sun went down. There were no spurts of commotion, no marvelous feats or near misses. Gene and I got to know each other very well but we never saw an elk, much less one close enough for me to hit. Afterward, he told me that a beginner bowhunter going for elk has only a 10 percent chance across a five- to ten-day excursion. My three days weren't going to cut it.

All the while our producing team was hearing rumors of hunters in a neighboring town who shot deer in their backyards out of the windows of their homes. Some slept with guns next to their beds, and, when they woke up in the morning, they looked out the window to see if there was anything to take a shot at. "If you shoot inside the house it doesn't make a lot of noise because it breaks the muzzle sound."[38] This hunting lifestyle seemed bizarre and yet perfectly American at the same time. But I was also told I was sure to get something for Antonia if I switched from elk to deer (Wyoming almost has as many deer as people)—which is how I found myself in Bob's house in the cute little town of Story, Wyoming, running, crossbow in hand, from the living room through the kitchen to a back bedroom for a better shot.

The culture that Bob exists in is the most foreign to me. It has a code—he personally won't kill does—but it seems all else is fair game. He hangs heads on walls, does not have a problem with trophy hunting (though he drops the meat off at food pantries), and seems to be having a feud with the local fish and game warden whom he says is out to get him. Not knowing the specifics, I have a feeling it's definitely Bob's fault. His funny, tough-guy schtick masks a cold, sober, lifelong passion, handed down from his father, for killing animals. His earliest memories "were bouncing around in the sagebrush" looking for animals.

My director/producer Marty Bleazard commented, "Walking into Bob's place, it felt…like walking into the ultimate divorcé's cottage, although one where the idea of decor was dead animals all over the walls." Bearish (a six-foot-three barrel of a man) and charmingly coarse with a handlebar mustache and a beat-up trucker hat, he knows he is a character—one with the affability of someone who has dealt with all kinds, guiding hunting expeditions for forty years. On the phone he told me he left the gate open for me and I smiled when I pulled up to his house and found there was none to leave open.

Almost immediately upon shaking hands in his doorway, we saw deer wandering through his backyard. Bob handed me a crossbow and led me to his back bedroom and an open patio door where a young buck was trimming his grass for him. The angle into the yard over his patio's wooden fence was awkward and I put a diamond-shaped notch in the top of the fence, which sent the arrow flying in some God-knows-what direction (I never did find it). The deer looked around quizzically at the noise and sauntered off. Not my finest moment.

Bob had a friend, John, down the street, who was casing his backyard as well, and we were on walkie-talkies so we could go back and forth between the houses whenever a deer was spotted. That house was where I stalked a deer down into a little gully about thirty feet off the kitchen window with my DP at my hip. My heart pounded in my ears as I raised my crossbow only to see a next-door neighbor on his lawn mower drive through my sights just behind the deer. This was the opposite of the calm, collected hunting Gene and I had done, but it would be a lie to say that this visceral, almost frenetic, style wasn't an addictive adrenaline rush. Back at Bob's in the early afternoon, I finally took down a doe. My arrow went through her and into the fence at the rear of the yard. She went back behind his woodshed to die. We gutted and washed her in the creek between him and his neighbor's property.

Bob was welcoming and friendly. In Marty's words, "His morals seemed to be in the right place, that place being Wyoming." However, hunting with him brought complexity to the hunting picture for me. I was very uncomfortable with calling what we

Gutting deer with Bob

did, what they do, hunting...but had trouble describing how it is any different from hiding in a shack next to a corn feeder or shooting from any kind of blind.

If hunting is an integral part of different subcultures, some subcultures feel much more comfortable to me than others. Hunting is killing, and just as people kill people for many different reasons, whether on battlefields or on neighborhood streets, they kill animals for many reasons and with many emotions. I don't think hunting can be thought of as a thing in itself, but only in the contexts in which it's embedded.

I was really interested in how other folks working on the show were feeling about what we were going through, especially if they came from different perspectives. Suzann, a field producer who is vegan, talked about how working on the show grounded her more than ever in her plant-based diet. "If I am not willing to slaughter to eat, then I shouldn't be paying someone else to do it for me," she said. "The philosophy behind *From Scratch* is exactly that: *If you want to eat this food, try getting it yourself.* This is the central notion I was drawn to explore along with David and our crew."

Gina, a co-exec producer, describes herself as essentially a vegetarian who eats fish from time to time but can't rationalize why she feels more comfortable with that. She's also ambivalent about consuming eggs and milk because of the animal suffering and environmental impact involved, but isn't ready to give them up. Gina talked about her respect for people "who hunt for food and have a deep respect and reverence for the animals they kill." "But," she adds, "it is brutal and violent. There is no way around that. If one does hunt for food, you will never approach meat-eating the same way again." And, she adds, "Most people eating meat don't hunt for food and most hunters don't hunt for food reasons. And most meat consumed is not hunted. There is no doubt about the environmental impact and the brutality in factory farming. And that is where most of the meat comes from." Her conclusion: "I'm just not eating meat."

So where did this leave me? About where I started. I wasn't ready to give up eating boar, deer, or other animals, although I understand my vegetarian and vegan friends. For me, my concerns are less about the killing; that's a natural part of the life cycle. But the number of animals that are consumed and the way they are raised, farmed, held in captivity, and fed…I have a problem with those. And I felt comfortable with Jesse, Gene, and their careful hunting ethics. And with the fact that I killed the boar and deer for food. But do I also think about how the boar looked when she died, and about the fact that she was a sentient expectant mother? Yes.

Round Scad, Patis: Philippines

My son's maternal lineage is of the Y-chromosome haplogroup, most probably originating 25,000 years ago in the fishing villages of the Nivkh people in Siberia, on the island of Sakhalin and along the Black Dragon River (the Amur). Meaning his mother's, my wife's, one thousandth great grandma was likely fishing for salmon along the La Pérouse Strait dividing what's now Russia and northern Japan. 23andMe, the personal genomics and biotechnology company, gives us an even more specific story. Karen's lineage is the group Y2, which split from Y1 and appeared 7,000 years ago among the marine-based hunter-gatherer populations of Nivkh, the Ulchs, Nanais, and other Indigenous groups around the Sea of Okhotsk and Kamchatka. Four thousand years ago, her hundredth great-grandma probably made her way to what is now Taiwan, and then, soon afterward, one of her descendants made their way down to the Philippines where, many generations later, my wife was born.[1] This is to say that my boy comes from a long line of fisherfolk.

Karen says that describing the Philippines is like aiming at a moving target. The Philippines sometimes appears so alone out there at the edge of the South Pacific with no one to the east 'til the

Americas. It seems to handle disasters with a solitary levelheadedness, with its typhoons, its floods, its earthquakes. But sometimes the map feels very crowded due to the Philippines' proximity to China, Brunei, and Indonesia with all the invasions and the geopolitical chess matches. Briefly, the Philippines was the Pearl of the Orient, only to be abandoned and carpet-bombed by its ally, the US (targeting the invading Japanese). The country went back under US control through the despot Ferdinand Marcos until it wrested itself away to the place it sits now, tenuously autonomous. Between war and natural disasters, the country is like an Etch A Sketch, shaken down and rebuilt every few years.

This can be seen in the language. Words are drawn from whomever was in charge at the time the object came into existence or arrived on the islands. Bikes are *bicicletas*. Trains are *trens* (33 percent of Tagalog words have Spanish roots).[2] Even the country itself was named after Prince Philip of Asturias, a region of Spain, by the explorer Ruy Lopez de Villalobos, in 1542. Vans are vans, buses are buses, toothpaste is Colgate. Kids of the '80s are named Maybelline or Pinky (the next highest number of loanwords in Tagalog are English). But the sun and the moon are from one of the archipelago's native tongues prior to the arrival of the Spanish and the Americans.

Boats are *bankas*, and fish is *isda*. Mackerel is *alumahan*, and seabass is *apahap*. And *galunggong* is round scad, which is what is used to make *bagoong*—fermented fish paste. The liquid by-product of the fermenting process, a watery, brown, very salty jus, is one of the most important ingredients in Filipino cuisine. It is also named in unborrowed Tagalog—it's the umami sauce called *patis*.

The fermented fish paste, bagoong, and its partner fish sauce, patis, are why I found myself at midnight off the coast of

Occidental Mindoro struggling to stand, aka getting my sea legs, in the dark, rolling South China Sea. The wooden slats were slick and difficult to get purchase on. The air was sweltry, with some sheet lightning in the distance lighting up far-off clouds. I sat in the damp, pregnant air, with gooseflesh caused by a breeze of the coming storm. Three days before, our trip literally started with a bang as thunder boomed over Manila and unleashed one of the fiercest rains I'd ever seen. The wet season began as we gazed out of our chrysalis with Margarita Manzke in her (and her sister Ana's) Wildflour Café and Bakery, eating prawn Kilawin and mango and *sumam*, chasing them with a *lumpanug* milk punch.

I first met Margarita (Marge) in LA in 2018 while hunting for some sourdough starter. This is a fermented dough that is traditionally used to make bread. I had asked around, and a couple of people I trusted told me that République's bakery made the best bread in town. République would later become one of Karen's and my special places to celebrate something with a wonderful meal (three birthdays, two Valentines, and counting), but as of then I'd never eaten there. Marge was extremely celebrated and awarded, one of the best pastry chefs in America. Her talent is Robert Johnsonian (my favorite dessert of all time is her mango passion fruit cream pie which simply hypnotizes—it tells you, "Eat the whole pie in one sitting"), and she's a three-time James Beard nominee, with cookbooks and over twenty restaurants in her and her husband Walter's empire.

But I figured it couldn't hurt to ask. So I strolled up to the crowded pastry counter, cleared my throat, took a shot, and was met with silence. Then, "You want a sourdough loaf?" I shook my head. "I'd like to buy some starter." The waitress was confused and went to the manager. Both looked perplexed and the waitress glanced back at me to point. I waved. To elucidate, I have a secret weapon. It's my face. People think they know me because I'm vaguely recognizable. People can't place me, but they feel like we went to camp together or something (it's because of the movies *Big* and *Newsies*). They smile at me on the subway and nod at me in line for coffee. It sometimes gets me things or gets me out of trouble. Finally, the two of them came to a decision and the manager told me to wait. After five minutes, Marge emerged in her chef whites, a little flour in her hair, with a disbelieving "What are you asking for??"

I explained how I wanted to bake bread and I'd heard hers was the best, so could I borrow some starter? It may have been the audacity, or the strangeness of the request (or she thought she knew me from camp), but she agreed. "Come back at four a.m. when we are baking and I'll give you some." I left with a skip in my step and a 3:30 a.m. wake-up set in my phone. Our meeting went down as planned, and I walked off into the cold LA night four dollars poorer, with some amazing starter wrapped in a dishtowel. Two years later I was back, but this time armed with a short film I'd shot about making a taco at Broken Spanish restaurant. I wasn't looking for her dough, but for her to make a dish from Sari Sari, her downtown Filipino restaurant, for *From Scratch*. In the middle of my pitch, when I felt her on the fence, I asked if she remembered someone coming by a couple years ago to buy some starter in the middle of the night. She did! "Well," I said, "that was me."

Anyway, it was Margarita and Ana who had gotten me into this patis mess: the Kilawin needed fish sauce. Ana told me that while Kilawin can be made in many different ways, she wanted to highlight fish sauce in particular. "It has become an heirloom recipe that has been passed down from three generations. So the condiment also holds a special place in my heart and I try to use it when I cook wherever possible." Their extended family owns Lorins Patis and had graciously allowed me to walk through the process of making it. Though, I will say, Marge, ever smiling, with an astral shower of freckles on her grinning face, did tell me, "It's not gonna be easy."

And so we set out to catch galunggong. With the storm not yet upon us, stars were shining through, and a bright moon illuminated our crew hustling around. How we fit sixteen people onto that boat, I have no idea. The banka, named Shammah, one of King David's mighty men in the Old Testament, was a double outrigger (one thin, central hull with two planks of bound bamboo on either side for stability),[3] long, thin, and low on the water and all angles. The outrigger is the first type of oceangoing vessel ever developed and allowed the Austronesians, my wife's foremothers, to expand from southern China/Taiwan into the South Pacific between 3,000 and 1,500 BCE.

While 5,000 years ago they were paddle- or wind-powered, these modern versions are usually outfitted with secondhand and reconditioned diesel truck engines converted for marine usage. The fifteen-meter boat was divided by two masts made of a single piece of wood connected to the hull by metal wire. The inside was painted bloodred, while the outside was white with blue trimmings—it looked sharp and well maintained, only marred by random cans of gasoline, which sat loose on makeshift shelves. Lights for attracting fish, or the plankton they feed on, were up front on poles that could be swung out over the sides. Belt drives for winches to haul nets were installed in the rear under a tented area. With all the paraphernalia, it looked like a water bug bristling with legs and antennae scooting around on the sea. Two large nets with a tight weave like mosquito netting were draped between the main hull and the four outstretched arms that held on to the outriggers. The nets were attached at the corners by ropes for liftnetting, dropping the net a certain amount and then pulling it up to catch fish on the upswing.

Earlier that day we had arrived full of confidence at Sablayan Adventure Camp, a lovely diving hotel on a small bay. Coconut palms, rice fields, and water buffalo dragging carts greeted us down the narrow, peach-colored dirt road leading to this far eastern beach. Some cinder-block homes or wooden hovels appeared along the drive, but mostly it was greenery, with foot- and moto-paths that looked like ditches heading to homesteads in the forest. At a stop, I noticed a man had stepped out of his hut, with a pig rooting and chickens pecking around at his feet. The moment felt as if it could have been from any time in the last 500 years until he raised a cell phone to his ear and a plane soared over-head. The hotel wasn't American high-end-luxury lovely; casual and rustic, it consisted mainly of concrete bungalows. But each room had an overhead fan (I heard rumors of a couple of air-conditioned rooms) and mosquito netting, for which I thanked God because there was malaria on that side of Mindoro. The grounds were manicured—mowed lawns, though, behind the bungalows, there were extra rebar and piled rocks, and the jungle crept onto the property. The main hotel building was thatch-roofed with no walls, and had an open eating area where we could all come down to meals of fresh-picked fruits and some grilled fish and rice. And we had patis on the dinner table alongside some *datu puti*, vinegar spiced with hot peppers.

After the meal, we walked onto the sand and into the bay that was shallow for a long way out. The water was warm. And as the sun dipped into the sea, we were out there playing in the waves. Then Jorge, my father-in-law, called from the shore and we went and dried off and I left to meet the fishers that we were going

Bankas at Sunset in Mindoro

out with that night. We had bought the night so the boat's only mission was to catch the fish for our patis.

Jorge, my field producer and fixer for this episode, was born on Luzon, in Manila. He spent his young adult years traveling the many islands, verifying bank loan collateral for local businesses. Vetting remote mines and lumberyards and their equipment, dealing with bribes of fish and *lechon*, and being protected by armed guards was quite the adventure until my wife reared her newborn head and Jorge had to grow up. After three years he moved his family to California, where he has been ever since. We had been discussing his role in this episode as soon as the show had gotten picked up. He handled most of the local logistics and translation on- and off-camera.

Jorge and I made our way down the beach past bankas pulled up on the sand and feral dogs sniffing through beached trash.

Someone was burning garbage up the way; the smoke was black-black and, when it twisted towards us, the breeze smelled toxic, like hot plastic. When we met the captain—a wide-faced man flicking the ash off a Pall Mall, the conversation quickly turned to the bright, full moon. He felt it was unlikely we would catch anything because during a full moon, the moonlight diffuses the lure lights on the boat. It also penetrates below the water, causing fish to remain deep—to remain far enough in the dark that larger predators can't see their silhouette and strike. There are myriad things to consider—not only the moon, but also ocean temperature; rainy, cloudy, or clear weather; sea currents;[4] and, in recent years, overfishing and environmental tenuousness.

The captain said that it had generally become harder and harder to catch fish—he had to go further and further out and had to stay out longer, and sometimes came back with nothing, but he had come to live with it. According to the Center for Strategic and International Studies in 2019, fish stocks in the South China Sea had fallen by 66 to 75 percent in the previous twenty years. So we had heard versions of the captain's story from others over and over again. Changes in "catch per unit effort" measured how fishers have to spend more time and more fuel to bring in shrinking amounts of fish. I worried that without the fish there would be no patis. My molehill was made from mountains—I was about to learn that emptier nets were a symptom of a much larger issue.

Round scads, for which we were going out to fish, are related to pompano, jacks, and horse mackerel. They are about twelve inches long on average, and are green and white and shaped like a cigar (they are also called cigarfish). The meat is firm and oily, with a strong, mackerel-like flavor. In the US, they are mostly used as bait fish. While they spawn far offshore, they spend the rest of their lives in shallow seas, the neritic zone between the shore and the drop-off of the continental shelf. And, lo and behold, the water around the Philippines is all neritic zone.

We left the dock and joined a flotilla of boats headed out for night fishing. The Occidental Mindoro province is so remote that its claim to worldwide fame was as the place where a Japanese soldier hid out until he surrendered twenty-nine years after World War II ended. The Philippines, an archipelago of 7,100 islands, sits between the South China Sea to the northwest, the Philippine Sea and the rest of the Pacific to the east, and the Sulu and Celebes Seas to the south. Mindoro is close to where Chinese naval vessels are harassing Filipino fishing boats as China and the Philippines struggle over fishing rights in the area.

* * *

I had never heard of the South China Sea until shortly before I first saw it, which goes to show my parochialism. Covering about 1,400,000 square miles, it is strategically located, bordered by, among others, China, the Philippines, Taiwan, Vietnam, Malaysia, Brunei, and Indonesia. Political, economic, and military control of the sea is fiercely contested, in no small part, because of its shipping and fishing importance. It is the second most-used sea-lane in the world, with an estimated third of the world's maritime shipping going through it. The sea contains a third of the world's marine biodiversity, produces about 12 percent of the world's fish catch, and is the fishing grounds for more than half the fishing vessels in the world.[5]

In the Etch A Sketch nature of the Philippines, even the sea's name is contested. The name South China Sea originated with Portuguese traders in the 1500s interested in trade routes to China. In Chinese, it is called South Sea; Vietnamese call it East

Sea. The Philippines used to call it the South China Sea, but as tensions rose with China, the Philippine government started to call the parts of the sea within its Exclusive Economic Zone (EEZ, 200 nautical miles from shore) the West Philippine Sea.

Chinese territorial expansion—creation of artificial islands and related maritime claims—is threatening to the Philippines, as well as to Vietnam and other countries bordering the sea. Even before this expansion, China (and Taiwan) and the Philippines (along with Vietnam, Malaysia, Brunei, and Indonesia) have clashed for years over Chinese claims to much of the South China Sea under China's so-called "nine-dash line." The first maps showing the nine-dash line (originally, it was the "eleven-dash line") were created by Chiang Kai-shek's Republic of China government in 1947 before it was forced onto Taiwan and replaced by the People's Republic of China on the mainland. Since then, both Taiwan and the People's Republic have insisted on the validity of the line, and both rejected a 2016 arbitration decision under the UN Convention on the Law of the Sea (UNCLOS) that declared it invalid.[6]

The fundamental problem underlying the fishing disputes in the South China Sea, both among and within countries, is the drastic decline in the number and size of fish to be caught. Overfishing by the big, industrial fleets—Chinese, Filipino, Japanese, American, Canadian, and Australian—is threatening the very existence of the fish stocks. At the same time, critical habitats have been disappearing; coral reefs will likely become almost extinct by 2050 if global warming continues at its current pace.[7]

As a result of the overfishing and degradation of habitats, there is cutthroat competition for the remaining fish. There is money to be made as fish (along with rice) is the main Filipino staple food. As the medium-to-large commercial Filipino vessels get smaller catches, they increasingly fish illegally in massive numbers within the rich coastal "municipal" waters that extend fifteen kilometers from shore, which are supposed to be reserved exclusively for the small boats of the artisanal or subsistence fisherfolk, who make up perhaps 85 percent of Filipino fishers. This, in turn, threatens the ability of the small-scale artisanal fishing families to survive.

When I asked Ana if the fishing issues affected Wildflour, she said yes. "We do still carry both local and international fish and seafood dishes and products…but obtaining supply at the quality and volume we need has only become pricier and more difficult." She added that it's caused by the exportation of a "huge chunk" of what little fish there is left. "This has resulted in the price of fish to be volatile and to have been on an upward trend over the years."

As the competition for the dwindling supplies of fish intensifies, fishers often use destructive practices such as dynamite, coral-damaging bottom trawlers, and *muro-ami* nets, in which divers pound coral with rocks or pipes to scare fish into nets. These, of course, aggravate the problem. Some of these practices are illegal, but much of the fishing in the Sea, in the Philippines, and elsewhere, is captured in the phrase IUU—illegal, unregulated, and unreported.

Much of the threat to poor fishing families has come from policies of Philippine governments and international agencies that promoted foreign investment and export capacity in the fishing industry. In the late twentieth century, the government invited foreign fishing corporations to fish in its EEZ waters, allowing them to repatriate profits without paying taxes. The Asian Development Bank and other sources supported government construction of ports, increasing fishing and export capacity. But the effect was that foreign fishing boats were taking more fish from local waters than Filipino fishers.[8] Government policy toward foreign vessels since then has varied from permissiveness to prohibition, both in rhetoric and in practice.[9]

Interestingly, these problems are not confined to the Philippines; the Chinese narrative mirrors them, even with China's much greater power. Chinese fishers claim they are harassed and fear efforts to create fishing bans and sustainability efforts, even as China has ignored the UNCLOS arbitration. Clearly, the countries bordering the sea are far from finding a way to collaborate to enforce common rules and restore sustainability, even, perhaps, through separating a common interest in sustainability from issues of sovereignty.[10] So the fish continue to disappear and the communities that depend on them continue to become more and more unstable.

In the Philippines, this instability—exacerbated by climate change-induced rise in sea level—takes the form of millions of fisherfolk, already one of the poorest groups in Philippine society, abandoning the coast and heading into Manila and other cities, further destabilizing the country and contributing to urban crises, rising crime, alcoholism and drug use, and, perhaps not coincidentally, authoritarianism.

One of the responses to this instability in the Philippines, and elsewhere, has been creation of marine protected areas (MPAs). In the Philippines, these started on the small island of Apo, where a fishing community, with help from marine biologists from Silliman University, created and guarded a marine sanctuary, a portion of local fishing grounds in which there would be no fishing. Not surprisingly the fish thrived, and there was "spillover" into the surrounding waters, so the fishers didn't need to go as far out to catch their fish and the CPUE tripled. Over time, the sanctuary and surroundings became a center for "coral reef tourism," which brought additional money into the village.[11]

Eventually the Philippine government set up a national marine sanctuary program with hundreds of sanctuaries around the country. Grace (her name has been changed for her privacy), an environmental activist in Manila, told me, "We have over 1,000 MPAs here, but many are paper parks. MPAs are among the few proven conservation systems to actually work." Norwegian marine researcher Portia Nillos-Kleiven studied MPAs in the Philippines and found that besides those that exist literally only on paper, others are "nonfunctional" because they are of limited quality, while some are very effective. She wrote that ingredients for successful MPAs are initial technical support from a university or other outside organization and strong local buy-in, including participation of community organizations and funding from the local government. When they work, the MPAs reverse fishing communities' race to the bottom (sorry, folks) and create centers for sustainable fishing, preservation of coral reefs, and ecotourism, which in turn provides alternative sources of income.[12]

Lots of MPAs have now been created around the world; but before we get too excited, less than 3 percent of the ocean is highly protected, while scientists estimate that 30 percent is necessary to restore biodiversity and adequately rebuild fish stocks.[13]

When I asked Maria, an older activist, if she thought that the country could fix some of the larger fishing issues, she seemed doubtful. "The only thing I've ever seen the country come together over was Marcos leaving. And then it went right back to the way it was. If you ever thought that the rich were gonna help the poor and solve larger problems, that was the one time." She added, "I thought maybe COVID would've helped unify the country, but instead the rich hoarded vaccines, the poor people took the brunt of it."

I wondered if a younger activist felt the same way, so I asked Grace whether overfishing issues might unify the country; she echoed Maria, saying that achieving unity would take something devastating akin to an apocalyptic disaster. She also said that what from afar looks like Filipino "levelheaded" responses to typhoons and earthquakes is actually the opposite. Rather, she said, the government barely helps its people. "There was a typhoon and then a whole city was basically drowning. They were on roofs and stuff. And then it went viral that their mayor was vacationing on some private island when all of this was going down." I jokingly asked if he was named Ted Cruz. With national elections coming up when I spoke with her, Grace said, "So far nobody has declared any environmental platform yet, and nobody has discussed their plans on the environment." She did praise one government official, Gina Lopez, who had been secretary of the Department of Environment and Natural Resources. "She started a really good program cleaning the canals in the city. She was really the one leader that we had that genuinely cared about the environment and did something about it." What seemed like a glimmer of hope ended with, "But then she tragically died."

There are NGOs focusing on preserving the seas, the fish, and the fishing communities, and there have been victories. PaNaGaT ("Fishing" or "Fisherfolk") is a network that promotes sustainable fisheries. Danjugan Island, notorious for illegal fishing, has become a nature tourism site thanks to Philippine Reef and Rainforest Conservation, Inc.[14] In 2021, the Philippine Tuna Handline Partnership became the Philippine's first fishers' organization to achieve certification to the Marine Stewardship Council's internationally recognized standard for sustainable fishing. Significantly, the process of achieving certification was sparked by the European

Union threatening to ban fish imports from the Philippines if it didn't effectively combat IUU fishing.[15]

Gregg Yan, founder of the Best Alternatives Campaign, and a leading advocate for sustainable fisheries, identifies three core strategies that could make a major difference: ensuring that MPAs are properly managed, using technology to monitor fishing in deeper waters, and expanding sustainable aquaculture. He notes that aquaculture already has surpassed fishing in the wild and says that the means exist to make it ecologically sound through adopting low impact, extensive (rather than intensive) farming and recirculating aquaculture systems.[16] Needless to say, to bring these to scale would require a high level of government commitment, politically, administratively, and financially.

When I asked Ana if she thought she and Wildflour could have an impact on sustainability, she was positive and mentioned some of the same management solutions as Gregg. "We try our best to work very closely with organic farmers and those in the fish industry to bridge the gap between farm/fishery and market. Even in small ways, by highlighting the quality of our local fish (local sardines and bangus being among some of our more popular items), we hope that we can contribute to a growing demand for local fish products, and this would in turn encourage care and sustainability for our fisheries and communities to progress amidst adversity."

But it seems like bringing about change is all on NGOs and local communities, with little support from the government. And while the government gives lip service to sustainable fisheries, it is actively repressing and killing other environmentalists, especially Indigenous peoples in the mountains. The British human rights group Global Witness said that at least 166 "land and environment defenders" were killed between the time that Duterte took office in 2016 through 2020. In 2020, twenty-nine were killed, the highest in Asia and third highest in the world. Global Witness adds that "opposition to damaging industries is often met with violent crackdowns from the police and military."[17]

* * *

At a certain point, we stopped and the flotilla kept going. Everyone who had been squatting and chatting quietly sprang into action. For no reason, I expected the fishers all to be in some kind of uniform, but everyone was dressed no differently than folks I'd seen at the market or on the back of a trike motorbike— US-brand T-shirts (one announced a faded Cleveland Cavs championship), various colored shorts, and flip-flops or barefoot. Only the captain had pressed pants, sneakers, and a polo shirt. It was a family affair. There were a few younger kids (maybe aged thirteen), sons and nephews, who were nimbly flying up and down ladders into the mast, in preparation, unhooking the nets and booms for release into the sea. Or that's what it looked like they were doing. But truthfully, I had no idea what was going on on the boat. And bothering the captain with questions seemed like a bad idea. A dozen people were running around the skiff like there was a house fire. And I was just trying not to get in anybody's way or fall off 'cause it was really narrow and there were waves making the thin workspace scary. The boat randomly jumped like a dog happy to see ya.

Each pitch of the boat brought up something I'd read. The original outriggers, ones four-to-ten meters, were very stable, but as they scaled up today into trawlers with the same design, little attention had been paid to any performance calculations or naval architectural analysis. Subsistence poverty means no engineering school; skills are mostly handed down generation to generation.

Most bankas are built by local boatbuilders without the benefit of boatyards, modern equipment, power tools, paper plans, or formal design process. And with no conventional plans for the larger boats, "the presence of outriggers has a definite effect on the heave, pitch, and roll motion of the craft as compared to the hull without an outrigger. Reports show a high percentage of capsizing by these motorized banca boats."[18] The captain noticed my pale face and came over and spoke to me in some dulcet tones. Though Tagalog is Greek to me, I smiled and nodded. Then held tightly to the mast, knees pressed to my chest, trying to look calm.

One thought kept floating at the top of my mind: In a world actively discussing "frontline" workers, fishers are at the top of the list. Fishing is considered to be the most dangerous occupation in the world. The International Labour Organization reports 24,000 deaths per year.[19] Falling into the sea and drowning seemed right up my alley.

Once nets had been lowered into the water via booms, we had another round of waiting. I had asked to try to be involved, so they handed me a rope and I pulled alongside everybody, only to end up staring at an empty net. Literally nothing after hours of fishing.

Each empty pull added to my slow panic attack. One net on the opposite side of the boat had three anchovies, which I kept with the hope that we might be able to use them. I only needed a small amount of sauce. Then a three-hour pregnant pause as we motored back to the dock. The ride home was long and quiet as I sat, three anchovies in hand, fingers crossed.

They were useless for the patis. Marching up from the dock in the dark, we made our way to an open-air processing plant owned by Lorenzana Food Corporation, the makers of Lorins Patis. And right away the manager looked at the small fry and shook her head sadly. She did say I could jump in and help her staff, as another boat had been more successful than we had and they had a truckload of fish to get into barrels to head out in the morning. So a little after three a.m. I stepped into large blue waders, put on a hairnet and rubber gloves, and got to work shoveling scads (*ahh that's what they look like*) into a tub and then shoveling salt in after them.

* * *

Humans learned long ago that salting preserves food. People all over the world have salted foods for preservation for thousands of years. Although it's not known when salting started, it is known that Egyptians, for one, were using it for preservation as early as 2,000 BCE. Salt draws up and replaces the water in food; this osmosis leaves the food lighter and removes the environment that microbes need in order to thrive. Furthermore, high concentrations of salt directly kill the pathogens.[20] The United Nations' fish salting 101 report advises, "A concentration of between 6-10 percent salt in the fish tissue, together with the drying effect due to loss of water, will prevent the growth of most spoilage bacteria".[21]

Salting meant food could be stored on ships for long journeys; as Paul Greenberg, author of *Four Fish*, commented to me: "Salting was how you got protein from one place to another without it spoiling."[22] Filipinos traveled extensively both on inland waters and by sea long before European colonization, reaching Siam (Thailand), China, and what is now Indonesia in large, wooden balangays. Salting also made possible the European journeys that led to the colonization of the Philippines and much of the rest of the world. Now, of course, fish aren't salted, fermented, and dried as much as they once were. Mark Kurlansky, author of *Salt: A World History*, told me that salt had the greatest decline in economic value of any commodity with the introduction of refrigeration.[23] More recently, health concerns have targeted salt.

My mother-in-law, Anne, uses patis not only as a condiment but as a salt replacement in Filipino dishes. Her mother, Thelma, says Filipinos add it to *pancit, sinigang, nilaga,* and most other soups. When I asked Thelma why she uses Rufina, her favorite brand, she said, "It's the best you can find in the States, taste-wise," though when I asked her if there is a taste difference among brands, she shrugged and said no. However, Anne argued that there were different flavors, to which Thelma agreed—that there were lighter and darker brands which corresponded to different levels of umami. Patis tastes like a super-salty soy sauce without the depth. At first sip it's shocking, like the salt water my mom made me gargle for a sore throat; but, after a moment, a subtle flavor slinks in. The sly fish remnants make the salt not so bold as to be off-putting; they dress it up a bit. Jorge mentioned that some brands add spicy peppers, others calamansi juice. This latter is called *patismansi* and, when I tried it, it added a limey tang and brightness which I preferred to plain patis. Patismansi and the spicy pepper brands are usually not cooked with, but used only as a condiment.

Patis is a simple recipe. Generally fish is mixed with salt in a 3:1 ratio and left to ferment for anywhere between three months and two years. The fish's digestive enzymes break down its own flesh during the fermentation; fermentation is much quicker when the guts are left in. The process leads to the fish-sauce taste.

Karen's "Tita" Pam agreed with Thelma that patis brands are pretty similar, but she did point out that there are other fish sauces that are used in Filipino cooking. Similar fish sauce to patis is made all over East Asia—it's *kecap ikan* in Indonesia, *nam pla* in Thailand, *shottsuru* or *ishiru/ishiri* in Japan, *nuôc mâm* in Vietnam, *budu* in Malaysia, *ngapi* in Myanmar, *yeesu* in China, and *aekjeot*

Patis making

in Korea; Southeast Asia is particularly noted for fermented fish condiments, while Northeast Asia (China, Korea, and Japan) mostly uses fermented beans.[24]

Fish sauce made through fermentation is not unique to East Asia. Ancient Greeks used fish guts to make *garos* sauce in what's basically the same process. Garos likely evolved into ancient Rome's *garum* sauce and *liquamen*. Needless to say, like today's patis and other East Asian fish sauces, the process of making garos or garum stank. The outcome, however, was mild and tasty. Pompeii was known for making garum, and jars of what may have been kosher garum were found in the ruins.[25] Sally Grainger, a student of garum, says she thinks liquamen, used in the cooking process, probably tasted like the Vietnamese *nuoc mam nhi* and garum *sociorum*, the condiment, like Japanese *ishiri*.[26]

* * *

The heavy lifting was backbreaking, and the thick, fishy air was suffocating—the rubber waders didn't help. I was dripping sheets of sweat. After mixing the fish and salt with our hands to fully integrate them, the group of us wielded our shovels again to fill two barrels with the mixture. We put these on the back of a large truck, which bounced off, disappearing into the night. The barrels were making their way over to Luzon. We would follow in the morning by ferry to meet them at the large Lorins bottling plant to continue the next steps of the process. In the meantime, it was time for some needed shut-eye.

I won't go into detail about almost missing the ferry. Or the ATMs that didn't accept my bank cards, or the emergency call to Jorge's sister, Pinky, to wire us some cash to pay the hotel and to pay the bribe to the customs officer so we could get on the ferry. I'll leave that for another day. I will say we got to the fish factory in the early afternoon, just in time for the end-of-the-day shift.

Entering through a large metal gate, I was immediately struck by the half-rank, half-delicious smell of salted, fermenting fish. There is an underlying trash aroma to fish (contrasting to other meats, which are pretty odorless). This smell comes from the breaking down of trimethylamine oxide, which is common in the skin of ocean fish (freshwater fish and other meats don't have nearly as much). This oxidation creates amines, which are stinky. But this ripe funk, when combined with salting and fermentation, becomes a little briny—a pungent, sour smell that actually makes your mouth water. The closest thing that I compare it to is that strange pull of stinky cheese. We geared up—back into the hairnet, facemask, boots—and stepped into a tray of chlorine to enter the main building and the huge warehouse holding giant tubs of fermenting fish.

Walking through the rows, we opened up tanks from various dates to see the fish breaking down across time and to taste the patis. Under the metal lids, the broth was murky, inky black, with swirls of brown and lumpy gelatinous fish parts like phantoms suspended ghostly, just under the surface. The little ponds reminded me of how the Dagobah swamp in *The Empire Strikes Back* looked (and probably smelled). But the taste was a different story. Each one on the timeline had a slightly unique flavor, but the mildest, and my favorite by far, were the two-year-old tanks—the end of the fermenting road, the type we would be bottling later. We stopped our stroll at the two barrels I had a hand in. They sat next to a half-filled tank. I tried lifting the barrel myself for shits and giggles and couldn't move it an inch. With three other folks who knew what they were doing, and who would put some CrossFit trainers to shame, we topped up the tank.

Now it was time for me to grab some patis for Marge and Ana and head back to Wildflour. In Filipino style, the manager generously handed me two crates for the chefs and my family.

Back in Manila, I met the chefs at the flagship of the Wildflour cafes, a restaurant which wouldn't feel out of place in Greenwich Village or Beverly Hills. Tita Pam, who spends half her time in

Marge and Ana at Wildflour

NorCal and the other half in Makati (one of the posher areas in Manila), told me that the success of Wildflour was strangely surprising. Could an upscale coffee shop with European pastries do well in a place where it's not a meal if there isn't rice on the plate? Turns out it was something the growing middle class was looking for; that demand supports seven Wildflours and spin-offs like Little Flour and Wildflour Italian, which was where we set up shop to cook.

While all the dishes were very simple, they also felt luxurious. A milk punch made from blended mango, coconut milk, coconut sugar, and coconut moonshine; a sticky rice and mango dessert with coconut sugar wrapped in banana leaf and steamed; and, finally, the prawn Kilawin. Kilawin is similar to ceviche. It's a snacking food usually eaten when drinking. The main theme of the meal was how many ways we could use coconut; one of the important ingredients in Kilawin is coconut vinegar. Calamansi juice is also one of the unique flavors here. If lemons, limes, and oranges all had a baby, it would be this tart little sweet citrus. It's used often in Filipino cooking as a meat marinade. In this case we poured a half a cup of calamansi juice and three tablespoons of coconut vinegar over two-and-a-half cups of uncooked shrimp. We minced up a head of garlic and a shallot, and a couple bird's eye chilis and added them to the mix. Lola Thelma adds coconut cream and ginger to taste, but we did it traditional and tart. Finally, some pepper and a teaspoon of patis was added as a salt replacement. It's all tossed in a bowl where it marinates for an hour or so.

Between sips of my cocktail, I munched on the prawns and mulled over the experience:

How the most overwhelming and complicated ingredient, patis, was only one small part of the larger whole. How many pieces must fit together to make this meal. How many interacting ingredients come together to create a food culture. How much time it must have taken for Filipino cuisine to evolve—layer after layer! While cooking the meal with all the piles of ingredients, the sack of rice, the coconut sugar, the mangos, the prawns, the coconut moonshine, I saw the tablespoon of patis in its place in the center of the table. And what a joyful, delicious puzzle it was part of. But I kept returning to the empty nets and the portending of disaster. I couldn't get away from how much of the food culture is dependent on…fish. The future of an entire country pegged directly to this single food source. And yet the fish are disappearing. How do I write about my experience here without it feeling so dire—part of me wanted to soften it because of my family, which wouldn't be true. Do I write about my fears that, much like Croatia's oyster beds, it will get much worse before it gets better? This would only lead to discussing the consequences. How more people would migrate from the fishing communities to the cities, followed by more unrest, followed by an empty sea, followed by more regional conflict. This thread ends with questioning whether human life will continue on this planet.

Could I write about hope? I thought about the hard work and the luck that were the backstory to the tablespoon of patis that were essential ingredients in the Kilawin. And I hoped that our empty boat had not been a foreshadowing for the future. I found a glimmer in the fact that more of the world's consumers are and will continue to demand sustainable seafood. That unions of conscientious people can change the economics of overfishing. It is also possible that the countries bordering the disputed South China Sea could work across differences, realizing that humanity staying alive requires, in anthropologist Anna Lowenhaupt Tsing's phrase, "collaborative survival."[27] I rather hoped that the fisher families that I met, together with the NGOs and other forces in Philippine civil society that are fighting for sustainable fishing, the health of the seas, and the well-being of coastal communities will overcome the odds and prevail. When I later asked Gregg Yan if he was optimistic, he smiled and said yes, because *homo sapiens* are smart and can solve the problems that confront us with the will to solve them (and, he added, the will to solve them equitably). I hope he is right.

Potatoes:
Peru / Utah

AT A QUECHUA WEDDING IN THE ANDES of Peru, the couple is dressed in vibrant, almost neon, colors of the mountain peoples, the embroidered *monta* cape, the bride in a knee-high *pollera* skirt, the groom in traditional, handwoven pants (though today sometimes he may wear new jeans instead). The bride's hair is neatly braided underneath the upturned bowl-like *montera* hat sitting on her head. Over the three-day affair, the wedding party dances amongst confetti, eats alpaca meat, drinks beer, and chews on coca leaves. It's a joyous time of the joining of the two families. It's also a relief for the bride, for she has passed the potato test.

Traditionally, before a Quechua bride is going to marry, she is given the gift of a brownish/purple, lumpy potato by her maybe-mother-in-law and is asked to peel it. How well she does represents how good of a cook she will be for her husband. This potato is called *Lunchuy Huacachi*, meaning "make my daughter-in-law cry," and its shape reminds one of a particularly chunky Botero figure or a fist-sized blackberry. If she removes more than the skin, too much of the cortex or pith, she can't get hitched.[1] Not exactly the greatest wedding gift.

The custom is disappearing, but the symbolism underscores the potato's importance in Peru. If you can't peel a potato here, you aren't worth marrying.

I thought about this as I held a potato in the kitchen of Lima's Central, brainchild of wildly talented chef and food ethnographer Virgilio Martinez and the world's fourth best restaurant according to the "World's Best 50 Restaurants." [2]

In the Central kitchen, looking down at a hybrid of the *puka papa* (red potato) and *papa púrpura* (a purple-fleshed tuber eaten by Incan royalty) which I had harvested in the Sacred Valley of the Andes, I obsessed about how I had messed up. This food lab restaurant's menu is built around the altitudes of the country's varied microclimates. I was here to reproduce a meal I'd had with Virgilio a week earlier that consisted of three dishes—one coastal, one Amazonian, and one Andean. The original Andean dish I was to replicate was composed of a variety of roasted potatoes laid over stones and pebbles of *arcilla*, edible Andean clay. But I hadn't been able to find most of the potatoes. It was December, too early in the season (the harvest starts in May) for the *pumaqmaquin* (*puma paw*) potato or the *quwi obispo* (guinea pig with skin the colors of a bishop's robes) variety and too late for *kuntur warmi* (woman with the colors of a condor's neck) or even the less-appetizing sounding *quwi sullu* (guinea pig fetus). In a place where a person's value is so closely linked to their skill with a potato, my complete failure was not going to go over well.

Virgilio and his wife, Pia León, and his sister, Malena Martínez, also run Mater Iniciativa, the "scientific and social research center at the heart of [the couple's] restaurant empire." [3] Mater Iniciativa groups travel throughout Peru to gather and document local ingredients, and to encourage local people to save them from extinction. Their task is to preserve traditional ingredients and

Photo by Jared Paisley

Tasting potatoes and clay with Virgilio Martinez at Central

honor the relationship with the land. Mater Iniciativa engages with younger people who may see "modern" as "better." Mater Iniciativa hopes that by providing a market for the traditional foods, it can provide reasons for Indigenous people to maintain them, bringing in income and helping to maintain the cultures to which they are integral. The groups have gathered hundreds of ingredients and put them on the menu at Virgilio's restaurants in a myriad of ways. Malena says, "Right now we are focused on accessing herbs and fruits which are getting lost because people aren't producing or gathering them—they are simply dropping to the ground and rotting. People are less interested in local ingredients and more interested in potato chips. It's crazy, but true."[4]

Before arriving in Peru, I hadn't given a second thought to harvesting a potato for myself, dismissing it as much too unhealthy. The potato I knew was the common russet that tasted great any way you cooked it, as long as it was fried. Who even knew there were this many types of potatoes? Peru is home to over 2,800 native varieties of the more than 4,500 varieties in the world, most of which have Peruvian origins. The season, the location, even the altitude changes everything about potato varieties. Here, each elderly woman bringing a full sack down from the mountains to market is likely carrying a one-of-a-kind breed on her back. On top of that, a week in, given the time constraints, I hadn't been able to make the fourteen-hour ride down to Puna, near Lake Titicaca, for the edible clay ("*chaco*") which was traditionally used to leach the poison out of wild potatoes.

Poison out of potatoes? My meal was going to be a disaster.

And it had all started so promisingly.

Leaving Central to start my potato mission seven days ago, I had known Manuel Choqque Bravo was the man I had to see. I had heard rumors about him from a number of people in the Peruvian food world. The "potato whisperer," breeding potatoes away from the bland, large, modern varieties into rainbow-colored, healthy, smaller balls of flavor. Most notably, I had heard this from Virgilio himself. When I had cut into the delicious misshapen lumps in his roasted potato-and-*chaco* dish and they opened like periwinkle and pink geodes, Virgilio had given all the glory to Manuel and to the Incas.

Manuel was trained by his father, who had been trained by his own father, and he by his father before him. He earned an agricultural engineering degree from Universidad San Antonio Abad del Cusco, and he lives and works at an experimental center at the National Institute of Agrarian Innovation in Urubamba, a small town in the Sacred Valley, an hour from Cusco (which just happens to have been the ancient center of the Incan empire). A trip to the area would also let me do a little digging into the agriculture of fifteenth-century Peru. As my LATAM flight breached the gray clouds of spring over Lima, I saw the peaks of the Andes, and I was on my way to discuss the history and future of arguably one of the most influential crops in human history. Yes, one could say it's been at least as influential worldwide as wheat, corn, or rice—the humble potato has been responsible for enormous changes over the past five centuries.

* * *

Potatoes were one of the major elements in the so-called Columbian Exchange following European colonization of the Americas. American crops such as maize, tomatoes, and potatoes were introduced to Europe and Asia. The Exchange brought Asian and African crops such as rice, coffee, and sugarcane to the Americas, along with the unwilling migration of millions of enslaved Africans.

Potatoes from Peru helped to end Europe's massive repetitive famines that dominated life in Northern Europe through the eighteenth century, doubling Europe's food supply. At one point, potatoes made up the entire solid food diet of about 40 percent of the people in Ireland, and 10 to 30 percent of the people in the Netherlands, Belgium, and Prussia. University of Chicago historian William H. MacNeill argued that by allowing the rapid growth of the European population, the potato permitted European nations to take over most of the rest of the world between 1750 and 1950. [5]

Of course, there was a downside to this heavy reliance on the potato as a subsistence crop—when it failed, the results were catastrophic. The Irish potato famine of 1845–1849 was caused by the fungus-like *P. infestans* attacking the "Irish Lumper," the sole variety grown in the country.[6] The "Great Starvation" is well known for causing the deaths of a million people and the emigration of at least another million. The Finnish famine of 1866-1868 was known as "the great hunger years." Caused by a combination of very cold summers and very wet autumns, the failure of the potato crops led to about 8.5 percent of the population dying of hunger—20 percent in the hardest-hit areas.[7] It also led to massive migration, though not as immediately as in Ireland.

In both cases, the core problem lay in the cultivation of potatoes as a monoculture—reliance on one variety of potato—although the human effects were greatly exacerbated by social and economic factors such as governments indifferent to peasant suffering and poor communication and transportation systems. But this type of monoculture historically hasn't been an issue in the Andes, the birthplace of *Solanum tuberosum*.

Cusco, and its cropland in the Sacred Valley, is one of the oldest continually-inhabited regions in the world. As I stood at 11,000 feet, even in the morning chill and with a brutal altitude headache, it wasn't hard to understand why. The area, an ancient lakebed with natural routes leading off to surrounding regions, was an advantageous spot from which to rule. Clouds swirled atop the peaks which surround the valley bowl. Cusco, the ninth highest city in the world, is one of the most stunning, with red-tile roofed, whitewashed colonial Spanish buildings, some of which stand on the iron-gray and ochre-red structures of the imperial Incas—only nobles were allowed in this town.

Three rivers, the Huatanay, Tullumayo, and Chunchul, deposit the valley's fertile soil. The valley and its surrounding Andean slopes created the perfect microclimates for growing potatoes. The high peaks, low valleys, short rainy season, and frequent droughts make the Andes a great testing ground for different varieties. Food and dining journalist Camper English writes, "Potato plants evolved in regions with long dry seasons, so, as an underground tuber, a potato stores energy to make it through the season. Potatoes can even grow in regions where no perennial grasses can survive."[8]

Because of the short growing season, the Incas developed an ingenious way to take advantage of the environment in order to grow as many types of plants as they could in a short amount of time, a strategy still on display at Ollantaytambo, a town and archeological site at the opposite end of the Sacred Valley from Cusco. I decided to stop there before visiting Manuel.

Ollantaytambo became the Incas' provisional capital when Cusco was sacked by the Spanish and before the Incas were forced down the east side of the Andes into the Amazon. Ollantaytambo today is known as the place you catch the train to Machu Picchu, but more interestingly, it considers itself to still be a living Incan city. My guide, Klever Marca, informed me that the town motto is, "We are still here!"

The Ollantaytambo archeological site is an incredibly advanced agricultural site masquerading as an Incan religious temple and military base. A temple of the sun sits on the top of Cerro Bandolista hill, with forts saddle bagged next to it, all overlooking a bottleneck in the valley. Below the temple's stone carvings of the three *pachas* ("worlds") of Incan belief, a tiered farm is laid out in the shape of a female llama (the ceremonial center as the head, the storeroom below positioned as the womb).

On the hillsides, the Incas used chiseled base stones jigsawed tightly on top of one another to form the terraces and hold in the dirt. Those stones soak up heat during the day, raising the ground temperature by 5–8°, and leach out the heat slowly to keep the soil warm at night, allowing for farming on hillsides and the growing of plants transplanted from lower altitudes. After hiking up the steep stairs alongside the tiers, I turned and stared out across the valley at storehouses, known as *quolqas*, perched on sheer cliff ledges. The fierce winds hit the high Andean peaks and shoot down, freeze-drying potatoes there for later use in a dish

called *chuño*. *Chuño* can be translated from Quechua as "potatoes passed from ice to the sun." Five hundred years before NASA
freeze-dried food for the astronauts, Incas were stomping potatoes
into paste to remove the skins and water to dry them on the side
of cliffs for eating decades later.[9] With this 360-degree view in the
foothills of the Andes, I got the picture of an intricate machine of
food growing and preservation, with the potato as fuel.

Klever mentioned that the site still produces food and is
actively farmed on the lower tiers. Could I get my potatoes for
my meal here? "No, they have already been harvested."

Moray, an Incan site only sixteen kilometers from Ollantaytambo, seems to have been built purely for scientific agricultural
trials, no military forts or temples needed for this open-air laboratory. The walk starts up on a cliff, from which, peering below into
a depression in the hill, you see concentric circles, resembling a
rock quarry overgrown with grass, each terrace approximately ten
feet deep, sitting one on top of another, rising up and out about
a hundred feet. This layout, together with the relationship to the
wind and sun, creates a difference of 27° between the bottom-
and top-tiered circles. The Incas grew food here that came from
all over their empire, transferring soil from different growing
regions hundreds of miles away into each tier. Their next steps
were even more incredible. Moray is believed to have been used to
breed potatoes and other plants to survive at gradually higher and
higher, colder and colder microclimates. For example, the Incas
would take the lowland-growing Amazonian purple potato, the
sachapapa, the *dale dale*, and the *michucki*, and seasonally move
them incrementally higher and higher until they could survive at
altitudes far higher than natural, sea-level plants now surviving at
the tops of the Andes. In the 500 years since the Incas ruled these
mountains, this vast apparatus that expanded potato varieties has

shriveled. But Manuel has taken up the mantle of continuing this experimentation, fighting the force of capitalism's "make it cheaper" symptom: erosion of heterogeneity.

From Ollantaytambo and Moray, I was also able to see the road to Urubamba and, thus, the path to Manuel and, hopefully, to the potatoes I needed for Central. After thirty bumpy minutes, we pulled into Urubamba, and coasted up to Manuel's. Through the brick-and-stone gate across a deep yard, under a tarp, stood a man with a large grin. His dark, floppy hair framed a wide-open, friendly face that belied the gravity of his mission. He was smiling at his two dogs that were chasing each other across the yard. These weren't the legendary street mutts of Peru, but pure-breds—a Dalmatian and a German Shepherd. Two dogs bred over centuries, loved by a man who has spent the last fourteen years breeding fifteen original potato crops into more than 300 varieties. In front of him, a picnic table with a basket piled with potatoes. My Quechua nonexistent and my Spanish only nominally better, we used a translator. Like a patient professor, Manuel led me through his background and the science behind what he was doing.

Ancient wild and early domesticated potatoes contained bitter poisons, glycoalkaloids, to dissuade animals from eating them. When the potatoes were wrapped in clay and tossed into a fire, these poisons dissipated. Later these poisons were reduced by purposeful breeding of the plants, and Manuel said that I didn't need to worry about that with today's potatoes. He brought out some legendary potatoes like the puma's paw and then unveiled what he was working on—evolving the popular white potatoes into colorful, nutritious, tasty potatoes. Years ago, his father doubted his decision to try to do this, and was outright against the idea that potatoes could cost $1.50 a kilo when the going rate was 25 cents. And he was almost right. Before the big-name chefs like Virgilio came calling, Manuel's decision was a disaster. "When I undertook in 2017 to harvest about thirty tons…I had no market in hotels or restaurants. I took my potatoes to the local market, and nobody wanted them. I explained to them about the color and they thought that it was bad; they thought that these potatoes were difficult to peel and not pleasant to cook. It was a very hard year. In that year we discarded…all thirty tons, feeding my cattle and pigs. Nobody wanted to buy. The supply chain didn't understand it."

Slowly, with the same patience and conviction it took to explain his thought process to me, Manuel knocked on the doors of hotels and restaurants. The buyers came around. He made the market for a healthy, delicious potato. After he sliced each of his breeds open to show me the incredible colors, he spoke about the antioxidants and minerals he was putting back in—represented by the colors I saw. His red and blue potatoes

Photo by Jared Paisley

Manuel Choqque Bravo with a Lunchuy Huacachi

are rich in anthocyanins, flavonoids, and chlorogenic acid, anti-oxidants with anticancer and glucose-lowering properties; they are more healthful than the white potatoes that we are far more familiar with.

After an aside from Manuel about the *oca*, another tuber he is now working with, I had to get going. So I asked if I could go dig some potatoes up, and for the first time his smile dropped. He explained that I had missed the season. I could have these potatoes in front of me, but there weren't any in the ground. Now this was trouble—my mission on the show is to harvest the food myself. Did he know anyone who was growing potatoes like him? He shook his head. Then, to lift my spirits, he asked if I wanted to try some of the potato wine he was working on. After three glasses and the purchase of four bottles for which I was going to need another suitcase, we shook hands and I headed out. Potatoless.

Luckily, I was in the Sacred Valley in Peru, the birthplace of the potato. We put out some feelers—"in desperate need of potatoes in the ground"—and within a day heard back from two family farms that had early (late?) potatoes just ready to harvest. That afternoon I was wading through a field of green potato stems peppered with white flowers. They weren't one of the varieties Virgilio had asked for, but at this point I was grateful for what I could get.

* * *

In Utah, on another shoot, I encountered another potato, an 11,000-year-old, native North American tuber. In January 2020, I was speaking about *From Scratch* at ChefDance, a culinary event that coincides with the Sundance Film Festival in Park City. I was staying at The Lodge at Blue Sky, and Yuta, the restaurant at the Lodge, became a clubhouse of sorts for the speakers and honorees—Martha Stewart would walk over to take pictures of your breakfast; Alice Waters was holding court with her team at dinner. All of us hunkered down in the warmth of Galen Zamarra's kitchen. After a particularly tender short rib, I paid my respects and found that Galen had been the chef of New York City's Mas Farmhouse, one of my all-time favorite restaurants. He had moved out to Utah for the opportunity to work in conjunction with the onsite, women-led Gracie's Farm, which employs a "no-till" method, working the land by hand instead of with modern farming equipment, and to cook with hyper-local ingredients. He was living the *From Scratch* life that I only get to experience on my show.

Galen soon joined me at Karen and my table where I roped him into agreeing to do an episode, and we began to discuss a possible menu. The back-and-forth lasted the four days we were there—every time I came down for a meal. He told me he wanted to include a rare ingredient in the appetizer that he hadn't used before. As an homage to his new home, he thought boiled, then roasted, Four Corners potatoes would make a great pairing with trout. As its name suggests, this potato is found at the intersection of Utah, Arizona, New Mexico, and Colorado; Galen told me it was a plant domesticated by Native Americans that had only recently become available to restaurants.

Six months later, back in the kitchen for the tasting, crunching on a nugget of dense, nutty flavor, I wondered why I had never heard of this potato before. This delectable veggie was so unlike what I knew to be a potato. The Peruvian potatoes and the Four Corners potato are a contrast of opposites. The high Andes versus the low desert of the southwestern US; a foundational food source versus one nearly lost; large, meaty, rainbow-colored spuds of various shapes compared to tiny, tan marbles. Compared to the russet, the southwestern *Solanum jamesii* has twice the protein, zinc, and manganese, and three times the calcium and iron;[10] it can be cooked for hours and still retain its integrity. Where had this been all my life? It became a mystery to be solved. Thanks to Galen, I was introduced to people who had been working for quite a while on this riddle, part of the answer to which, sadly, is a painful snapshot of North American history.

Galen introduced me to Lisbeth Louderback, curator of archeology at the Natural History Museum of Utah and an assistant professor at the University of Utah, and to Bruce Pavlik, director of conservation at the U of U and Lisbeth's husband. They had stumbled across a wild cluster of potatoes outside a dig at an 11,000-year-old archeological site in Escalante Valley in southwestern Utah. Lisbeth and Bruce then connected me with Cynthia Wilson, then director of Utah Diné Bikéyah's (UDB) Traditional Foods Program, which is farming the potato back into Diné life in the Navajo Nation. Cynthia has a master's in dietetics and clinical nutrition from the University of Utah. As director of UDB's Traditional Foods Program, she planned, organized, and implemented traditional foods policy, educational programs, community roundtable discussions, and tribal cook camps with the Navajo, Hopi, Ute, and Zuni cultures (known as the five finger earth people). The program's goal is to increase Native food access and usage to reaffirm connections with Mother Earth by the involvement of elders and reteaching the traditional food system to younger generations for health and wellbeing. I cavalierly invited myself down to meet with Cynthia to discuss the potato, but was met with reserve on UDB's part. I could only interview Cynthia after agreeing to take a thirty-five to sixty-minute Mandatory Cultural Sensitivity Training required of non-Native media people.

The training was a wonderful example of exactly what it was called: sensitivity training. After countless times of being burned by non-Native media people who knew little and cared less about Native perspectives, UDB insists that people who want to interview staff members sit and listen to what the world looks like from the Diné perspective. If we wanted something from UDB, namely an interview, UDB wanted something from us, namely respect. And an understanding that some rules are different. For example, non-Native journalism usually calls for maintaining a distance between interviewer and interviewee—Diné value reciprocity. Non-Native scientists get excited about identifying potatoes as 11,000 years old; Diné have no problem with that, but they themselves refer to the potatoes as having been there "from time immemorial." The Diné are fighting to protect sacred ancestral lands of Bears Ears and are glad when they have allies, but want the allies to recognize that all of the land has been taken from them, so it is not a "favor" when it is protected from further desecration. And Mormons should not be celebrating "Pioneer Day" on July 24; the newly arrived Latter Day Saints were settlers on land that was not theirs.

Down in Escalante Valley, standing next to the archeological site, North Creek Shelter, in 117° heat, Cynthia and Lisbeth were giving me a crash course in the last 11,000 years as I tried unsuccessfully to find some shade. The site was cliffside, the area outlined with a black string. In the tan, sandstone wall face were hints of old carvings now weathered almost beyond recognition. But the find I was more interested in had been beneath our feet— *manos*, handheld stones used to grind raw foods against *metates*, long stone slabs covered in starch granules. This spot, partially protected by an overhang in the rock, had been a recurring home, with at least seven distinct occupations, for Native peoples for millennia. When studying the site, Lisbeth had been expecting seeds and nut fibers; the starch was a surprise discovery. "The earliest of these potato granules were found on tools dating to between 10,000 and 11,000 years ago. During both these periods, the people living at the site are believed to have been hunter-gatherers. The presence of these starch granules shows that they were grinding potatoes into flour and exploiting a food source that archeologists had not previously recognized as part of their diet."[11]

Lisbeth had heard rumors that the valley used to be known, by Civil War-era cavalry, as Potato Valley. Northwest of Cedar City, the valley is composed of desert and xeric shrublands and gets less than ten inches of water a year—the perfect climate for a plant that holds its energy underground in a tuber, dormant through droughts. This gave Lisbeth and Bruce something to look for.

And one day it happened. Bruce was walking a stone's throw downhill from North Creek Shelter when he spotted a small group of low-lying plants, dark brown in color, with greenish/blue leaves. A botanist, he recognized those as potato leaves.

Cynthia, Lisbeth, and I walked down the same path to find the same group of plants. Without their help, I would not have seen them at all. They are unexceptionable ground cover plants. But this shy plant very likely is the oldest domesticated potato in the world, and the oldest domesticated plant in the western US.

There are lots of them in New Mexico and Arizona, but in Utah they are found solely at archeological sites, meaning they were likely brought there, thus pointing to domestication.

Where did they originate? Bruce told me that *Solanum jamesii* is among the 111 or so species in the genus *Solanum* that form tubers. It is completely distinct from the Peruvian potato (*Solanum tuberosum*) and its 2000+ variations (yellow, purple, white, etc.). He said that although the evolutionary history of these plants is still being worked out, there is no evidence that they have ever shared genes or even come close geographically. The Four Corners potato probably originated in Central America, while *tuberosum* is strictly Andean.

They even have different numbers of chromosomes. Bruce explained that diversification in *Solanum* started two million or so years ago, leading to distinct diploid types (i.e., having only two sets of chromosomes) that include the Four Corners potato lineage. *Solanum tuberosum*, on the other hand, is a tetraploid (having four sets of chromosomes) and may be of more "recent" origin, perhaps only 15,000-50,000 years, though that is still unclear.

When I reached down to dig some potatoes up, Lisbeth stopped me. There was another grove that she wanted me to see that had more plants and where I would be able to collect what I needed. Moments later, I was in my car following her to an undisclosed site on state park land. The wild potato is rare in Utah, so I wasn't allowed to film the journey because too many people might disturb the clusters. The wild potatoes are now so hard to find that the locations are a carefully guarded secret. The long-term drought in the Four Corners area has made it even harder. In fact, knowing that I needed to locate it for my meal, Lisbeth and Bruce went out to water this cluster of wild ones so I was sure to have them.

After a grueling hike in the broiling heat, we came to an old oak grove. The cool shade instantly changed my mood. Under a layer of fallen leaves, the floor was carpeted with potatoes. Each stem stood over roots with five to twenty tiny tubers collected around a slightly larger mama, all bundled in thin, almost-gossamer roots. Harvesting in this picturesque cove, I thought about how this potato had nourished Native Americans from time immemorial,

The elusive Four Corners potato

and more recently Mormon migrants, Union soldiers, and even some locals during the Great Depression. I held human allies in my hand and was excited to cook them.

Cynthia's grandfather was a Diné medicine man who passed on a lot of knowledge to her mother, who is an herbalist and passed the values and teachings on to Cynthia. Cynthia, in turn, became a nutritionist who thinks that food is what connects everything—nutrition and health, the spiritual connection between the body and the land.

Cynthia described the traditional methods of cooking the potato. She told me, of the potatoes, "They are so tiny, you wouldn't peel the skin, so you eat them with the skin on." She continued, "Some elders say they were eaten raw, but they are usually boiled in white clay—*gleesh* (also known as kaolin)—so they are less bitter and more easily digested. They are not cooked in metal pots. Some people grind the potato to make flour or yeast. It's also been used in salads and soups. It's really filling. It's high in fiber and nutrients."

There goes that "clay" again. While not eaten with the potato here, the potato is cooked in pottery to combat the bitterness, reduce the toxic glycoalkaloids, and become edible. Such a symbiotic relationship wherever potatoes are harvested. I wondered where I could find clay, and, though I was never able to find white kaolin clay, red clay was all around us. With a shovel and Salt Lake City expert potter Clark Marshall leading the way, I pulled over to the side of Highway 189 outside of Heber City to scramble up the rise. Road cuts (as well as natural embankments like canyons or stream beds) are great places to dig. A few miles up the road in Henefer, red ceramic clay has been mined since 1913 by the Interstate Brick Company; it's been mined all over Utah by the Diné, Hopi, Ute, and Zuni cultures from time immemorial, because at some point along the way Native tribes realized that cooking the potatoes in clay pottery made them less bitter. After sifting and cleaning the clay, I spent the rest of the day learning how to make a pot at Clark's studio in SLC.

The Four Corners potatoes were a vital part of traditional Diné diets. The potato exemplifies the Diné's self-sufficient way of life before European settlement, and also that lifestyle's devastating disappearance under genocidal pressures. Cynthia told me, "The Long Walk, government rations, commodity food programs, food stamps, and for the Ute tribe having their children taken away and introduced to Mormon culture—all of these things pushed away our culture and took a toll on our community."

They were also an important part of the early Mormon settlers' diet. But they faded from most people's consciousness, both among the Diné and the European-Americans.

Cynthia said the potato wasn't something she knew about when she was growing up. "My mom had heard about this potato, but had never consumed it. So, I knew there was a wild potato that our elders had eaten, but I did not know how tiny it was or where I could find it." As Cynthia started investigating, she found that "The elders of today only hold a memory of this potato, usually of their grandparents using it." The elders, Cynthia said, "speak of *their* elders, who used it a lot more." In each of the conversations she had with the elders, "They were very surprised to see the potato again and wanted to grow it again."

For the Diné, wild foods serve many roles as a living, breathing being. They carry power and gifts, and there are certain plants that are male and female and acknowledged in ceremonial songs and prayer. Cynthia told me, "The significance is how we relate to these wild plants and honor them. They lived on this earth long before we have. The way we treat the plant is to provide an offering; there's reciprocity behind this. It comes down to kinship, being caretakers of the land. We should approach them in a highly respected manner, especially those coming from the mountain, our protector foods. How we approach it and consume it impacts the nutritional and medicinal qualities it gives us, not only for us but for the four-legged beings. But these plants [the Four Corners potatoes] are highly valued, even in our creation story."

I asked Cynthia what it means to her that the potato has such a long history, even longer than the known history of Peruvian potatoes. She told me, "It gives a lot of knowledge and hope to our people that this potato can stay dormant for so long and it's still here trying to live for us. All we have to do is restore our relationship with this plant. We can have rain again. We can have a healthy relationship with the earth. I see it as hope left for us from our ancestors to connect back to who we are despite the historical traumas that have shifted us away from these teachings."

I get a little schizophrenic after talking to people like Manuel, Virgilio, and Cynthia, and then coming home and driving down the road—any road—past Mickey D's and 7-Elevens. Because potatoes in their pure form are incredibly healthy to eat. They are rich in vitamins, minerals, and antioxidants; improve control of blood sugar; reduce the risk of heart disease; limit signs of aging; and are very filling, which helps with weight control. B6 vitamins in potatoes are critical to maintaining neurological health by helping to create useful brain chemicals, including serotonin, dopamine, and norepinephrine.[12]

Potatoes' resistant starch can help with digestive health.[13] They exist in thousands of varieties, which protects against the risks of monoculture. They are most healthy with the skins on. Dark-skinned potatoes are healthier than lighter ones. And as Manuel has shown, native potatoes of many colors are even healthier than white potatoes. Finally, potatoes can have deep cultural significance, connecting people with the land.

And what do Americans do with potatoes and how do we think about them? Just the opposite on all of these! Statistically, we mostly eat them as French fries (outside the house) and potato chips (at home and as snacks), both of which are incredibly unhealthy. They are high in calories, fat, and sodium, and, particularly when fried, high in acrylamide, which has been linked with cancer. They promote high blood pressure and may be tied to increases in heart disease. They don't fill you up, and actually make you want to eat more and more. We eat potatoes mostly without the skin, where the nutrients are, and we generally eat the less-healthy varieties. If you're eating fries from McDonald's, Burger King, or Wendy's, you're eating some of the millions of russet Burbank potatoes, which flow from monocultures around the world.

The "American Way" is not the inevitable result of "modern" life. For example, Finland's relationship with potatoes is what the

US's might look like, as a wealthy, industrialized nation, if the US hadn't gone down the monoculture and fast-food paths. Finns use around 140 pounds of potatoes per person per year (Americans eat about 110 pounds. The country that eats the most is Belarus at 392 pounds per person!). Finns' love for the potato has led to well over sixty varieties to choose from in supermarkets. Bags are color-coded to assist the shopper to decode which is the right type for soup, mash, boiling, or baking.

This came to mind while standing, holding my potatoes in the Central kitchen, discussing any number of the potato dishes Virgilio serves. As writer Elyssa Goldberg summarized it, "At Martinez's restaurant, he and his team employ more than fifty different techniques to prepare spuds. They purée them, fry them, dry them, and make infusions, thickeners, and jellies. They also ferment the skins."[14]

Back home I had a plan to introduce this new mindset into my own kitchen. There are ways to eat potatoes more healthily, in addition to growing your own. You can get heirloom potatoes of various colors. Don't fry them. You can boil them, or, if roasting, roast them whole. Something really healthy is to boil them and leave them in the fridge overnight, and warm them up the next day (or, if you are like me, eating them cold the next day with warm butter drizzled in the slice crevasse). The cold plus time cuts the calories by a third.[15]

After some internet investigation I found Hudson Valley Seed Company, an organic farm in upstate New York that is "committed to growing organically, sourcing locally and sustainably, and preserving crop diversity by selecting unique, rare, and hard-to-find varieties."[16] I bought a pound of Adirondack blue potatoes with inky skin and flesh and a pound of Adirondack red potatoes with bright red skin and pink flesh. I ordered four ounces of kaolin edible clay from Uclays.com, Described as easy to bite: "First is a crunch; then, when chewed, melts in the mouth, melts into a creamy mass. The taste is reminiscent of the chalk, which practically does not stick to the teeth. In appearance—a snow-white. The touch—smooth. Aroma 'after the rain.'"[17] A creamy, chalky mass didn't sound particularly appetizing, but it sounded useful in that it would help the process of "cleansing the body of toxins and radionuclides."[18]

Ingredients:
1 potato
4 ounces kaolin clay

The clay arrived double paper-bagged to keep out moisture, which I opened to reveal an egg-sized stalagmite. Placing this in a bowl, I added water and mixed it 'til it formed a pudding, which then got all over my hands as I layered it about one centimeter thick around an Adirondack blue.

After a good hand-washing, I poked a small slit into the clay and potato to let some future steam out. I set the oven for 450° and put it in. I had an hour.

While I waited for this to roast (and in a potato frenzy), I ordered one hundred Four Corners potato tubers off the internet to plant in my mother-in-law's garden.

Sixty minutes later, with the clay oven hardened into a bright white shell, I used a spoon to crack it open. The carapace came apart and fell easily away from the skin (after it cooled, I excitedly put it back in its paper bag for reuse). Poking the potato with a finger, I found it hot, and the upper side soft to the touch. On the underside the skin remained hard with some white stain from the clay. I cut the potato open and steam puffed out; so far so good. I mashed one half, skin and all, and began to eat.

It was really tasty, a smooth umami flavor. The potato taste is hard to describe; it doesn't taste like anything else. If anything, other things may taste like potato, because it is so elemental. This potato was almost creamy against the skin, which was patchy with crunchy bits where there were remnants of clay. And the little remains of the clay added an almost sweet (though gritty) taste. I knifed a tab of butter on the other half and the steamed, buttered ball of flavor had hints of all the potatoes I had in childhood summer lobster boils—but with crunchy skin! I set off to find my wife so she could try some. I cornered her in her home office, holding a small packet of skin filled with fluffy pith. It's safe to say she wasn't excited and, after biting, made a face and said, "Gross." I asked if it was the texture or the taste, and she said, "Yes." And then thought about it and said it was too chalky. Later at dinner, my two-year-old also didn't appreciate the edible clay (sans potato). He chewed on a tiny piece, nearly gagged, and wiped his tongue furiously, reaching for his cup of water. But when I asked if he wanted Dada to eat it, he said, "Yes!" and clapped with glee when I did.

Cod, Scallops, Salt: Iceland

CHEF GUNNAR KARL GÍSLASON looks Viking-ish. Tall, burly, and bearded. Yet, rather than brutish, a bubble of earthy, amiable charm surrounds him. I'd caught flashes of seriousness—when he was standing over the stove or concentrating on tweezing fried haddock scales onto a baked cod (or was it the other way around?), but his resting face was an impish grin. He gave off an aura of *gemütlichkeit*. You can almost tell he started in a restaurant as a dishwasher. And this man did not fail upwards, but earned his rise to becoming one of the top chefs in the world. Most every place he touched tongs—Denmark's Kommandanten and Ensemble, and now Iceland's Dill—received Michelin stars.

On meeting him in the small, front dining area of Dill, I sat down at a table dividing the restaurant from the kitchen. The open kitchen was a stage for his flair as a master of ceremonies. Behind me on shelves were pickling jars where local herbs (some self-foraged) like chervil, birch shoots, juniper berries, and dill floated, refracting the light of the front window. Gunnar was moving around the prep station, manning the stove, and walking me through the recent rise of Scandinavian cooking. He said that harvesting ingredients himself adds to the experience: "If I go and

Cooking with Gunnar at Dill in Iceland

pick it, the story that I will tell the guests is always going to be greater, and I will always cook it and serve it with more respect than if it was just brought here by a delivery guy." A little twinkle hit his eye, "With all due respect for delivery guys."[1]

Slicing, fileting, grilling, plating, he talked about the local fish ("We have the best fish in the world"), the just-as-impressive lamb (on an "island with more sheep than people"[2]), and the evolution of taste in this unique landscape where chefs adapted techniques developed in old Europe to use local ingredients in traditional recipes not found anywhere else (rotten shark, anyone?). He was at the height of his powers, not only in creating the meal but also in walking me through the cooking process. Technical genius and talent, mixed with knowledge, joy, and pride, is quite a combination. And it all came together in the salted cod hiding in another's scales and scallops sauteed in smoked butter that sat steaming before me.

For the smoked butter, we stopped at a family farm a few hours from Reykjavik. The enormous barn, dwarfing the family home, was on a slope leading down to the sea. It was made of three large, connected bays protecting this rural family's livestock of cows and sheep. Tucked by the wide, flat water in a tall fjord, the house and the barn and the sheep grazing alongside in the summer sun were picturesque. But seasons change. I thought about what it must be like in January, with the wind howling and the snow whipping around in the twenty-four-hour night, with no one else around for miles, as well as about what people go through to have some "freedom" and a little land to call their own. Even in summer, the sunlight was measured here: We were at the edge of the Arctic. Caring for animals in bucolic places is hard work, but in Iceland it seems extra tough—a true struggle to survive. The matriarch came out to meet me: "I heard you are smoking butter." She was in her sixties, whipcord thin, with deep crow's-feet etched on her face. But her eyes were bright and she had the healthy look of someone who spent their days outside. As we headed towards the barn, a cloud passed over the sun and the wind picked up. I pulled my hat down and zipped my jacket and I—who has known comfort most of my days—thought life here seemed tenuous, at best.

Moving past the rows of stalled cows (I already had various types of milk in the show's "pantry"), I was headed towards the sheep. The long bay had a low, slanted ceiling; we needed to duck under the anchor beams. There was no pretense here, no bright red-painted walls or unused space for a nap in the hay. This was purely utilitarian, divided neatly stall after stall, and the walls outfitted for warmth—chinks filled with a mix of straw and clay. The crew rounded a corner into the next building, a different configuration called a bank barn. It used the slope of the hill to have two levels, the upper (more a ramp than a floor) to toss hay down to the animals below. We entered above the few sheep and three-month-old lambs not out on the hillside lunching. Just what I needed. Over the guardrail I went and jumped down below with my pitchfork in hand—looking for just the right one. And there it was, a perfect size. A large, dried patty of stomped-on, urine-stained, hard-caked sheep dung. A couple of these and I'd have what I needed to smoke the butter.

There is a saying in Iceland: If you see three trees together, you have a forest. On the long drive from Reykjavik out to the Westfjords I saw not one. It's hard to wrap your head around the empty, open expanse. Trees give context to your own size, but there—with only the volcanoes and glaciers and fjords to measure yourself—you just feel incredibly small. The midnight sun, the pale blue sky with a fiery glow on the horizon, looked over rocky windswept fields. There were no forests because the Norse settlers cut them all down and, in doing so, almost ended human life on the island.

Early settlers saw the rich soils and old-growth forests that covered 25 to 45 percent (and new evidence points to even more) of the country and went to work planting and chopping. The birch, mountain ash, and willow trees were cut down to build and heat homes, build boats, and smelt metal, but also to make way for fields of barley and meadows for livestock. Early settlers brought along their seeds and pigs and cows from Norway and the British Isles. But this wasn't Norway or England. The deep soil and forests were different from home. Here they stood on a fragile landscape that hadn't seen people before. The equilibrium was quickly upended, the trees came down, the soils eroded into the seas, and the Middle Ages grew too cold for planting.[3] Only about

2 percent of Iceland is now forested (and that's mostly because of serious tree-planting initiatives since 1990). Gone are most of the cows and pigs, as they became unsustainable. And over time, even some of the fish stocks collapsed. The Atlanto-Scandi herring fisheries dropped by 99 percent by 1970.[4] Gone is most of the agriculture, as the short season, rocky ground, and intermittent volcanic eruptions make growing food haphazard—80 to 90 percent of food is imported. Norse ghosts now look down on a very different landscape.

In the absence of trees for energy, Icelanders had to become resourceful, and there was where the dung came in. Without trees to heat homes or cook, they turned to what they had in great supply: shit. But they aren't alone; more than a quarter of the planet—over 2 billion people—use the dried plant material in animal dung for energy.[5] What started as necessity evolved into taste and a food culture. *Hangikjöt* is the classic Icelandic Christmas dish of smoked lamb; it's also eaten by many as the Sunday meal as well. You can use birch or peat, but sheep dung is the traditional fuel. Gunnar incorporated the smoke into his seafood dish, so here I was collecting the poop to infuse the butter.

After walking out with my treasure we headed down the road to meet the son. He led the way into a field towards the smokehouse. I asked if he ever used cow dung for smoking. With a smile on his lips he said, "No, no, no. Only sheep dung. Cow dung?! Now that's just disgusting."[6]

As we moved across the meadow, the smokehouse looked like a hump in the earth, covered with turf, like some kind of old burial mound. It was only when we tramped around to the front that we found a door that opened into the dark inside. Poking my head in, the smoke burned my eyes. Through a haze I glimpsed shelved cuts of meat, hanging legs of lamb, and fish. "We also smoke trout and salmon."

I looked back at the farmer's son, "It doesn't smell so great in here."

He replied, "It smells lovely."

Luckily, it was too dark to shoot in, so we set up our smoke in the open air on the hilltop next to the smokehouse. Unlike lamb, which is smoked for up to two weeks, butter takes on flavor very quickly. We laid the butter, some tinder, a large glass bowl, and the poop out on a slate slab. I used the tinder to light the crusty pie. Once the dung was billowing I placed the dome over it to collect smoke. Then I placed the smoky bowl over the butter. While we waited, I asked if smoking butter was traditional. "No, it isn't." Totally Chef's unique riff on an Icelandic tradition.

I noted how strange the smell was and he agreed. "It is very strange."

I said, "But nostalgic for you."

"It's the smell from the kitchen at Christmas time."

After about five minutes, the farmer's son said time was up.

Why had I gotten myself into this mess? Reluctantly I took the lid off in a puff of stinky smoke.

"Should we taste it? Is that what goes on?" I was kind of afraid.

The farmer's son leaned down to take a whiff. "Now that is the smell you want!"[7]

I leaned down and sniffed the butter. *That is the smell you want?!* Uggh. Was the funk coming from the butter? I got a pinch, took it on my tongue and...

It was actually good. Quite good. It brought me back to the meal I ate at Dill, and I now knew why Chef's scallop dish popped the way it did. I'd had sauteed scallops before, but not like Gunnar's, never ones in smoked butter. Here in the field, I had been afraid to taste because of the noxious smell coming off the smoldering poop. But the butter itself smelled like a campfire and had a nice charcoal accent to it. I said the last part out loud and the farmer's son nodded in agreement with a big smile on his face.

* * *

We were fishing the Westfjords—if you picture Iceland like a lamb, this would be its screaming head. Heading to the town of Flateyri and its fjord, which are surrounded on both sides by steep mountains, to get there you had to wind your way along a coastal road for hours. In and out of fjords, with only a few short-cuts through mountain tunnels. The bar in Flateyri was empty and no one was staffing the little shed that was a hat store, so I knocked on doors to chat with locals about the goings-on around town. At the end of town, closest to the mountain, I came across the wife from a married couple of shepherds. I asked what it was like living in this small town. "Everyone knows when you go to the bathroom."[8] She explained how they hadn't been here for the avalanche in 1995, which destroyed twenty-nine homes and killed twenty townsfolk,[9] but the neighbor's roof had ended up on top of her mom's house. She pointed to the avalanche dam that had been built into the mountain above the town like a giant capital "A" that would now channel snow slides to either side of the town. While there was no snow up there now, I could imagine the winter drifts piled up until they finally came down in a roar… but now diverted, saving the town winter after winter.

I asked why a young couple would end up here at what felt like the end of the world. She said they had come back from Reyk-javik for the self-sufficiency the town allowed and to have a more sustainable life with their garden and their sheep. A fierce environ-mentalist, she spoke wholeheartedly about overconsumption and living a more authentic existence. It did look extremely fulfilling, maintaining a home in this rough environment. And her description of her son's life—the bike riding, the fishing, the herding, the freedom—came out of a storybook.

I had surprised her while she was grinding down mutton to store for the winter, which was kismet. My guide to these parts was Dill's sous chef, John Peterson. And if you are lucky enough to have a chef around, you put him to work. I bought ten pounds of mutton later that afternoon from her husband, so John could make his version of shepherd's pie. The subtle sharpness of lamb makes it my favorite meat, but I'd heard that older sheep taste overly wild and overwhelming. I'd never tasted mutton, as it's hard to find in America, so here was my chance to try it. In my anticipation I hung around the stove like a fly, "trying" to help out, but John shooed me from the kitchen. He had a mantra passed down from a mentor: "Food is like music. Nirvana was a three-piece band and they still kicked ass; you don't need more than three or four elements to make a dish work. Therefore make each element shine on its own." And shine it did. What can I say about the meal besides how exceptional it was? A perfect dish for the place and moment. The mutton was done just right, with the powerful flavor moderated by the creamy potatoes and sweet carrots and sauteed onions. Someone opened some kind of alcohol, but all I remember is the dish. The group had argued about the size of the purchase—ten pounds is a lot of meat—but we licked the Pyrex clean. Unsurprisingly, John now runs his own kitchen at a fishing lodge in Hofsa on the east coast.

We, the crew, all sat in the dining room of our Airbnb stuffing ourselves with this savory layer cake of flavors, with the late-evening sun like never-ending twilight coming through the windows in this renovated wooden house, days from "civilization." We

John and his Land Cruiser checking out Flateyri

talked about the remote town and the conversation with the shepherds about their authentic existence. John said Icelanders generally share this mentality. "There is pride in accomplishments (here), and having a self-sustaining life."[10] This was one of the reasons he moved from Greenland.

As I got into my kayak the next morning to fish for cod and haddock, the fisherman from this little town of 150 told me I could use a fish from his quota. Flateyri sits on a hooked cape in the Önundarfjörður Fjord. The weather was surprisingly mild for one of the northernmost towns on the planet, due to the sea I was about to enter—the offshore Gulf Stream brings warmth. I paddled out of the sheltered marina. And *wham!* The current was in a fierce rush and paddling was tough, the waves choppy even though we were somewhat protected by the other side of the fjord directly across from us. The fjord did, however, create a funnel pushing us back from where we came. Returning home from our trip was gonna be a breeze, but getting to the salmon aqua farms we were gonna fish around wasn't a given. The buoyed, circular structure never seemed to be getting any closer.

When I complained, the fishing guide told me about a swim race that had just been run, from one side of the fjord to the other. My jaw dropped. Every year it commemorates a rogue cow, Sæunn, who in 1987 escaped from a slaughterhouse and made it across from Flateyri over to the beach on the opposite side in Valþjófsdalur. When the townsfolk went to go get her back, farmers from Kirkjuból in Valþjófsdalur valley heard about her pluck and bought her.[11] She lived happily ever after (for six more years). Now, annually, in tribute and as a tourist attraction, people make the one-and-a-half mile swim. As I watched the current rip past me, looked up at the church Kirkjubólskirkja on the distant shore in Kirkjuból, and put my hand in the freezing water, I thought about how living at the top of the world with not many people around (no one to tell you what you are doing is bananas) makes you do crazy things.

And there definitely weren't many people around. Flateyri started in 1792 as a trading post and then, in the second half of the nineteenth century, became a base for whalers and shark fishermen and has had a long history tied to the fishing industry with a few hundred people calling the town home. But recently it has been in decline. When I asked why, some locals mentioned the avalanche, which led to an exodus as many residents found continuing to live there too painful.[12] Others pointed to government fishing rules which they felt had dried up jobs. To counter the collapsing fish stocks, Iceland instituted a cap on how much fish could be caught.

It was these limits the townsfolk seemed to be bristling at. Here was what seemed to be a direct conflict between local needs and the greater good. Did requiring fishing to become more sustainable damage local economies? My initial reaction was that everyone was probably disgruntled because limits were being put on their catch—but if it was saving the fish, then it was a good thing. But after doing some research and speaking with a local environmentalist, it came to seem a hijacking had occurred! There was a crime with no crime scene, no police tape to mark the spot, just empty towns. It turns out it wasn't the fishing limitation itself that was the problem, but how it was laid out and who profited from it. And thus I was introduced to the total allowable catch (TAC) and the individual transferable quota (ITQ).

* * *

Fisheries (the fishing grounds and the processing plants in the fishing villages) became economically important on the coasts around 1900 and attracted people from more isolated areas of the country. Fishing boats became motorized early in the twentieth century, and the fishing fleet expanded greatly in size and technology after World War II. From 1930 to 1968 is often called "the herring adventure," an adventure that ended in 1968 with the collapse from overfishing of the herring stocks. Fisherpeople moved on to other species, the fleets were improved, and the territorial waters were extended to fifty and then 200 miles. And stocks started collapsing again. Following warnings of overfishing of cod, the government established a TAC for cod in the late 1970s. Yearly TACs for other species were introduced in the '80s.

The ITQ was introduced in 1984 and a comprehensive ITQ was made permanent in 1990 in the Fisheries Act. Under the ITQ, quotas within the total allowable catch were given for free to fishing-boat owners based on their relative catches over the three years prior to its introduction. The "transferability" feature was key: Original quota owners and subsequent buyers could rent or sell their shares fairly freely, or use them as collateral, creating what has been called a "fishing stock market."

The goals of the TACs and the ITQ were to limit the total amount of fish that could be caught, eliminate the boat race to catch the most fish, and provide incentives for protecting fishing stocks for the long term. The ITQ was also designed as a way to make fishing fleets more efficient, as efficiency—rather than just more fish—would mean more profit, and as a way for less-efficient owners to leave the business by selling their quotas.

There seems to be universal agreement that the combination of the TAC and the ITQ has worked as hoped to preserve fish stocks. "Currently, none of the commercially harvested species in Iceland is considered to be threatened due to overfishing,"[13] according to a report from the Organization for Economic Co-operation and Development in 2017. From an ecological point of view, this is an amazing turnaround and a model that lots of other places can be (and are) looking at. Iceland now also wastes little of its fish—98 percent of each fish is used, with "by-products" being used for fish oils, collagen supplements, or innovative products such as medical plasters for wounds.[14]

But the economic and social impacts of how the ITQ was set up have been a lot less positive. Although the Fisheries Act says that fish in Icelandic waters are the "common property of the nation," the Act actually transformed fish from a "common good" to a "private good" (of course, the fish may see the whole discussion very differently). The fortunate boat owners who were awarded the right to harvest the fish struck it rich; nobody else who depended on fishing for their livelihood did. Villages that were dependent on the fleets and the fish they brought home for processing got depopulated when quotas were transferred and new owners moved local fleets elsewhere. The Act has contributed to an intense concentration of the fishing industry: Environmental entrepreneur and film/TV producer Rakel Gardarsdottir told me in January 2022 that ten families and two or three large companies now own the whole quota.

Although the Act has been amended to try to make it a little fairer, the fundamentals and the bitterness remain and have played out in Icelandic politics, not least in the long and contested campaign for a new constitution. The demand for a new constitution rose out of the economic collapse of 2008, and regaining public control of fishing resources has been a central feature from the beginning. The Constitutional Council, composed of people who were not professional politicians, was appointed by the prime minister and drew up a draft with broad public involvement—the process was often referred to as "crowdsourcing the constitution." Over 66 percent of voters approved the draft in a 2012 referendum.

Article 34 establishes rules for permits related to natural resources, including "marine stocks" and "other resources of the ocean." It insists on "full payment" for use of the resources and time limits for permits, and it states that permits "shall never lead to a right of ownership or irrevocable control of the natural resources." In a complementary vote, 82.5 percent of voters approved the statement that they wanted "natural resources that are not privately owned to be declared national property."[15] The proposed constitution was submitted to the Althing (the parliament), where it has sat for ten years, resisted by those who would lose ownership of the quota and other interests. Despite this, it retains its popularity, with an October 2020 poll showing 54 percent in favor, 21 percent opposed, and 25 percent ambivalent. And Rakel seemed to be speaking for many others in expecting its eventual passage and reassertion of the "common good."

* * *

We finally did make it out to the salmon farms at the mouth of the fjord. Because of all the food in the farms, other fish like to congregate around the nets. After some false starts ("Cod damn it!") I netted my haddock and cod, which was nothing compared to the six fish my guide caught. There are definitely fish in these waters.

The next day was for the shellfish. I'd dived before but only in bath-warm water with pretty fish. This was dry-suit scuba in Arctic waters, where you put warm clothes under a sealed suit. Only your hands and face are in the elements, and they are freezing. To top it off I have trouble equalizing my ears deeper than ten feet or so. Early childhood battles with ear infections literally left scars and so a teenage open water scuba test ended in failure. Unable to leave the depth of a pool, I wasn't able to get my diving certificate, which added some mordant humor when I noted there was an extra mouthpiece and tube connected to my tank in case I had to save my guide. We would be in serious trouble if it ever came to that. Diver Simbi Hjalmarsson of Dive Westfjords seemed unfazed by the inappropriate power I held even after I struggled to stand with the tanks and only got to my feet with his help. This wasn't going to go well.

But wading into the water changed everything. I sank below the surface and the sharp sting of the cold woke me, firing off the euphoria that comes with it. Cortisol was released from my adrenal glands, providing pain relief and a sort of high, giving me confidence. Followed by beta-endorphins and norepinephrine and, dare I say, joy. Below me was a silt and rock bottom with waving yellow sea plants. With my green net bag in tow, I started pulling myself along, looking for food. Simbi says seals sometimes join the divers who are after the same thing—scallops and clams and uni. The week before he had seen a large, dark shadow not far from him—what he believed was a whale passing up the fjord while he was harvesting.

The only thing missing was the shellfish. The dull rocks and sediment looked empty. And then Simbi waved his hand over some silt, fanning it into the current, and pointed to a rock that wasn't a rock but a clam. An ocean quahog, the longest-living animal in the world. I put that in my bag. Then I saw a scallop and that went in, then a sea urchin, then another clam, and so on. Once you wrap your head around what you are looking at, the piles of shellfish below the water, you realize there is so much food it's almost shocking. Vídir Ingpórsson, who runs a seafood exporter out of the Westfjords, says that this area is one of the last unpolluted places in the world. "We are a green zone, the west, with no industrialization. [...] It's only seafood companies." All the jobs, "everyone's salary, come from seafood." Vídir says the seafood industry in Iceland originally just fed and gave jobs to locals "to catch protein to feed their families and to live, but then it evolved into an export industry."[16] I asked Simbi if there was a quota on the mollusks. He said collecting by hand had no limits. We went deeper into the cold and, surprisingly, my ears popped with the gradual descent.

But then it happened. Something grabbed the bag that was tied to my suit and I lurched to a stop, stuck floating under fifty feet of water, in the dark. Not made for this, I immediately lost my shit and my heart started racing. That's when I knew I was going to die. There was a button on my suit which, if pressed, would fill the suit up with air and shoot me to the surface. I thought about pressing it but was conflicted. What about the bends? Rising to the surface that fast could force nitrogen from my bloodstream into large bubbles and kill me. I reached for it and my hand

Diving for shellfish in Iceland

hovered, mulling what was a better end—decompression sickness or whatever was behind me in the deep. Counting to ten to calm myself I slowly turned with my flashlight to see…my bag caught on a rock. I reached back and untangled it. But while I wasn't dead, I now needed to pee badly, and this suit was sealed and I was dressed underneath in clothes I liked, so, sadly, I had to slowly rise. Breaking the surface, my bag raised into the air in triumph, thanking the universe no one had seen my near-suicide, I swam back to shore.

Sitting on a slight, grassy rise at the water's edge with Simbi and Vídir, we went through the bag to taste. Raw shellfish was never my cup of tea, but the scallop was delicious and the bright orange uni (which I was told were the urchin's gonads) were creamy with tasty dairy and egg-like flavors. Vigor explained that the same receptors that responded to cannabinoids were also triggered by sea urchin. "Eating this is like smoking weed?" Whether it was the uni or coming down from the swim, I was truly mellow. The only disconcerting moment was the quahog, which was

174

spawning. With a grimace, I watched Vigor wipe off the foaming gelatinous sperm before we tasted the clam muscle. I definitely wasn't as excited as this clam was.

* * *

Iceland is powerful. Under the ground lies energy to spare, and 66 percent of the country's primary energy use now comes from geothermal sources.[17] Geothermal energy heats 90 percent of Icelandic households and generates 25 percent or more of the country's electricity, a percentage which has grown by over 1,700 percent since 1990.[18] Geothermal has been used for decades to heat greenhouses, where Iceland can even grow tropical products such as bananas—and it's now being used to recycle plastics through extreme heat.

Although Iceland is doing exciting things, it is not unique in its potential access to geothermal energy. While some sources are site-specific, it has become apparent that geothermal energy can be developed practically anywhere, and it could become the major source of virtually clean 24/7-reliable, renewable energy. In a 2020 article in *Vox*, climate reporter David Roberts described it as "an inexhaustible, dispatchable, flexible renewable energy source" that is close to breaking through in solving technology issues, with the result that "the vision of a fully renewably powered world seems less and less utopian, more and more tantalizingly within reach."[19]

I was going to use this geothermal energy to make sustainable sea salt for my dish at Dill. So I headed out of the Westfjords towards Reykjanes Peninsula and Saltverk, a local salt factory. The peninsula sits on the mid-Atlantic rift where the North American and Eurasian tectonic plates meet (or, in this case, separate, as they are drifting away from one another). Geothermal pools, lava flows, and earthquakes are all common. It's here that tourists come to swim in the famous Blue Lagoon spa, all powered by a geothermal power station in Svartsengi.

Salt is vital for life. We need it to survive, but our bodies don't make it. So we have to find it in our environment. Luckily, planet earth is rich in salt, particularly the oceans. In hot countries, sea salt is made naturally by the oldest method—evaporating sea water with the power of the sun. When I was harvesting salt in Malta, the famous Gozo pans were just concrete pools that trapped the high tide. By the end of the summer the water was gone, having left behind piles of crystallized salt. But in colder countries the water has to be boiled away, and that is what I was doing here at Saltverk, using volcanic heat, the sustainable power under our feet.

I hopped out of John's beat-up, bright-red Land Cruiser and got right into the work. The manager, Petar Stakic (a Serbian national who immigrated for work and has run the place for five years), met me in the field outside the factory and took me down to the water's edge to check out the pumps taking water out of the ocean and pipes taking 206°F water from a hot spring underground. The shore was steaming where the spring came out to meet the ocean. Both the PVC pipes led back up to a tank house in a shed on the hill. The shed is a two-story high wooden structure with cloudy plastic panels in lieu of windows. On the ground floor is a large water tank, and as we made our way up the interior stairs, that's when it hit me. The heat. Opening the plywood door and stepping onto the scaffolding above the pool was like opening the lid on a pot of spaghetti. A thermometer on the center post read 38 degrees Celsius (104°F), and it was a muggy 38 degrees. I immediately started sweating. You could taste the salt in the air; white powder crusted everything. There were salt stalagmites and stalactites hanging everywhere.

Below us, piping ran through the tank of sea water, called the concentrating pond. Those pipes hold the hot spring water as it weaves its way around until the sea water dissipates, increasing the salinity from its natural 3.5 percent to 20 percent. At that point, the salt and water brew is moved via a brine pump to the salt pans in the main factory, where we headed next. Not so dissimilar from what I saw in Gozo. Those rectangular crystallizing ponds in the main factory were where the concentrated near-boiling happens, generated by the heat from the geothermal spring.

Saltverk wasn't the first to try this method—a Danish king built a salt factory on this very spot in the eighteenth century but abandoned it, according to Saltverk founder, Bjorn Steiner Jonsson, because it caused his iron to rust.[20]

Saltverk's website proudly says, "Geothermal energy is the sole energy source used, which means that during our whole process we leave zero carbon footprints on the environment and no CO2 and CH4 emissions." Salt crystals form on the surface and then sink to the bottom. Watching the science occur in real time was relaxing, until Petar handed me a very large shovel. I needed to get that salt from the bottom. Wearing a hairnet, gloves, and an apron, I dredged the bottom of the pool and came up with a heavy shovelful. These shovelfuls went onto trays, where we looked for any inconsistencies and then racked them on top of each other. The first batch of salt taken from the pans is the highest quality, and Saltverk calls it blue salt. Unlike grains of salt that are derived from mining and chemical processes, the sea crystals produced through this method form into flakes.

"It's a good workout," I commented to the worker shoveling next to me. He stared at me like I was an idiot. Maybe doing this day-in and day-out wasn't the trip to LA Fitness I imagined. I wheeled my trays into the drying room. Here is where the salt spends the final twelve to sixteen hours of the five-to-seven-day process. Waiting for me at the end was Petar holding a paper sack of blue salt to bring to Dill (I also bought a bag of smoked salt to bring home to my wife). Petar said Gunnar was a regular customer, as are many European Michelin star chefs. I was struck by the fact that it is not only sustainable and environmentally friendly but also a great business model, because they didn't have to pay much for their energy (a small fee to the city covers their use of the public spring).

And that was that. With only seaweed left to forage I headed back into Reykjavik. John drew me a map with an "X" marking the spot for good sea truffle and sandwort on a beach within city limits. The wind was brisk and the rocks slippery, but I made my last harvest. With a bit of sadness I realized this journey was over—it was just me bringing back the ingredients and the final cook that evening and then a flight home in the morning. Gunnar and I cooked together and then he treated me and the crew to a wonderful meal.

I was going to miss this place. Journeying the world puts your face right into the problems overwhelming humanity and the planet. It was invigorating to see all that has been done—reversal of overfishing, virtual elimination of waste in fish processing; exciting uses of geothermal energy; planting of trees in a treeless land. And it was invigorating to watch the continued effort of Icelanders to get it right—to demand the restoration of a common good and equitable sharing of its benefits. And most invigorating of all was the confidence of the people I met that they will overcome the obstacles and achieve both sustainability and equity. If they do, they might just end up being a Norse Star for the rest of us.

Saying goodbye to Chef, we all went out into the Reykjavik Friday night. Some didn't make their flights home in the morning.

Goat, Barley, Honey: Kenya

IT WAS 4:20 A.M., AND STRANGE SCREECHING, hooting sounds next to my tent jerked me out of sleep with a start. Hyenas had found the bed of branches by the river's edge where Simon and I butchered the goat, and they were ecstatic with bloodlust. Over the last week, I had gotten used to the other wild noises, the loud, eerie rattle of colobus monkey troops; the male frogs trying to out-sing one another for the love of a female; a bark/bleat of a zebra on the forest border. This was a bit different and set my teeth on edge, reaching down with a finger into my primitive brain. They sounded like death.

I lay there, still, holding my breath, eyes wide. Taking mental notes. More chittering and cackles echoing across the water at 4:24 as the hyenas splashed down the Sand River. Elephants passed by the riverbed at 5:03. Mostly, I heard my heart beating hard, my ears straining for the hyenas' return. When the sun came up, I left, bleary-eyed, to go find Uhuru, so we could pack up and head to meet Shaman Parmuaat Ole Koikai in the Forest of the Lost Child.

I had come here to make a meal. I was in Kenya collecting ingredients on instructions from Chef Ariel Moscardi. Ariel, born and raised in Ecuador and trained at Le Cordon Bleu, came to Kenya as a tourist in 2017 and stayed. He owns Cultiva—a farm-to-table restaurant in Nairobi, where he fuses new flavors with ancient ingredients from the bush. There is mystery in the meals. I didn't recognize most of his ingredients, but even the ones I knew, such as goat, were prepared in ways I'd never known before—goat-heart tartare with sweet beetroot dust; pureed peppers; artichoke; and pumpkin seeds formed into tiers. Ariel's meals are swirling with unusual textures and tastes. Most meaningful of all, Ariel draws on his own background to influence his menu. Goat is a staple food for the Maasai, and slaughter is conducted ritually, he says. He adds, "Of course, where I come from, the Mayas, the Aztecs, the Incas, had ritual offerings to the gods, and the sacrifice was to eat the heart."

Ariel's meal not only sent me on the journey for a goat shank and heart, but was filled with local twists on dishes I thought I knew such as beer and crème brûlée. We would be harvesting other tentpole ingredients from local farms, on the African plains, and in primal forests: barley, *khat*, sausage tree fruit, medicinal herbs, and the root of a shrub that tastes like vanilla.

We traveled first to Mount Kenya to visit Tamalu Farm to get barley for our stew and khat and sugar cane for our cocktail, among other ingredients. Famed Kenyan paleoanthropologist and conservationist Richard Leakey had agreed to talk with me and had thrown in the use of his plane as well, so we figured we might as well use it. The Kenya Forest Service has been working towards restoring the country to 10 percent forests, the level at independence, up from 7 percent; it works with conservancies and communities that live next to the forests to achieve this. Toward this goal, Tamalu, a ten-acre site on the slopes of Mount Kenya that was originally a flower farm, became an open-source demonstration site of regenerative agriculture in 2019 managed by L.E.A.F. Africa (Linking Environment Agribusiness & Forestry). Farm supervisor Sven Verweil told us that regenerative agriculture "increases biodiversity, enriches soils, improves watersheds, and enhances ecosystem services." The key strategy at Tamalu is agroforestry, the planting of forests that are integrated with crops and livestock on the same plots of land. Tamalu is starting with alley cropping, planting crops between rows of trees. Sven and farm manager James Thiong'o are planting forests of African redwood, Elgon teak, silver oak, African cherry, and African juniper. They are interspersing cash crops, including those I needed. When I arrived, I realized I had hit the jackpot: They had all the beans, herbs, artichokes, squash, pumpkin, beetroot, kale, garlic, ginger, and turmeric Chef might want. And the barley, sugar, and khat.

Tamalu follows the Brazilian agroforestry technique of "syntropic" agriculture. Developed by Ernst Götsch in Bahia, syntropic agriculture works with nature and mimics early farming. As trees grow from seedlings, they help to restore the soil and provide shade. Two months after planting, the farmer can harvest vegetables, and then, fruits and grains. "Each plant needs not only soil, fertilizer, and water, but microclimatic conditions to develop," says Götsch. "When farmers understand it, they create biodiverse ecosystems that offer each plant a life bubble, with no need of poison and fertilizer." [1]

Sven gave me a tour of Tamalu and explained syntropic agriculture and its practical impact on reversing environmental degradation and combating climate change. Then he handed me off to James to grab most of the produce I'd need. Along the way, James pointed out medicinal trees ("my people [whom I believe are the Kikuyu] use that for prostate cancer"), flowered artichokes (not harvested, but being used to regenerate the soil and support bees), sugarcane, and khat (also known as *qat*). We grabbed barley from a testing plot and, racing a rainstorm, hopped back on Leakey's plane to make our way to the borders of the Maasai Mara National Preserve. As we lifted away, I looked down at the little human-made forest hiding the fruits and veggies, and then to where small figures were running this way and that, preparing for the storm. Checking out Tamalu and agroforestry filled me with a fighting spirit. A farm like that accomplished a lot—countered the drawbacks of monoculture and, because of that, didn't have to use pesticides. It integrated trees, valuable soldiers in the climate-change fight, and created jobs. Small, non-mechanized farms can be local economic hubs for a community. It all felt so intuitive.

As we broke through the clouds and crossed the Great Rift Valley, the Mara revealed itself. The brush and trees, then the snake of a river and moving dots that grew into animals as we descended—elephants and zebra and wildebeest traveling south to Tanzania. Ahead, a dirt runway was cut into the bush like an orange scar.

Ariel's also the head chef for Royal African Safaris (RAS), so we devised a plan for how I could forage in the wild. I would piggyback with the safari, but instead of following the great migration that the park is famous for with the other tourists, I would make excursions to find my ingredients.

"Safari" means "journey" in Swahili. My childhood images of safaris were mostly gathered from movies, which always seemed to show wealthy white hunters in pith helmets shooting lions and having illicit Hemingwayesque love affairs. Some things are different today; some are not. For one thing, in Kenya, tourists can look and take pictures but can't harm the animals. Some safaris still cater to the super-wealthy and super-entitled; others are less expensive, though hardly cheap. Tourism, much of which is safari-based, is a huge industry in Kenya; in 2019, over 2 million tourists brought $1.6 billion into the country, providing foreign exchange and supporting jobs.[2] Many of the safari and other hospitality jobs are of the "paycheck-to-paycheck" type, and there are charges that much of the "real" money goes to tour operators and leaves the country.

Peter Sylvester, a partner differentiating RAS from other safaris, says, "We are aiming to get to 90 percent of the tariff staying local. In many of the existing luxury safari models, adjusted for international capital and equity payments, less than forty cents stays in the country, and probably less than five cents of those into the local economy."

I couldn't harvest in the national park, so while other tourists would be in the Mara watching lions, I would be foraging and harvesting in conservancies that bordered the park.

The conservancies surrounding the Maasai Mara National Preserve, which is reserved for wildlife, were created in response to crisis. A million wildebeest, and hundreds of thousands of gazelles and zebras, annually migrate from the Serengeti National Park in Tanzania to the Maasai Mara Preserve in pursuit of water and grazing land.[3] But this migration is threatened by human settlement, increased cattle grazing and cultivation of crops, and the building of infrastructure. While no one lives in the Preserve, the population of the areas around the Preserve grew by 400 percent just during the period 2010-2020, while the numbers of large animals on the Kenyan side dropped by more than 75 percent. The Kenya Wildlife Conservancies Association (KWCA) says that Kenya, overall, has lost 70 percent of its wildlife since 1990.[4]

More than 14,000 Maasai landowners—many of whom had found themselves individual owners as a result of legal, political, and economic forces that undermined the Maasai's age-old nomadic pastoralism—have formed fifteen conservancies bordering the Preserve, setting aside land to provide refuge to wild animals, in conjunction with safari operators.[5] The landowners get paid for the set-aside, essentially being paid not to farm or graze cattle on it. The safari operators get the benefit of higher concentrations of wildlife. The income from tourism and philanthropy is shared between the operators and the landowners. According to Daniel Ole Sopia of the Maasai Mara Wildlife Conservancies Association, an average of $7.5 million gets paid annually to participating landowners.[6] Of course, all is not always sweetness and light—there are often intense disputes over who gets what share of the money and who gets jobs; but, overall, it seems to be a win-win, not least for the wildebeest, gazelles, and zebras.

The Chef's cocktail, a *pombe* (beer) made of herbs, honey, khat, sugarcane, and *muratina*, was the main reason for the foraging. Muratina is a local alcohol made from the *Kigelia africana*, or sausage fruit. Found in the savanna, the sausage fruit is propagated by bats; is eaten by baboons, elephants, and hippos; is deadly poisonous to humans when raw; and grows up to thirty pounds and three feet long. The fruit resembles a large sausage and gives its tree its name.

I went with Uhuru, managing director of RAS's Mara unit, to climb a Kigali tree just outside the Mara Park elephant fence, though halfway up I realized there was no way I was reaching the fruit. The six million years of evolution away from our ancestor shared with chimpanzees hamstrung me. Plus, the lower fruits had already been taken by opportunistic elephants. I climbed down and found some on the ground, though they had been nibbled by something. We ended up tossing sticks and rocks to bring the hard fruit down—Uhuru could pitch for the Mets. Then we went off to boil it fifteen times—no one was specific with a number (it ranged from three to fifteen), so I felt better to err on the side of not dying. Uhuru promised to be the taster.

But our fruits were too small and too young. Chef took one look at the foot-long, green gourd and sent me back out. Turned out that Indi knew of another tree that might just have fruit. Indi, an RAS partner, is one of the continent's most qualified guides, having completed the FGASA (South African) and KPSGA (Kenya) certifications. She is the only female Gold-Level guide, the highest KPSGA qualification, one of fewer than fifty active Gold-Level guides in Kenya. Indi's also a certified walking guide with a heavy-bore .458 rifle, which she brought along in the Rover and on our walk—just in case. There are only a handful of those certificants, as Kenya banned sport hunting in 1977.

As we walked, she talked about how hard it was for a woman to rise up through the ranks and how it took her much longer to achieve her levels than if she were a man. "There are only two handfuls of female guides in the whole country, because it is a

Indi and David on foot in The Mara

very male-dominated industry." There are always more questions for women: "As a woman, can you carry a firearm, can you walk safely, can you drive, or can you be able to stay six months in the bush?" "It was much later that I got into working because I had to get qualified first." Knowing how much harder it was for her to get where she was ironically made me feel very comfortable out in the bush. Underneath the smooth, easygoing Safari guide patter, she was a tough cookie.

Indi's tree was exactly what the chef ordered. So many fruits underneath I didn't even have to climb; huge, three-foot-long gray tubes that had to have been thirty pounds each littered the grass. We found one without any nibble marks straight off and I flipped it over my shoulder. Though I did notice a jackal carcass in the tree next to us that had been more than nibbled (by a leopard, Indi said). Ariel was very pleased with the fruit of our labors.

Ariel adds khat leaf to the brew to give it some real punch. Khat, which I had grabbed at Tamalu, is a stimulant, a drug akin to speed that is chewed all over Africa and the Middle East (it may have originated in Ethiopia). It also doesn't taste so great. But if you chew it and immediately suck on sugar cane, its dance partner in the cup of muratina at the bar in Cultiva, it is tantalizing. The drink was an adventure in my mouth—the tastes weren't easy, but the speedball push-pull aftereffect was almost euphoric. While WHO doesn't consider khat addictive, I definitely wanted to harvest some more after the tasting.

For the honey, I went with several local Maasai men to visit a wild hive in the Sacred Forest. Upon arrival, I had to be introduced to the elders, forest guardians, and the shaman, also known as the *laibon*, as access to the forest is subject to their invitation. The Maasai culture is a gerontocracy—one that reveres its elders. As Uhuru said, "obviously those who have survived so long in a tough environment must have done something right." The shaman is the most important figure in the Maasai religion, guiding the community through divination and prophecy.

Heading into the Forest of the Lost Child, I was also asked to shut off my phone. There was to be no GPS on the trip, to keep the Sacred Forest a secret. I was told the story of the chief marketing officer of a huge American tech company who refused to give up his phone; he was finally reluctantly convinced, and by the end of his journey understood that places like this need to be protected.

The Sacred Forest is the spiritual center of the Purko Maasai, the largest Maasai section. This land is high, misted hills, thick with vegetation like a botanical garden greenhouse, and wet with old growth trees—huge strangler fig trees you can't wrap your arms around that spill white milk when poked (Shaman Parmuaat told me this sap was the only female aphrodisiac in the forest). Pencil cedars and Afro olive trees form the forest canopy and all kinds of medicinal berries and flowers that don't even have scientific names yet hug the ground. I tried a berry that Parmuaat said cures stomach aches. After taking a bite of the bitter red berry I asked how the cure works. I was told that it makes you vomit and shit diarrhea. The next twenty minutes were a little tense.

This forest was rich, the soil sticky and loamy. The lowlands are arid and wild, while those highlands are the productive areas all the way to Sudan and Ethiopia. Wild animals make their way through the farmlands and into the hills, too; baboons come to the small lake edge at dusk along with zebras. Elephants are sometimes seen through the trees, rare, like ghosts. And there are buffalo up there, arguably the most dangerous animal in Africa. As we walked, foraging, the buffalo scat got fresher and more frequent, like something out of a horror film. Thankfully, the guardians brought along their spears.

The Maasai double-sided spear is a formidable weapon, and each warrior would carry two into battle. It's one of the reasons the Maasai were so effective as an army, their grip on a tract of land ensured good pasture for their livestock. Coincidentally, this also stopped the European trading caravans and explorers from reaching the interior of this part of the continent. This protected many of the cultures that make up modern-day Kenya from the horrendous ravages of slavery. While now the face of Kenya (especially for the vital tourism industry), Maasai have always only made up 2 percent or so of the population.

The next stop was honey. It was surprisingly chilly; everyone had reached into the depths of their bags for the odd sweater. I had on a couple layers topped by my raincoat. Not the Neil Simon's "Africa hot" I'd been expecting. We were traveling through upland mesic and Afro-Alpine forests. My crew wore hats and even a fingerless glove or two. We'd woken to a light drizzle. People had the sniffles. One producer was nursing a cough and a sore throat. We all slowly made our way out of camp down into the valley.

The caravan stopped halfway down the mountain at a small encampment half-hidden from the road by a copse of flowering jacaranda. Hopping from the Land Rovers, we pushed branches aside and were met by smoke. It was traveling blacksmiths. The actual craft of forging steel and making the tens of thousands of spears needed to defend the Maasai was undertaken by a group of "blacksmiths" loosely descended from an Iron Age West African migration into East Africa. As such, the blacksmiths remain socially/culturally distinct within the Maasai. Next to the Sacred Forest is a neighboring community, whose lineage allows them to be blacksmiths, and they are next to a rich iron ore deposit. You can actually see the metallic, dusty hills as the ore sits near the surface.

We'd stay the afternoon to watch clay furnaces and makeshift bellows melt the ore while the local master blacksmith (a retired doctor taking up his father's mantle) pounded metal into swords and spears. I bought my wife an iron necklace and my father a throwing mace reserved for elders.

Afterward, the Maasai elders and I continued down into a small glen where the buzzing of bees got and kept our attention. African bees have a bad rap. Here in America they are known as killer bees. Yet an African lowland bee or savanna bee sting is no more potent than a European bee sting. The problem is that African bees send out ten times the guard bees, hundreds in response to a threat, and will pursue that threat for a greater distance—up to a quarter mile from the hive. The hive I was approaching had around 80,000 bees, and the average lethal dose for a person my size is 500–1,100 bee stings. But, in truth, those bees had more to worry about from us. If I were to try to get the honey from them in the wild I would likely destroy their hive. Instead, one of the beekeepers we were with was going to take me into the village to see a hive he had designed that the Maasai are now using to deter elephants around gardens.

As we left I glanced back; the bees' nest sat up in the hollow of the standing half of a fallen tree, disturbed by some illegal logging. The logging site was still active; there was fresh sawdust around some cedar stumps. The shaman and other guardians whispered amongst themselves and gave angry glances when they noticed it. A logging site up here without their permission was a very serious problem. Later, Peter told me that encroachment into the forest has been getting worse. People have been putting up fences and taking down trees. The Shaman Parmuaat would report a violation and the trespassers would be arrested, but, more than likely, would be released the next day when a call was made from a powerful ally. Illegal logging is big business. The UN reports 70,000 hectares of Kenyan forest are lost every year to illegal logging. Some of the logs are used for charcoal and local use, but most of the logging is backed by large criminal syndicates sending high-value logs to Asia. The elders end up using their local sway to combat the logging more than relying on government help. They also try to give these local poachers other jobs. One of the beekeepers we were traveling with used to earn money in black-market timber.

At the hives in the village we were one bee suit short, so that meant we kept a car close for me to jump into in case anything happened. The beekeepers lit a native mushroom on fire to smoke and calm the bees. Not quite calm enough, it seemed, because I ran away with three stingers in my head and hid in the car. We did get our honey, though, which was important as it jump-starts the fermentation of the muratina. As with any beer, the muratina needs time to brew and ferment, so we started the process out in the bush. After boiling the sausage fruit and adding some medicinal berries for health and honey for taste, we uncovered the jug and waited for *Saccharomyces cerevisiae*. There are more than 150 different species of single-celled fungi that we call yeasts, but there is one in particular that's the yeast used for baking and brewing. It's unusual in that it's tolerant to very high levels of alcohol/ethanol so it can be used to ferment sugary fluid and create ethanol (which is actually quite poisonous). It creates this ethanol to ward off competitors—basically to kill the other bacteria yeasts in its surroundings to have free rein on the calories in order to reproduce.

The yeast isn't airborne. It doesn't produce spores. So how does it get into the jug if people don't put it in? Likely through insects. All noncommercial yeast starts with bugs; in this case, probably Kenyan paper wasps (the American paper wasp is vital to the US wine industry). Wasps with saccharomyces yeast in their belly will arrive to begin the fermentation. In the wild, a fermenting sap will attract a bunch of organisms, other yeasts—a conglomeration as soon as it's open to the air. But then saccharomyces comes in and raises the level of alcohol to wipe all the microscopic critters out. Cheers to that.

* * *

Then it was time for the goat. Buying a goat from a Maasai is complicated, made more so by the fact that goats, along with cattle, are part of Maasai culture's currency and thus any transaction needs to include the day's goat/Kenyan shilling exchange rate. But it's not a goat-shank barley stew without one. So the first order of business was to meet up with RAS Maasai crew member William Sekeri. In the Mara, he took me to his *boma* (a Swahili word for a livestock and community enclosure, probably from the Persian for "a place where one can dwell in safety") to barter for and slaughter a goat.

Goats were one of the first animals to be domesticated, possibly preceded only by dogs, with evidence in Iran dating back 10,000 years. Providing milk, meat, and fiber, goats have been particularly valuable for nomadic pastoralists such as the Maasai because of their adaptability.[7] They can eat a greater variety of plants and survive in a wider range of environments than either sheep or cows.[8] Although goats' intensive grazing can damage vegetation and soil stability, they are popular because they have short gestation periods, give milk in all but the worst droughts, and can eat almost anything.

There must have been a mix of fifty or sixty goats and sheep in the pen and I couldn't tell the difference. I knelt to get some goat milk (for the crème brûlée), only for a couple of five-year-olds to laugh and tell me that it was a sheep, and that the goat was the one behind me. I had informed the kids who were teaching me how to milk that I already knew what I was doing, but without their big, wooly coats, these sheep were making me look really bad. The young milking tutors loved it, and there was lots of shared giggling and pointing at me. I was saved by Uhuru, who motioned that it was time for the bartering to begin.

I'd met Uhuru, otherwise known as Daniel Kiarii, when I first arrived in the Mara and he shook my hand just outside the entry flap of the mess tent when I came for a morning coffee. Tall, solid, with tremendous patience and a lively sense of humor, he had been a sea of calm as the camp sputtered to life. A one-time bartender, TV repairman, and secondhand clothes smuggler who didn't even know how to put up a tent when he started in 1986, Uhuru had the air of someone who had seen and handled it all. I'd started looking forward to his tales of derring-do around the campfire at night. Born at midnight on December 12, 1963, the eve of Kenya's independence (thus his nickname), he had a nose for the dramatic. Like the time he smuggled a bundle of clothes across the border in his youth by wearing them all at once. There were run-ins with rebels as well as with aggressive hippos and lions and wild dogs—each story ending with escape by the skin of his teeth. Having already done the impossible and taught me to drive stick on a grumpy old British Land Rover ("if you can't find it, grind it"), this goat barter was gonna be a breeze for him.

We left through an opening in the acacia branch fence and William's father, one of the elders, pulled a goat out by a back leg and started haggling. William interpreted for me and his father, who was dressed in the legendary Maasai *shuka* (red-checkered robe), until Uhuru stepped in and took over. At that point it got real. When I asked if he had done this before, Uhuru said "only in a market, not a village." But he seemed pretty sure of himself. Uhuru was happy with the animal, "a big he-goat." During the bartering, though, he was loud and confrontational, with lots of "whoa whoa whoa"s on his part. William's dad seemed nonplussed. I watched the back-and-forth like a tennis match. Then it abruptly stopped on a dime—with smiles all around. Uhuru slapped my shoulder and I took the goat by the horns.

Maasai diets are over 50 percent vegetarian, including maize, roots, honey, and tree bark, and Maasai raise goats, sheep, and cattle primarily for milk and blood. Milk and blood can be harvested daily, while an animal's meat can be harvested only once. Milk is drunk fresh and in tea and is used to make butter. Blood is a valuable source of nutrients. Fresh milk and fresh blood are sometimes mixed for a ritual drink or to be given to the sick.[9] Milk or a milk/blood mixture is fermented to make a yogurt-like drink. Boiled blood is used in soups and stews and to accompany *ugali*, a maize-based porridge. Meat, sometimes mixed with blood and ugali, is primarily eaten at special occasions such as births, circumcisions, weddings, funerals, and TV hosts preparing a meal for a chef.

Fascinatingly, despite having a fat-heavy diet, Maasai traditionally have few heart problems and generally do not have high blood pressure or high cholesterol levels. It's not clear why they are so healthy—maybe genetics, maybe a high level of low-intensity activity. It's also not clear yet whether as many Maasai move into cities, and their diets become more "modern," their health will deteriorate.

When meat isn't needed, the blood is normally extracted without killing the animal. I saw this extraction on a cow. Using a small bow, an archer shoots a half-moon tipped arrow from a yard away as a group of men hold the animal still. Blood spurts out and is collected in a gourd until dirt and dung are pressed to the wound and the animal stumbles away to live another day.

The dairy and blood food sources have influenced Maasai culture in no end of ways. The need to maintain a viable food supply is paramount. Herds must always include a number of animals that have just calved. But cows and goats conceive only when reasonably well-nourished. Given the presence of lions, leopards, and hyenas, they must be guarded while grazing, driven to water, and housed inside the village's walls, and while being moved to fresher grazing areas. The family and village structures have been set up around this seminomadic pastoralism. The *boma* is a microcosm of this. Thorny branches are used as an outside wall. The family homes are just inside the wall and circular, thorny-walled animal pens that house the sheep, goats, and cattle are in the center—literally at the center of village life. If a lion or leopard were to get over the first wall, the Maasai have put themselves between the predator and their livestock.

Collecting the goat in the Boma with, from left to right, William and William's father, Uhuru

Simon Tira, my Maasai guide during the ritually conducted slaughter, was born in Talek and raised in a traditional Maasai family boma. His childhood was a mixture of looking after the family cattle and attending the local school, from which he graduated with a good command of English. Working for RAS for seventeen years, he is a confident, stout man, with a round, easy-to-smile face. He effortlessly carried the goat chest-high in his arms from the Land Rover out to my tent, handed it to me with a plop, and the goat stayed pretty docile. Head up, the buck was glancing around warily, neck swiveling for danger—not knowing he had already pulled the short straw. We took him into a little grove of green African milk trees at the edge of the sand and laid him down in a mattress of branches. Simon assured me that "goats are handled all the time," so ours was not immediately distressed by being turned on his side and sat on.

Simon showed me how to wrap a hand over the mouth and nose. The goat is knocked unconscious through strangulation, which is achieved by putting a knee into the chest and closing off the nostrils. The process was surreal—I was choking a living thing out with my bare hands. Staring straight ahead at the camera, I was able to look away from what was happening on the ground—to disassociate myself. A little dazed, I held on to the squirming animal. Simon told me I was doing well, obviously trying to build my short-lived confidence.

Two sides of my mind were wrestling with one another. One of them was aghast with what we were doing to the goat. This felt almost criminal. But the other voice was louder—this is how my hosts do things. It would be easier, more merciful (in my mind), and less personally distressing to just cut the goat's throat and walk away, but this ritual has been passed down for at least 500 years. So I bit my tongue, shoved the goat advocate into a small corner of my mind, and tightened my grip. I felt more for Wesley on sound who had a boom mic and headphones on and heard each groan and useless gasp. Jared, the DP, couldn't take his eyes off—we were filming and he was gritting his teeth. He later said he tried to stay on my face, keeping the strangulation hidden by the branches. Peter said that this is "quite quick and arguably more humane than other methods," and my mind flashed to American slaughterhouses. It seemed like forever. For two to three minutes we held the goat and forced the air from his lungs until he shuddered into unconsciousness. And, once again, I realized that when I'm eating meat, I am ultimately responsible for an animal's death, whether I kill it directly or simply have it arrive on my plate.

Once the goat was out, Simon unsheathed the long blade all Maasai men carry at their hips and went to work. He opened up a flap of skin along the side of the neck to act as a cup. He peeled it from the muscle and, with the tip of the knife, pierced the jugular vein. The trick was to drink the blood out of the flap as fast as it was flowing in and not get put off by the heat, smell, and sound effects. Peter explained, "Usually an experienced blood-drinker goes first, when the flow is fastest, and then hands over politely for those of us just getting our whistles wet. It's a precious and important part of the traditional diet." After Simon took his fill with "Yum, very sweet," I leaned in and drank. Definitely more metallic than sweet.

From the start of the goat day, our cultural differences kept bumping up against each other in my head, particularly around food. Watching the bloodletting with the bow and arrow as everyone held the struggling cow down, the blood spurting into the gourd of milk, where it was swirled and drunk, made my stomach turn. And drinking this pulsing blood wasn't much different. As writer Amy Fleming says, "Humans may be omnivores, but we're damned picky omnivores. One nation's succulent horse fillet is another's scandalous counterfeit beef."[10] Taste is built over time and molded by many streams, including communal and family norms, environment, and genetics (everyone's taste receptors are slightly different). And it begins before we are even born, as fetuses develop a predilection to what our mothers eat. It all makes for one of the most personal of orientations. Whether in Kenya, Tokyo, or Des Moines, some of the food will be regional and seem foreign to an outsider. And the visitor's reaction is sometimes visceral. I remember driving through middle America—Casper, Wyoming, to be exact—where my crew and I balked at the Rocky Mountain oysters at a late night meal. Trying to be as open minded as I could only went so far, as taste cannot be legislated. My first thought after hearing that Simon mostly just drank milk and ate meat was to ask, didn't he get bored of that? And my second was how that was such a Santa Monica thing to think.

The whole experience seemed so foreign to me, but then I thought of kosher and halal slaughter, both of which involve cutting the animal's neck for it to bleed out with an accompanying blessing. And Catholics drink blood every Sunday.

While I took the heart and shank back to Chef, I gave the rest of the goat to RAS's crew. RAS hires and trains from within the community, Peter says, providing jobs to people who are often unable to get employment in the more structured hospitality business. A white Kenyan, whose father opted for Kenyan, rather than British, citizenship at independence, Peter argues that RAS's business model supports local economic development and social justice by designing camps that are designed, built, and repaired locally. Hiring Maasai allows for most of the inputs, including food, to be local, assuring that more of each dollar spent reaches the local community, creating a sustainable circle.

The crew, nearly all Maasai, stood around the goat roasting on an open fire and a pot of boiling offal. In order to get more nutrients, the goat stomach and intestines, still filled with the goat's last meal, are made into a soup where the half-digested plant fibers (and some dung) are cooked—the previous grazers having already done most of the work. The RAS crew shared their meal with me, sawing off one of the most delicious ribs and cutting a mouthful of goat intestine that will never leave my nightmares. Once the meal was over, singing, dancing, and the famous Maasai jumping contests began. We jumped 'til the sun went down.

* * *

The next day, as we moved from the grassland savanna towards the Sacred Forest, we began to pass small homesteads, fenced acreage with one home, owned by Maasai who had left the pastoral life to farm or go into other jobs. The pastoral commons has been collapsing under multiple intense pressures, including the growth of the cash economy, leading many Maasai to shift to small-scale cultivation and, in some areas, to participation in the conservancies that seek to counterbalance the fencing in of the land. Many other Maasai have become landless after subdividing and selling once-communal land in order to raise cash. In the 2017 election campaign, opposition presidential candidate Raila Odinga said, "Years of neglect and abuse is forcing them to trade in their birthright for survival."[11]

Drought, polluted water sources, environmental deterioration, population increase, and physical infrastructure construction have contributed to making pastoral life harder, as have government policies that consider nomadic pastoralism "retrogressive and unproductive" (and often aim to take the land from Maasai in corrupt deals with powerful interests). Other changes include increased educational opportunities; if young people are in school, they are not available for herding. And there is the attraction for young people of participating in Kenya's "fast economy," although this glitter often turns out to be illusory.

We were going overland from the national park up into the Lolita Hills. This six-hour journey over rough roads took us through the nascent stages of Maasai sedentary life, including villages that now house businesses, schools, markets…and motorcycle traffic. Cell phones on every ear and a TV in some houses. The "fast economy" I'd been hearing about from Peter and others had four key elements: communication, banking, motorbikes, and TV. From a few hundred thousand telephone landlines, Kenya now has the highest percentage of smartphones in Africa. In a 2017 poll, 80 percent of adults reported owning a mobile phone (50 percent smartphones and 30 percent basic phones).[12] Only about 40 percent access the internet, but 96 percent of those who do, do it through a phone.

Kenya's Safaricom's M-Pesa was the world's first "PayPal." About 72 percent of Kenyans over fifteen have a mobile money account.[13] Their phones provide access to a cheap, secure, and instant phone-to-phone money transfer system. Kenyans were able to skip the need for a bank account or debit cards.

The number of registered motorcycles, now called *boda bodas*, has skyrocketed from 53,508 in 2004 to 1,147,403 in 2016.[14] For the price of a cow, one can travel on the same footpath used to go to market. Boda bodas complete a trade network, allowing produce from the most remote places to get to market quickly. The network was further enhanced by the growth of a national airline, linking those footpaths to jets and the world. Peter says, "Since there are pretty lax license requirements, it has also meant that there are some very busy orthopedic surgeons."

And finally, television. The availability of cheap satellite television meant that the "consumerization" of traditional societies, and the will to "improve" lifestyles and keep up with the Joneses, arrived concurrently with phones, finance, and transport. Peter shudders "to think what watching the Kardashians might do to one of the most resilient cultures on earth."

* * *

Richard Leakey also gazed into Kenya's future with his fingers crossed. His plane put to good use, and my trip almost done, it was time for the moment I'd been anticipating. *The Making of Mankind* had been in my parents' bookshelves while I was growing up and I had read *Wildlife Wars* as an adult. The moment didn't disappoint. Meeting with Leakey was inspirational. Just the number of books in his house alone and the house itself with its great windows, a huge fifteen foot-by-ten foot ancient rock painting on the living room wall, and its view perched on the Rift cliff at the outskirts of Nairobi. It's just down the path from the site of Leakey's planned Museum of Humankind. And the man himself, standing tall in spite of being physically humbled by his amputated legs and serious health battles. He was like a walking encyclopedia, intellectually vibrant and such a force.

The ninety-minute interview was a deep dive into human history, the politics of fossil hunting, and the sly battles between scientists all trying to put their stamp on the discovery of the earliest humans. There seems to be some serious pride—as well as fame and potential money—at stake for individuals and nations in finding the first bone, fire pit, burnt oyster shell...

We talked about early humans and food. When I asked about the importance of fire, Dr. Leakey surprised me with what he thinks may have been an even more important advancement—the

Dr. Leakey interview at his home overlooking the Rift Valley

development of the cutting edge. He told me that people, like other primates, were foraging in the forest and the savannas, including leftovers from predators. He didn't think meat-eating started with the ability to make sharp edges, but "I do think at a certain point early humans in the savannas of Africa were probably breaking up rhizomes (tubers) and sugars.... If you smash them around, they're perfectly manageable in the mouth and you can get a reasonable amount of nutrition, as long as you haven't got a toxic one."

At some point, banging with stones led to creation of edges that could cut tubers or meat. A dead wildebeest is too tough to tear with fingernails or teeth, but a sharp edge lets you cut a chunk away, and then to carry it home. "If you can cut off two or three pounds of meat, you have good packages of food that you can share." The access to "packages" of high-end calories enabled growth of much larger brains and the ability to grow more slowly, because the community could afford to stay in one place while it was being fed. "And so," he concluded, "I think that the cutting edge was probably the most significant thing humans did to become human."

As the interview wound down we got into the state of the modern world, and he seemed less assured. It was surreal listening to someone be concrete about a prehistory of more than three million years but uncertain on the next twenty.

At the height of the initial COVID wave, Leakey spoke about bush meat and about environmental devastation. Whether in Nairobi or other cities around the world, he said, very poor people can't afford to get protein from stores, but they can buy bush meat very cheaply on the black market. So they eat rats, squirrels, pangolins, or bats, enabling viruses and bacteria to jump to humans. "And COVID is exactly that—and there are many more viruses coming."

He went on, "If we could assure everyone at least one square meal a day, it would have a huge impact on the environment. But governments aren't so farsighted because, particularly in wealthy countries, wealth wants more wealth. Poverty doesn't want, but gets, more poverty."

* * *

And then I was done—back nestled in a dell on one of the Lolita Hills at the edge of the Sacred Forest in our little camp. Fourteen days had passed since arriving in Nairobi, and I had been transformed. My body was weary with nicks and scrapes, an acacia thorn here, a bee sting or three there. But my mind was alive and racing. Ariel and I had just completed the final cook using the ingredients I'd collected. Standing on a hill with a sunset streaming through a layer of darkening clouds, the wind whipping (with the dropping sun went the temperature), there was an epicness in the air. We cooked and drank and drank and cooked with such joy—the journey taken to get to this moment in each bite. The goat heart dish was different; not in layers, but divided à la a deconstructed poke bowl—then mixed on the plate—but just as good. The cocktail wasn't near as satisfying as Ariel's—too young and mottled with random herbs. The drink didn't have the clarity of purpose (to get one high and drunk) that Ariel's had back at Cultiva (it also was a funky, off-putting color). But the shank and barley was stunning—Ariel himself said it was better than the one he made in the restaurant. This dish was made to be cooked on a hill in the wild with the sun setting and the goat melting and the barley burning black on the bottom of the pan (Ariel called it *le souk*, as it's known to the French). Ariel said, "The magic ingredient is the forest, the crystal mountain, and Parmuaat." To cook great food with someone and then share it over wine has few peers.

We found our way down to the communal campfire—and people began to arrive. Almost everyone we had worked with over the course of the trip came driving or strolling up the hill in the middle of the forest to share one last drink, chat, and hug. Parmuaat had saved a special gift for me before I left: a rolling of stones, a fortune telling. Next to the fire he laid out a mat and opened a bag of rocks. This was a moment I had been hoping for since I'd heard he'd predicted a Trump victory ahead of the 2016 election.

Shaman Parmuaat reading stones in Kenya

I first asked about the future of the forest. With the fencing and logging I worried that this enchanting, vulnerable place might not last. "Will the forest survive?" I saw Peter and Uhuru glance at one another. The stones were rolled and Laibon Parmuaat spoke. Uhuru translated, "The forest will survive."

I felt a weight was lifted for everyone around the fire. On that positive note I asked a daring question, putting Laibon Parmuaat's reputation on the line. It was September 2020, and the US presidential election was two months away. "Will Donald Trump win the presidency for a second time?" With sparks spitting from the fire and floating up into the night, with what felt like Laibon Parmuaat's natural sense of drama, he rolled and rerolled the rocks, looking for some meaning and an answer. Minutes ticked by. He mumbled. Uhuru translated: "He will not win." I hooted with joy! "He's not gonna win." I smiled, but Shaman Parmuaat raised his hand with more to say and Uhuru jumped in to cut my exuberance off. "But there will be trouble."

Trump lost and there was trouble.

Maybe there's hope for the forest.

Porcini, Chanterelle:
Finland / Whidbey Island, WA

I AVOIDED MUSHROOMS WHEN I WAS YOUNGER—the sourish taste and funky smell of the store-bought button/cremini mushrooms had the consistency of packing Styrofoam. Are they supposed to squeak when you bite them? I'm not surprised that people are now using specially grown mushrooms as an environmentally friendly packing peanut. In the back of my mind was also something I had read about certain mushrooms being poisonous. So why chance it?

Enoki were my gateway drug into eating mushrooms. When I tried them, clumped together, swirling lazily in the Japanese hot pot meal *shabu shabu*, I was hooked. The little heads popped when bitten, they took on the flavor of the sesame sauce I dipped them in, and they just looked fun. Later, I learned that the strange, stringy stem and bright white color only develop when grown in the dark with low oxygen levels—the stem stretching upwards in search of air. In nature they are squatter, thicker, and colorful. Whatever the reason, they led me down a path to liking mushrooms by just realizing the sliced grayish ones of my youth were not the only mushrooms in town.

There are 70,000-100,000 known varieties of fungi—they are their own set of branches on the tree of life; the fungus kingdom is different from the plant or animal kingdoms, though fungi are closer to animals than to plants. There are likely anywhere between 2.2 and 3.8 million species of fungi overall.[1] Mushrooms are the sex organs that are produced by 16,000 different kinds of those fungi; by analogy, they are often referred to as "fruits," producing the spores that allow the fungi to reproduce.[2]

When I think of Finland, I think of porcinis. I sometimes think of forests (there are many; it's the most forested country in Europe) and mirror lakes (also lots). Of dipping into the vicious Baltic waters (freezing) after a sauna (suffocating). Or sitting outside Ekberg 1852 cafe (magical), unchanged forever (it's the oldest bakery in Finland), eating sugary, buttery, berry-filled Alexander pastries (fattening), and sipping coffee on bright summer days (imagine winter in LA). I think of fly-fishing in the two a.m. twilight, and the best chowder, and my eighteen-month-old son pushing his fingers together, signing *more! more!* until he got another spoonful of the salmon soup.

But, mostly, I think of mushrooms.

Mushrooms were in the fish broth for which Chef Jari Vesivalo of Olo in Helsinki was sending me out to forage ingredients. But figuring out where to go and what to get was proving complicated due to cultural differences. To start, having a conversation with Jari was awkward. His expression whenever I spoke was severe and pained, as though my words were so weighty that they hurt.

I would compliment his dishes (the velvety, poached pike perch slices, paper-thin circles with frozen droplets of spicy horseradish cream and the taste of the forest in the pine ice cream with wild strawberries and honey), some of the most unique and tasty I had ever experienced, and he would listen balefully. He never nodded

Jari in Olo

in agreement, or raised an eyebrow. I told a joke about praying for trout, not my greatest (but trout jokes are always a little fishy and I was pulling trout all the stops); he didn't laugh. There were gulfs of time between when my sentences ended and his would begin. So I filled the space between us with my American patter. Later,

I heard that, generally, Finns hate interrupting people, so they wait awhile to respond. And they don't like small chitchat—they wanna get down to business.

* * *

I was in Finland to see how food fits into Finland being the world's happiest country per the UN Sustainable Development Solutions Network's annual World Happiness Report[3] and being routinely cited as having the world's best education system.[4] Turns out much of modern Finnish life is the result of conscious decisions, mostly since the end of WWII, which might not have seemed at all predictable.

Finland was ruled by Sweden from medieval times until 1809, when Russia defeated Sweden and Finland became a semiautonomous part of the Russian Empire. Alexander I designated it a grand duchy, with the czar as the duke. So, it had separate rules from the rest of the Russian State, which worked to its advantage. Alexander I allowed the duchy to maintain its own legislature, the Diet (although he soon suspended it and it stayed suspended for about fifty years), religion (Lutheranism), estates represented in the Diet (nobility, clergy, bourgeoisie, and peasantry) and most of its own laws. Having gained about a third of Swedish territory, the czars set about to neutralize their new subjects' hostility to Russia. Until the 1890s, they allowed and promoted the development of Finnish identity in order to reduce the influence of Sweden and of Swedish, which had been the language of education, business, government, and literature. In 1863, Finnish joined Swedish as an official language, which was a big deal.

Finnish cultural and national identity grew throughout the nineteenth century. Finnish folk poems were brought together in epic form in the *Kalevala*, with versions published between

1835 and 1849; the first Finnish-language novel was published in 1870; and the period 1880-1910 is referred to as the Golden Age of Finnish Art. A national style of architecture developed, and the Finnish pavilion (separate from Russia's) attracted a lot of attention at the 1900 Paris World's Fair. What the czars hadn't planned on was that the development of a Finnish identity did weaken Swedish influence, but also laid the groundwork for Finns eventually to reject Russian efforts at control as well.

In 1899, Czar Nicholas II issued a Russification manifesto, eliminating much of Finnish autonomy. He asserted his right to make laws without the Diet's consent; introduced Russian as a third official language; and disbanded Finland's army, subjecting Finns to conscription into the Russian army. His policies generated intense opposition, including draft resistance and the assassination of the ultra-nationalist governor-general, Nikolay Bobrikov, in 1904. A national strike in 1905 forced a temporary retreat by the czar and the Diet was reformed as a unicameral parliament elected by universal suffrage. Finland thus became the first country in Europe to grant women the right to vote, and the first in the world to grant all women and men the right to vote and run for office.[5] But the czar kept dissolving the parliament and, in 1910, moved all important decisions to the Russian Duma.

Meanwhile, the overwhelming majority of Finns lived hard lives in poor, rural areas. During the Famine of 1866-1868, known as "the great hunger years," an estimated 150,000 more people died than would have if potatoes and other root-vegetable crops had not failed and conditions for the wheat crop had been better. The government in Helsinki was slow to respond and when it did, poor communication and transportation meant a lot of people who needed help didn't get it. From 1890 to 1914, over 200,000 Finns emigrated to the United States alone, for reasons ranging from poverty to political opposition to avoiding conscription. In the early twentieth century, infant mortality was high—about 12 percent of children died before their first birthday.

In 1917, following the Russian Revolution, Finland declared independence, which was granted by the Bolsheviks in accordance with their policy of self-determination for the peoples of the former empire, though they may not have expected people to take advantage of it. A brief, bitter, bloody civil war broke out between Reds and Whites, as a similar civil war was beginning in Russia. In Finland, the left was defeated by the right-wing Whites who were aided by the Germans and led by General Gustaf Mannerheim, who was to become, with breaks, Finland's dominant military and political leader from then until after World War II. Following the civil war, over 20,000 revolutionaries were executed or died in prison camps. Many leftists held Mannerheim responsible for much of this retribution.

Although the conservatives won and intense social, economic, and political divisions remained, reformist social democrats maintained input into government, even as communists were repressed. The 1920s saw steps to reduce inequality such as progressive taxation, expropriation of large estates and creation of smallholdings for tenants and landless laborers, and the institution of six years of compulsory education. A social democratic government in 1926 granted a general amnesty to civil war prisoners.

Tensions between Finland and Russia continued. Some Finns supported a "Greater Finland," which would have included Russian Karelia; Russians worried about how close the Finnish border was to Leningrad. Finland was generally in the German sphere of influence. However, in the 1939 Molotov-Ribbentrop treaty, Germany agreed that Finland should be moved into the Soviet sphere. When Finland rejected Soviet demands, the Russians attacked, beginning the Winter War.

The Finns showed surprising strength against a much stronger Red Army, and the Winter War helped unite the country, especially because it got sympathy—but little help—from outside. Finns were able to maintain independence but had to agree to a peace treaty that gave up large amounts of land, electrical power, and industrial capacity to Russia. Finland subsequently joined forces with the Germans as the Germans planned the invasion of the Soviet Union, which led to the Continuation War. Again, the Finns were able to hold back the Red Army, but by 1944, it was clear they had to negotiate a ceasefire and eventually a peace treaty, which included heavy indemnity payments and necessitated resettlement of 450,000 Karelians from the land that was ceded to the Soviet Union. However, once again they were able to keep their independence. Mannerheim, as commander-in-chief of the army, marshal of Finland, and then president, managed to keep a distance from Hitler and Nazi policies—even while allied with Hitler—and to keep the respect of Stalin and Churchill even while fighting them. Much of Mannerheim's long-term and historical reputation, across political lines, came from his ability to maintain Finnish independence against all odds, even in defeat.

So, by 1945 Finland was not in great shape. How did it get to where it is now, an advanced economy, with healthy people who spend leisure time in nature, and an education system that people from all over the world come to learn from?

The next steps of the story begin with the effects of the resettlement of the people from Karelia and the indemnities. The government opened up forests to give the new settlers land and to produce timber for their houses and toward meeting the indemnities. Silviculture (what a cool word for the growing and cultivation of trees!) became a major feature of Finnish life and economy.[6] The indemnities were to be paid in industrial goods, machinery, locomotives, and freighters; these were things that the Soviet Union needed in order to rebuild, and part of the arrangement was that the Soviets would continue to buy the products once the reparations were completed. The Finns paid off the indemnities by 1952 and then had access to the Soviet Union's market, and to other international markets, having developed diversified industrial capacity at a breakneck speed.[7] This helped to convert Finland into an industrial country, with a rapidly rising standard of living.

With help from a strong labor movement, the social welfare system expanded over time. In 1944, preschool health clinics were established, resulting in a decrease in child mortality. Free school lunches and child benefit payments were instituted in 1948. Free dental care for everyone was put in place in 1956. In the 1970s, free comprehensive schooling expanded the education guarantee from the 1920s. By 1990, Finland became the first country in the world to guarantee public daycare for children under age three.[8] Parents get 164 days each of parental leave at 90 percent pay (single parents get the combined total).[9] University education is free, and most students receive additional financial aid.

Fundamental changes in the education system were phased in from 1972 to 1979 with dramatic effects. Finnish schools don't select, track, or stream students during their basic education. Finland prioritizes playful childhoods over standardized testing. Its school years and school days are among the shortest in the industrialized world. And it is universally recognized as having one of the world's best education systems with the best student outcomes. By 2003, and then again in 2006, Finland ranked first in reading and science and second in math in the

Program for International Student Assessment (PISA), a world-wide study that evaluates educational systems by assessing fifteen-year-olds' student performance every three years.[10] Although its positions have dropped since then, it has remained highly ranked. The education system is marked by 10 percent random sampling tests in all subjects in ninth grade (rather than universal testing in grades three through eight in reading, math, and science, as in the United States). This frees up lots of time and energy, and reduces stress on students, teachers, and parents. Teachers are held in high regard and are well-prepared and well-paid.[11] Small class sizes facilitate working with students of varied skills within the same class. There's also a lot of emphasis on play and outside activities.

When I visited a school (which included watching cooks make and serve delicious food), I wished my son would be able to go to school in Finland. What a difference the decision to make education joyful for teachers and students alike makes! Something that struck me was the high status of teachers and the competition to become a teacher, as well as how much they reportedly enjoy their jobs, in contrast to the US, where fewer people are entering teaching and current teachers are leaving their jobs in droves. Columbia University Teachers College's Sam Abrams, who has studied Finnish and American schools extensively, quotes a member of Parliament who said, "We had no choice. In Finland, we have our timber and we have our brains. That is all. To become an economically modern nation, we had to have very good schools, which meant we had to have very good teachers."[12]

Beginning in the 1970s, Finland also moved dramatically to improve diet and fitness. According to Pekka Puska, director of the National Institute of Public Health, "In the 1970s, we held the world record for heart disease.... The idea then was that a good life was a sedentary life. Everybody was smoking and eating a lot of fat. Finnish men used to say vegetables were for rabbits, not real men, so people simply did not eat vegetables. The staples were butter on bread, full-fat milk, and fatty meat. "[13]

The government saw a massive health problem and took steps to intervene. The interventions worked and the country is now far healthier. The reversal started in 1972 in North Karelia, the country's least healthy region, with a massive community-based intervention that utilized positive individual and collective competitions and incentives. Nationwide legislation and policies included a ban on tobacco advertising, changes in meat and dairy subsidies to emphasize protein rather than fat, pressure to produce low-fat milk and to make domestic vegetable oil widely available, and encouragement to grow locally produced berries. Finland now produces lots of different climate-suited berries, has reduced salt intake, and has one of the lowest smoking rates in the world.

In addition to changing diet, Finland reversed a trend toward physical inactivity. The health results of these changes have been dramatic. The number of men dying from cardiovascular heart disease has dropped from about 800 per 100,000 in 1971 to under 300 in 2017; the number of women has dropped from just under 400 per 100,000 to just over 100. The age at which people die from heart disease has also changed dramatically. In 1971 nearly 25 percent of people who died were of working age, while in 2017, fewer than 10 percent were. The median age for those dying was sixty-five for men and seventy-three for women; in 2017, it was seventy-nine and eighty-eight.

* * *

Mushrooming is a pastime for the Finns, supported by the government, though some rely more than others on it for income. The right to forage is literally written into Finnish federal law. It starts with the Everyman's (sic) Right. Everyman's Right (*jokamiehen oikeudet*), also known as the Right to Roam, is an integral part of Finnish culture and legislation. While some other Nordic countries have similar rules, Finland's are the most expansive.[14] Finland's Right to Roam goes back hundreds of years in common practice but was codified into a series of laws over the past seventy years.

Under the Right to Roam, you may:

- walk, ski, or cycle freely in nature, except in yard areas and in such fields, meadows, or plantations that could easily be damaged
- stay temporarily in areas where roaming is allowed—you can, for example, set up camp relatively freely, as long as you maintain a sufficient distance from people's homes
- pick berries, mushrooms, and flowers
- angle and ice fish
- boat, swim, or travel on ice

You may not:

- disturb or cause harm to others
- disturb or cause damage to birds' nests or their young
- disturb reindeer or game animals
- cut down or damage living trees
- collect dried or fallen wood, twigs, moss, or similar on someone else's property without permission
- light open fire

- disturb the privacy of people's homes by camping too close or by making too much noise
- leave litter
- drive motor vehicles off-road without the landowner's permission
- fish or hunt without the relevant permits[15]

Legislation in 1969 funded the National Board of Forestry to train mushroom advisors, a program which still continues. In 1981, Finland passed a statute on edible mushrooms and drew up a list of commercial species.

Looking over these rules, I thought about how incredible it was that the country collectively agreed that everyone would allow neighbors—no, strangers!—to forage and fish on "their" land. Finns incorporated into law their basic human desire to engage with the outdoors, to take a breath, to walk freely in the woods, to play in the water. How amazing that they were able to combine free time, reduced stress, a social safety net, and strong food traditions into wandering and foraging in the woods, often on a daily basis. My thoughts kept returning sadly to how far my country is from Everyman's Right. Could Americans ever accept these rights? Would they resent the obligations? Can we tear down our "No Trespassing" signs? Can we even all agree to treat the places we've set aside as parks respectfully?

Finns spend time in the woods, whether it's the Helsinki suburban housewife who fed me rye bilberry pie while showing me her mushroom-dyed pillows, or the supermodel/hotelier who took me for a hike to find toadstools for Jari. Both of them walked eyes to the earth in open pine forests, sometimes hiking into new terrain but mostly retracing well-worn steps to a spot they already knew would present a bounty of mushrooms. For some low-income—and especially immigrant—families, selling mushrooms can be an important part of their income. But in my mind, Finland and mushrooms, porcinis (or, as the Finns call them, *ceps*), are also tied together in a more symbolic way.

In general, mushrooms are hard to put your finger on; they grow out of the detritus of the past; some, porcinis particularly, have a symbiotic relationship with the natural world around them. Mushrooms don't need light to grow. Beneath the ground, mushrooms have a wide network of filaments, called mycelial threads, that absorb nutrients.[16] I found myself fancifully comparing mushrooms and Finland and the ways in which they are similar. There is a remarkable sense of togetherness about the Finns—a filament connecting everyone, so to speak. The Finnish identity is very strong. I have met third generation Finns in the US who still speak the language. It is almost a tribal identity.

I imagine Finland as having emerged relatively recently from centuries of foreign rule and rural poverty, hiding almost underground until it was time to fruit. A friend commented to me, "Most people here, although they drive modern cars on freeways and sit in offices, are only two generations removed from the old subsistence agrarian society."

Helsinki is a strange fruit. A melancholic dream. The foggy skies. The denim sea. Helsinki feels like it's keeping secrets. The buildings look like they're ripped from Le Carré novels or Ludwig Bemelman's *Madeline*. Finland as a whole feels eerie, with its strangely manicured forests, gray and a little subdued. Hua Hsu wrote in *The New Yorker* that "the mushroom is at the end of the known world because it's hard to find, a secret tucked deep in the forest."[17] This sounds like Finland.

Finland also feels very much a place that learned from lessons taught in kindergarten. Finns live to share, to clean up messes;

they practice basic sanitation, place value in keeping plants alive and rivers clean. There is a symbiosis with nature. But with both mushrooms/fungi and Finns it's more complicated. Both also decide how they want the forest to be—choosing which trees live and which die. Like porcinis, Finns love pines. Because of the importance to modern Finland of its forest and lumber industry, maintaining a renewable source of wood has been vital. Finns want to control nature and its messes. Anthropologist Anna Lowenhaupt Tsing discusses her visit to the managed natural pine forests of northern Finland:

> I had thought of natural forests as packed with tall and tiny trees, all jumbled together. Here all the trees were just the same: one species, one age, neat and evenly spaced. Even the ground was clean and clear without a snag or a piece of downed wood. It looked exactly like an industrial tree plantation.[18]

Is a forest a forest if all the trees are the same type, in rows, and there is no "detritus" on the ground? (Since the Forest Act of 2014, the Finnish state forestry company Metsähallitus has shifted policy; it says it now practices twelve different methods of harvesting, including both even-aged and uneven-aged forestry, and gives more attention in certain sites to maintaining continuous cover.[19] It is also leading a complementary "rewilding" project to restore life to rivers, creeks, and lakes that have been rendered "ecologically dead" by past forestry practices).

Just as the Finns redesign the forests, mushrooms do as well. Mushrooms likely control masting, when trees with fungi partners hold back their seeds until they "fruit massively and all together across an area." Tsing argues that "surely mycorrhizal partners must have a hand in the timing of pine seed production."

Tsing goes on to describe the ways that pine trees and mushrooms coordinate with each other, saying that neither "can flourish without the activity of the other." She reminds us that collaborative survival requires cross-species coordination unmediated by humans. Porcinis, *Boletus edilus*, hang out around trees in clusters—they particularly like evergreens such as pines, and evergreens like them. Fungi excrete digestive acids that break down nutrients. The trees share in this "cooked" bounty. Fungi also transmit water into roots, and, by digesting dead trees, contribute to the forest's cycle of life.[20] In turn, they siphon off carbohydrates from the trees' roots.

Exciting research by Suzanne Simard in North America over many years shows that fungal threads link nearly all the trees in a forest and transmit carbon, water, nutrients, chemical alarm signals, and hormones among trees. Seedlings that are not connected to these threads are more likely to die.[21] Toby Kiers of Vrije Universiteit is one of a number of scientists who are showing that fungi are not passive conduits, but rather active players in the distribution of resources.[22] Mushrooms and fungi are the ultimate foresters.

As Tsing points out and Simard and Kiers's work also shows, "history" is not made only by humans, but by trees and fungi as well, each seeking to meet its needs. Tsing cites Lisa Curran as saying that forests exist only because of this symbiotic or ectomycorrhizal relationship between fungi and trees.[23] In fact, she argues that the reason there are plants on land rather than just in water is because fungi have always digested rocks and helped create soil, providing essential nutrients for plants.

Pretty monumental stuff. With humans' ongoing attack on the natural world, Finland, whose forests cover about 75 percent of the land and are steadily growing despite intensive harvesting, seems almost ectomycorrhizal in comparison. The Finns are working to keep the woods alive and, in many ways, the woods work to keep the Finns alive, or at least happy. It's a culture that privileges gathering foods from nature over eating packaged or prepared foods.

Mushrooms can be a bulwark against the slow, sedentary creep of modern urban existence. My first time foraging for them was with a most unorthodox guide. Saimi Hoyer, a former supermodel, said her love for mushrooming is part nostalgia for memories of childhood forest walks with her grandma, who handed down her knowledge. With hair almost as red as a strawberry and a wild, spritely demeanor, Saimi had turned her back on Milan and Paris and New York for health reasons and returned to Finland. In 2016, she purchased Hotel Punkaharju, the oldest hotel in Finland, in a building originally built by Czar Nicholas I. It sits in the Lakeland district near Lake Saimaa, the largest lake in Finland, the lakebed gouged out by glaciers 10,000 years ago. The hotel promotes itself as a cultural and culinary experience, which includes picking mushrooms with Saimi herself.

Entering a cathedral of majestic trees just downslope from the hotel, you would never know about the parking lot and gift shop and restaurant above. One is immediately enveloped in a wood with one hundred-foot-tall Punkaharju pines blocking the sun. You can feel the oxygen, hear the life scurrying around. Yet I had a strange reticence foraging here. This was not something you did in the city. My mom's voice echoed in my mind—"Put that down. You don't know where that came from!" This wasn't a farm or garden with some semblance of human control, but a wild place. Who knew what we might find? I mentioned how weird it felt looking in the woods for food. She stared at me in a way that reminded me of Jari and said, "It's the way things should be." So

I gave myself over to Saimi's expertise and dutifully followed her into the understory.

We hunted on stumps and under fallen leaves, but to no avail. Not a shroom in sight. She apologized and explained that it was a little early in the season—the rains hadn't come through yet. It was actually easier to find the wild European blueberries, known regionally as bilberries. I parked my one-and-a-half-year-old in some bushes and left him to gorge. It was easy to find the itsy-bitsy wild strawberries that Chef Jari wanted me to bring back to his restaurant for the pine ice cream dish—a tenth of the size of industrial strawberries, but ten times the taste. We found nettles for the fish broth; they itched and stung so I put on some rubber gloves. We found wood sorrel and wild onions, also for the broth, but no fungi. I wandered down to the shore, hoping to see a rare freshwater seal.

Then, ready to head home, it was only near the end of our walk that we happened upon a few porcinis/ceps by the side of the path under a pine. Sometimes nature decides—and gives a gift.

It was Saimi's hawk eyes that saw the brown caps which, to my eyes, were indistinguishable from the leaves and the dirt. We squatted down, closer to the warm, piney smell of the forest and the damp earth. The ceps weren't huge, only a couple of inches tall. I reached under to take the base; the cep base is wide and tapers upward towards the cap. I pinched it and pulled it out of the ground to get a better look. Because there were no snail nibbles, Saimi felt they were very new, maybe even having popped up the night before. Following her lead and using her special knife that has a little brush for mushrooms on the handle, I brushed the dirt off the cream-colored stem and trimmed the brown discoloration, then put them in a pouch, heeding Saimi's words that they should not be washed. "Fine, fine, whatever you say." I was ecstatic; I had foraged food in the woods! I had visions of now being able to survive on porcinis while lost and alone. But Saimi was frank—the nutritional value is pretty hyped. They are very low in calories, the hydro skeleton is mostly pumped up with water, so you can't go out into the woods and survive on mushrooms.

When I told her I was fascinated by mushrooms because of the chance of dying when eating one, I asked if she was ever scared. She replied in a gravelly voice, "I am not afraid." Then, in a blunt Finnish way, she added "because I only eat the ones I know." The good news is there are very few species that produce very poisonous mushrooms; the bad news is it may be the last mistake you make. Saimi said, "If in doubt, throw it out."

I brought my mushrooms (and berries and fish and horse-radish and pine needles) back to Helsinki and Olo and Jari. If he was excited to see me, he hid it. I didn't think he could get grumpier after our first meeting, but the dinner rush was headed his way and he was sourly speeding through teaching me how to cook the meal. Jari also didn't like that I hadn't been able to get a trout and declared we couldn't make the fish soup. I told him hopefully he could make do instead with a pike I'd gotten. Turns out he doesn't like working with pike.

But when he saw the mushrooms there was a grunt and a hint of a smile. He relaxed a bit. We would make a seared pike with mushrooms. He turned on the burner to heat the pan and put me to work trimming the mushroom's dirty bits. "No washing!"

* * *

A year or so later and on the far edge of another continent, I continued my education by foraging for mushrooms again. I was making a wonderful meal with Chef Matt Costello at the Inn at Langley. As per usual, with this hyper local restaurant, every seasonal ingredient was to be found within ten miles of the restaurant—and a dish needed mushrooms. Travis Furlanic of Whidbey Mushroom Tours guides foragers on Whidbey Island, north of Seattle; he has light-socket wiry, dark hair like mine, which he hides under a Gen-Y beanie, and has an unshaven Gen-Z look. He once ran a successful American Ninja Warrior training center for the televised agility competition, but walking on a highway, he got hit by a car, broke his legs, and nearly bled out on the side of the road. So he turned to the forest, like Saimi. But here is where his story and Saimi's differ. In Finland, Saimi runs a high-end hotel; in America, Travis's hospital bills sank him. While foraging for mushrooms is a hobby for Saimi, Travis runs a precarious business guiding tours and doing semicommercial picking. Although their circumstances are different in many ways, the contrast also illustrates the sharp distinctions between the Finnish safety net and the US tightrope walk.

Photo by Marty Bleazard

Chef Matt Costello at the Inn at Langley

Travis Furlanic of Whidbey Mushroom Tours with a white chanterelle

Travis drove into the trail parking lot (he asked me not to mention the trail by name) to meet me in his van, which he lives in as he tries to get his finances back on track. Rather than work low-paying jobs he hated, he thought he might as well start a tour company. He told me mushrooms and mushroom hunting, mushing as he calls it, felt like a lifeline for him. Whip-smart, obsessive yet humble, he kept apologizing for imagined slip-ups on camera. I told him that's what film editors are for.

Talking to Travis was like getting a computer download about mushrooms. We were looking for chanterelles—I'd heard of their legendary, bright golden color—and Travis knew a secret spot to find them. "You know, most people think about chanterelles; they're one of the most commonly eaten wild mushrooms. So people that come on my tours really like to find chans, but I love educating them on a lot of other mushrooms that have a far superior flavor." He pointed as we walked, spitting out some of the names of the 5,000 types of mushrooms in the Puget Sound area. He told me to put my plastic bag away, as it wouldn't let the mushrooms breathe. He handed me a paper one. As we meandered through the damp, a steady Pacific Northwest rain was falling. I began to feel he was leading me in circles, so I asked if his mushroom spots were secret. He grinned, "I'll tell people my oyster mushroom spots all day long, 'cause those are everywhere. I don't care. But my thirty-pound- (or more) a-year matsutake [the most expensive mushroom in the world] spot or chanterelle spot? No, you tend to keep those secret." I should have dropped breadcrumbs.

Thirty-five minutes later, perched on a log was a cluster of what I thought were chanterelles but were actually a poisonous lookalike, the orange jack-o'-lantern. Travis said chanterelles never grow out of wood. What we were looking for was actually the "white chanterelle," so not orange-colored. "Generally, a very dense mushroom. If you flip it over and you look at the gill surface (a lot of people call 'em pseudo-gills 'cause they're not typical, thin, blade-like gills), they're much more vein-like rather than rib-like in structure—the body is thicker." The jack-o'-lanterns were not gold so much as orange and had true thin gills underneath. Chanterelles also don't clump together. And chanterelles don't cause vomiting, nausea, abdominal pain, diarrhea, weakness, and dizziness, while jack-o'-lanterns do. "Other lookalikes to stay away from are the wooly chanterelle, which make most people sick, but still, at the same time, people do eat it, which is interesting. But I don't recommend it just because so many people get sick from it...some mushrooms are edible, with caution." I asked if it was like nut allergies and he just shrugged. "Nobody really knows why." Strangely, wooly chanterelles are considered toxic in the US but are readily consumed in Mexico.

Travis also stands by the "if in doubt throw it out" mantra for the people he guides. But he actually gets riskier himself, a little bit more ninja warrior. "If I'm gonna try a new mushroom, I have to cook it well and have a small amount...[so I] make sure that I don't have any kind of reaction and wait a good twelve hours." I looked at him in awe. That is the last thing in the world I would do. He self-taught as dangerous of a daredevil act as anything on American Ninja Warrior. Imagine the first time you walk into a forest ready to harvest and eat a mushroom with only a handbook as your guide. Even with Saimi and Travis leading the way there was a wisp of fear for me, that childhood terror peeking out of the shadows.

Travis told me, "There are four different types of mushrooms: saprotrophic, mycorrhizal, parasitic, and endophytic. The mycorrhizal mushrooms attach to the root system of trees and they have a symbiotic relationship with a tree. So a lot of mushroom hunting is hunting the tree first. Then there's the parasitic mushrooms, mushrooms that attack trees. The honey mushroom is one of these—it's the largest organism in the world and it's taken over something like 2,300 acres in the Blue Mountains of Oregon.

"Then there's saprotrophic mushrooms, like oysters, and they'll be decomposing already-dead material. Like this log here. Um, you know, there's mushrooms right now, growing through that log, decomposing it. "

A rush of adrenaline hit me as my eyes fell on a white cap peeking out among some leaves. I cut Travis off as he was explaining how oyster mushrooms cling to trees.

I pointed across the path in the other direction. "Is that one a chanterelle?!"

It had a small, beaten-up cap. True to its name, it was white, but with orange bruising on the edges of the cap. Travis flipped it over to look at the gills, which were thick like veins as he mentioned. Boom!! I was a mushroom hunter. But tragically I couldn't bring it back to Chef at The Inn at Langley. The problem with the mushroom was snail damage. Severely tattered, it looked too chewed-up to be presentable on a plate. Even though I was the one who would be eating it, I balked at the idea of eating snail leftovers.

But I was jazzed. I could see how hunting for these would get addictive. I already wanted to find a better one, a bigger one. I had a taste of the detective work, of the problem-solving. *Is this the area? Is that the right tree? What am I looking for? Will that kill me?* Travis liked to say, "You're looking under shrubs, you're looking where they might hide. It's like adult Easter-egg hunting."

We ended up in a streambed covered with thick moss. It was here that Travis said his secret "grove" of mushrooms was. I glanced around. Layers upon layers of different green surrounded me. Brown columns of trees held up some fog that had rolled through. The forest went up into hillsides to the left and right, affording a nice view up the slopes and under plants. And there, between the mosses and a few shrubs, under a little forest of ferns, were mushrooms. I scrambled, squishing and slipping on the wet, until my muddy hands and boots found purchase. I'd tracked them down, bright white, cup-like chanterelles, importantly a few without snail marks. I put them in my bag and left the rest like sentinels pumping spores into the mist.

As Travis and I walked back, we discussed how mushrooming had saved him when he was really struggling. "When you get into mushrooms, you get into mushrooms! People that are into mush-rooms...get obsessed, and they wanna connect and hang out and learn from each other and do fungus fairs. When I was laid up in bed, I didn't have nothing to do but be online. So I joined all these forum groups. It was a saving grace when I was lonely.... I was able to hang out with my mushroom friends.... I don't know very many bad people that are really into mushrooms, it's just a good community of people."

I told Travis about Finland's Everyman's Right and asked what he thought about its relationship to Finland being the happiest country. He said mushrooming certainly leads to happiness. It gets people outdoors, exercising and in the sun for vitamin D, which is good for your mood: "In the Pacific Northwest, people get the seasonal blues every fall with the rain, cloudy skies. A lot of people become depressed—no sunlight, nothing to do. But I get excited. It does the complete opposite to me. I'm like, yes, the rain makes me happy and excited for mushrooms."

This made me wonder how important the basic act of going outside to forage was in a country as far north as Finland, with so much fall and winter darkness.

Travis also was intrigued by the fact that foraging in Finland is allowed on private land. He agreed with the rule of no foraging in yards or farms and said, "If you can't see a house, it should be legal…. I saw a quote recently that said, 'If you are more well-off than others and you have more land, don't build a bigger fence, build a longer table.'"

This brought me back to a moment in Finland. A place where they are literally removing fences. The housewife who fed me the berry pie also had a garden I was harvesting from. She led me outside for some of the horseradish I needed for Jari. In a small suburb outside of Helsinki, she and her neighbors had no fences between their properties, and their gardens just flowed into one another's yard. I exclaimed out loud how amazing that was, and she looked at me quizzically, didn't say a thing, and went back to helping me get some horseradish out of the ground. I took her silence to mean it was just the way things should be.

Pizza:
Amalfi Coast / NYC

MARCO THE MOZZARELLA MAKER AND I did not like one another. He had a snarky, pretty-boy face that needed a punch. He definitely felt the same about me.

He was in his early twenties, with slicked hair and a tight T-shirt. A bicep tattoo and a cigarette box rolled up in his sleeve like he was an extra in *Grease*. I was middle-aged, paunchy, and not sleeping so well from jet lag. When the PR woman from the cheese factory introduced us, Marco gave me a curdled side-eye look from my head to my toes and went right back to forming a mozzarella ball. And this was the guy who was supposed to mentor me. I stood with a dying grin on my face. "Hey, guys, who wants to walk me through the process?" Nothing. Then snickers amongst the four men collecting curds from the tub of near-boiling water.

They were massaging cheese curds, handing them back and forth to each other until they were finally round balls like the ones you find floating in Tupperware at a deli on Arthur Ave. in the Bronx. I say they were snickering, but it was in Italian so I might have been mistaken. They could have been saying, "I love this American who wants to reveal our secrets to the world," but

I'll never know. I don't speak Italian and my friend, producer, and sometime-interpreter Suzann wasn't really paying attention to the dark waters that were brewing there. So I stood, fuming.

One minute went by. I glanced at my crew. Two minutes. What to do? The cameras were rolling and I was the host. This didn't happen to the host! I was there at Tenuta Vannulo buffalo farm and cheese factory in Paestum on the Amalfi coast to be taught the ins and outs of making buffalo mozzarella. Which I had to bring back, along with wheat, anchovies, and tomatoes, for a pizza I was making with Emanuele Liguori, at Antica Pizzeria da Michele in Naples.

Without the help of the *casari* (cheesemakers), I was just a guy in a plastic onesie and hairnet holding a bucket of milk.

I had come from milking a mama water buffalo (*Bubalus bubalis*, if you wanna get scientific) who was grumpy and ornery— she tried to stomp on my hand and kick Giuseppe, her farmer. These bovids weigh up to 1,700 pounds, and a kick can kill; buffalo owners have gotten trampled to death. But somehow I was angrier at the cheesemakers. Why was I even on this buffalo farm? Da Michele doesn't use buffalo mozzarella, only *fior di latte*, made from fresh cow's milk. But buffalo mozzarella was something I'd always wondered about. The first time I'd come across it in a grocery store, my mind pictured American bison being milked in some vast prairie. Later, when I learned the difference between bison and buffalo, I was still shocked that people would milk what was sometimes called the most dangerous animal in Africa—the Cape buffalo. So when I got to Italy, I knew I wanted to see this for myself and to make buffalo mozzarella. And that's when I realized I had been mistaken for years—it wasn't Cape buffalo people milked, it was Asian buffalo. These buffalo are domesticated, and their milk has nearly double the protein and calcium of cow's

Buffalo with her caretaker, Giuseppe

milk. But they also produce much less than cows. So the farm goes through lots of money keeping them calm, serenading them with Mozart, and massaging them with electric rollers.

Since no one would help me, I took my bucket over to the side and added the rennet myself, stirring it into the still-warm milk for two minutes with an up, down, and across motion, which I knew how to do from when I made ricotta in Sardinia and Malta.

Rennet coagulates or sets milk into curds for cheesemaking. Its compounds are found in the stomachs of baby ruminants—in essence, all young lambs, kids, and calves turn milk into cheese in their stomachs. Traditionally, animal rennet is a by-product from the killing of unweaned calves; calves are not killed solely for the rennet. The fourth stomach, which contains chymosin, the necessary enzyme, is dried so that it becomes solid, and then ground into powder.

There are now alternatives to animal rennet; 90 percent of cheeses in the US are produced by fermentation-produced chymosin (FPC), often called a GMO-product, though largely exempted from GMO-labeling (and there are some purely vegetarian, clearly non-GMO cheeses).

But in Italy you must use rennet. And not just any rennet. To make buffalo mozzarella in Italy, you must use rennet from buffalo calves at the same farm where you are making the cheese. Rennet helps set the milk best at a temperature of 35°C-43°C (95°F-109.4°F). Once a buffalo cow is milked, rennet is added to form the curds or, in this case, a large curd block, as the milk is gradually transformed from a liquid into a solid. Once it is set, it's cut into squares or ground down to release the whey, and dumped into heated water. The squares are stirred until they collect, knitting into larger strings. These bind and bind, getting thicker and thicker like white dwarf stars forming in the cosmos. After that they are hand-molded and cut with fingers into the famous balls. *Mozzare* means cutting by hand. That was what Marco and the guys were doing over there.

I went outside for a break and to let the milk set. Marco walked out for a smoke, and he stood across from me, looking smug. When I walked back in, I went to what seemed to be the first machine in the mozzarella process. Maybe this was what could grind the block of curd that was like concrete in my bucket? It was just inside the floor-to-ceiling windows that looked out to the courtyard where the tourists were peering in to watch these experts strut their stuff before going to the cafe for a smorgasbord of buffalo milk products. It was a hot Italian summer and everyone out there appeared ready for air-conditioning and delicious buffalo gelato and pizza *bufalina*. My being there kinda confused them. Who was the disheveled, sweaty, red-faced man fuming in the corner with his bucket?

I stood there facing the machine. What was it? What did it do? Would it make my cheese? My crew was perplexed, looking back and forth from the cheesemakers to my darkening mood. Marcos Efron, my director, and I usually had a hive mind, with lots of unspoken conversations. He caught my eye and shook his head. I ignored him. I mean, what did he know? He didn't make goddamn cheese. And I pressed the red button to turn on the machine.

That's when all hell broke loose.

After I turned on the machine—which was for grinding the curds down with rotating metal teeth—I raised my bucket to add the cheese block, and one of the younger cheesemakers raced over to stop me. We tussled over the bucket until we both dumped it into the machine together. At that point I looked back onto the floor of the cheese factory to find the cheesemakers all staring at me, open-mouthed. The kid who helped me dump my curds was a little shocked and sheepish. I put my bucket underneath to collect the now torn-up curds and headed over to the large tub of steaming water.

I was met there by my crew, the farm PR woman, and two very pissed casari. Everyone was very loud, talking over one another, waving their hands at me. The next step was to combine my curds in the water and stir them with a paddle. I picked one off the table, poured my curds in, and began to stir. The Italians were completely in disbelief. Two stirs put them over the edge. Marco grabbed my paddle with an "Enough!" But I held on. We struggled...and then I ripped it from his hand and banged it on the tub with a thump: "Back off!"

After I banged the large metal tub with the paddle like a gong, everyone stopped. With the reverberation in the air, the oldest guy there stepped over, told Marco to leave. And he started teaching me. One by one the others came over and started giving tips and pantomiming actions. Even Marco nodded as I produced my first ball. As soon as I showed that this was serious to me and what they were doing was important to me—in essence, showing respect for the work that they do—things switched. The farm's PR person came over to tell the fellas what I was saying. It became apparent that we had all been operating on different tracks. The mozzarella makers had thought that I was just there to watch rather than to make mozzarella with their help.

As things changed, I started comparing their cheese balls to mine on camera. I showed what it was supposed to look like, what an expert did, and then what mine looked like. The PR person translated, and the guys nodded along and even laughed with my play-by-play.

I was struck by the collaboration—at a number of moments along the way, more than one person was needed to get the job done. This final step of handing the balls back and forth to another cheesemaker across the scalding tub became a meditation in partnership.

I also think the other cheesemakers enjoyed the fact that the last step in the process used scalding hot water. They were used to, it but I was definitely not. The cheese has to be kept supple and soft while you're manipulating it. So the water that you're bathing it in is super hot and you're cooking your hands in it. The first time I put my hands in this bath, everyone was watching and kind of just smiled. I had to bite my tongue because I had been basically yelling, "let me do this," for the last hour. I think they loved watching my face. Probably made the whole misunderstanding worth it.

* * *

Naples is one of those places that you either love or hate. Dirty, with one of the highest crime rates in Italy, it hits you in the nose, especially when there is a garbage strike. When, a few years earlier, my wife and I stepped out of the train from Rome in our honeymoon glow, we noticed at another platform across the tracks an older gentleman leaning on a quad cane, embracing a young woman. I nudged my wife and said, "They are like us" (I'm ten years her senior). We smiled and took each other's hand, thinking of our future life together. Glancing back over our shoulders to get one last look at the sweet scene, we noticed the woman was jerking the man off. The group of passengers on our platform hooted and hollered their support. *Welcome to Naples, the city of love!*

Soon after that, we headed down into the subway system. I folded up my map of the city and put it into my back pocket. As I moved through the turnstile, someone bumped me as they went past. At that moment, two people became really disappointed. Me, because I no longer knew where we were going, and the pickpocket who now had a new but likely worthless map of Naples. *Welcome to Naples, get lost in it!*

But even with this introduction, I love the place. When the city passed a seatbelt law, T-shirts with a diagonal stripe across the front were sold on street corners. It reminds me of the Bronx of my childhood in the '70s and '80s. The graffiti and the honking cars and the grit and the pizza.

For a New Yorker, pizza is equally a staple and a point of pride, tied to one's sense of home and a statement of taste. Everyone has their pizza joint. It starts early up in the Bronx—from ages two to eleven, I went to Three Brothers on Kingsbridge Road. That set the tone for pizza; I was imprinted for life on a very cheesy, slightly salty, lightly sauced, crunchy slice with garlic powder and sometimes red pepper flakes. For some reason, I also grew to love bubbles in the crust. I'd pry them open, burning my fingers, and dismantle the slice inside out and backwards. Three Bros also did a mean meatball hero, but I digress. I recently visited after thirty-five years, and while they lost the "Three" under new owners (it's now just Brothers Pizza), they still do a respectable slice.

From eleven to seventeen (I moved), I went to Sorrento's by Jerome Park Reservoir, but it was known to my friends and me just as the "pizza place." It was a block from my elementary school, up from the supermarket and across from the candy store. Brick-faced on the outside with two big windows looking onto the sidewalk, on the inside it was brown, tan, and orange, and pretty spacious for New York, where most joints are slim to keep the rent low. It was wide and deep, with ten or so booths and tables for two. Italian boxers on the walls—mostly old, faded Rocky Marciano fight pics. It was the place you met up with friends after school, a meal you could afford without asking mom and dad for money (coins found in the cushions!). Generally these spots make good slices, because if they don't, someone will open a better one across the street.

As you get into your teens and branch out into the city, you realize there is a bit of variation coinciding with choice. You start to eliminate places. Teenage deliberation on a corner with other delinquent friends regarding where to eat. On any given day you might hear, "I don't wanna go there, the sauce is too sweet." "That's a $2.50 slice." "What's with the pineapple slices?" "Nah, the cheese is rubber." "The bottom is greasy, I'll spend the whole time napkining it off."

You begin to ask yourself bigger questions: "Am I a fan of brick oven?" "To Sicilian or not?" "Is white pizza pizza?" And it's tricky. Some pizza places are running cons. You'll get lured in by a cheaper slice or a huge slice or a large chain or a name that has the word "original" in it. But only for a bit; it all corrects over time.

There are too many good ones to get stuck in a rut. So, finally, you land upon a pizza joint, yours, one that you might even travel for from uptown to downtown or into Brooklyn, or, dare I say, Staten Island.

My "older brother" Ken Mattson treks in from Mahwah, New Jersey, to Arthur Ave. for his favorite slice at Catania's. When I asked him why, he talked about mouthfeel, what they do right, and what they don't do. "The dough is light and crisp, not too thin, and has a great chew to it and stability. The crust doesn't flop downward like most all other pizzas. The pizza sauce is not at all acidic...not too garlicky. It's kinda perfect. They use good cheese, not the cheap, greasy type, although cheese does give off a slight bit of grease." It was his childhood spot, and they have been using the same starter for eighty-five years.

So I was a bit confused when I was told in Naples that New York pizza wasn't pizza. "Nobody can do pizza like us. The real pizza is Neapolitan." I almost couldn't believe it. I asked the pizza shop owner standing out in front of his place on Via Tribunali if there was anything good about New York pizza. He said, "Meat." "In America, you can only do the meats well." Then he started talking trash about Roman pizza. "That's not pizza either; only Naples makes pizza."

But this was why I came to Italy, to Naples. To try and make "the best pizza in the world." In any given year, Naples is home to most of the top pizza makers. Over time that group changes slightly, but there's one that is always listed. Year after year, Da Michele shows up in "best of" lists by *The Guardian*, *Time Out*, *The Telegraph*, *AFAR*, *Lonely Planet*...and is one of eight pizza places in the Italy Michelin guide. These rankings kinda follow the format of Serie A, the Italian football league, where most teams stick around; but every year, two or three drop off into the Serie B league and are replaced by other teams coming up. In this scenario, Da Michele, which opened in 1870, is Juventus, the most storied of all the clubs. Emanuele Liguori, the head pizzaiolo, explains, "We make only two pizzas here because the Italian tradition says to just make the Margherita and marinara pizzas. So for the people of Naples, this tradition remains with us here. And we have continued to keep this tradition with us for over a hundred years…as was started by Da Michele."

And they are still slammed. I'd never seen anything like it. Every table filled and a mob standing, waiting for hours, outside. This goes on throughout the day until closing. And I get it. The pie there is a work of art. Crispy, thin-crusted, just the right amount of sauce—which is not too tangy or sweet or salty.

You could say Naples makes great pizza because it's the birthplace of pizza. But it's more complicated than that. There are lots of examples of the place of a dish's origin not being preeminent (Austrian croissants? Chinese ketchup?). But in this case, the Neapolitans are still crushing it. Maybe it's because they have pizza rules; less official than German beer purity or French wine laws, but just as strict. Associazione Verace Pizza Napoletana was established in 1984 to dictate what makes a true Neapolitan pizza. Rules include, but are not limited to:

1. The dough is made with just water, salt, yeast, and flour, and is left to proof for at least eight hours.
2. Preferably, the ingredients should be from Campania.
3. The pizza must be cooked, not using a baking pan, in a wood-fired oven, for sixty to ninety seconds.
4. The pizza should be round, with a diameter no greater than thirty-five centimeters; the crust has to be puffed up, while the center has to be max four millimeters thick.

The rules also say that the pizza should have the aroma of baked bread with the acidity of tomatoes and mozzarella; have a balanced flavor with oil mixing with the sauce; and be easy to fold. Most of the rules sound pretty reasonable, but then we come to one thing that horrified me: the bubbles. "Its color should be golden and with very few burns and bubbles."

I asked Emanuele, the chef at Da Michele, about bubbles. He explained that a bigger crust forms when the sauce isn't laid out to the very edge of the dough. Wheat is made up of sticky starch molecules. Pizza dough, like other leavened dough batters (or shaving cream), is a foam, a bunch of air-filled bubbles held together by a thick liquid; the tomato sauce is poured on top of this foam. Once cooked, it becomes a set foam. But when it's put inside the oven, the edge without the sauce, in direct contact with the hot air, rises. Sometimes there is a blob of air trapped in the dough and, when it heats, the air expands into the large bubble. The thin membrane of dough is strong enough not to break and thin enough that it crisps up and sometimes burns. Boom, the delicious dough bubble! Bubbles cannot be totally eliminated unless you put your sauce all the way to the edge of the pie, which Da Michele doesn't do. It's just par for the course in pizza making.

There is a direct connection between Naples as a working-class city and Naples as the birthplace of pizza. Pizza in its various forms has been a street food in Naples for centuries, as a flatbread with various toppings, even before the advent of pizza as we know it today. It was cheap and could be eaten quickly. For many years it never caught on in Italy beyond the Naples area, perhaps because it was seen as a poor people's food and because southern Italians had long been looked down on by northerners.

It was a big and now legendary event when, in 1889, Umberto I and his consort Margherita of Savoy, the King and Queen of

Italy, visited Naples and asked Maria Giovanna Brandi and her husband Raffaele Esposito, of Pizzeria Brandi, for several pizzas as a novelty. The pizza makers delivered three varieties, including one topped with (red) tomatoes, fresh buffalo milk (white) mozzarella, and (green) basil, the colors of the flag of recently united Italy. The queen declared it her favorite, and that was the origin of what has been known since as Margherita pizza—as well as of the modern pizza. Fittingly, considering how everything connected with pizza can generate heated arguments, there are those who call this a myth and credit Esposito's marketing skills for the general acceptance of the story.[1]

Meanwhile, from 1880-1920, millions of Neapolitans and other southern Italians were emigrating to the United States, and brought their demand for pizza with them. Lombardi's, the first licensed pizzeria in New York City, opened in 1905, using a coal-fired oven and a thin crust,[2] setting the pattern for the history of pizza in New York. Previous New York pizzas had been made at home or sold without licenses.[3] Italian immigrants continued to eat pizza as they spread around the country, but pizza remained largely unknown to non-Italians until the 1950s. Some say that it became popular as the result of returning WWII soldiers who had tasted it in Italy; others minimize veterans' impact and say it was mainly postwar changes in Americans' living patterns and pizzeria technology that made it an attractive fast-food and delivery item.

And then pizza spread back to Italy, becoming popular far beyond Naples for the first time, as part of the overall impact of American culture on postwar Europe.

* * *

So what is the secret to great Neapolitan pizza? Whereas in New York, they say it's the water, here they say it's the wheat. Italian wheat, and European wheat generally, is usually composed of softer varieties; American is primarily a hard, red wheat. Hard wheat varieties have more, and stronger, gluten. [4]

The origins of wheat, the world's most widely grown crop and a fundamental part of the diets of about 40 percent of the world's population, have been traced back about seven million years. A million years ago, emmer wheat[5], one of the ancient species collectively known as farro, came into existence. About 8,000-10,000 years ago, hybridization between emmer and a wild grass species led to the emergence of spelt, most likely in today's northern Iran. Spelt developed into "bread," or "common" wheat.

Extremely adaptable, wheat can be grown almost anywhere, except tropical lowlands.[6] It has been bred intentionally since the eighteenth century, at various times and places, for disease resistance, higher yields, and resistance to drought and heat. Based on Darwin and Gregor Mendel's work, breeding has accelerated since 1900, and has entered new territory with gene-splicing and the ability to sequence genomes. But I was about to learn from someone who is very deliberately behind the times.

I drove through the Italian countryside past ancient villages of wattle and daub, timber and stone, feeling like I was wending my way back in time. I was on a mission, headed towards the medieval hilltop commune of Caselle. It was midday when we would farm wheat under a bright, dog day's sun using certain time-honored tools and processes, the way the grain had been farmed hundreds of years ago. I was meeting up with Antonio Pellegrino of Associazione Pro Loco di Caselle in Pittari.

The town, originally a Roman fortress, is perched on Mount Pittari, in Cilento National Park, overlooking the Bussento River. As the fort inhabitants outgrew it in the 1400s, their houses spilled down the mountainside, clustered in a slapdash of urban planning. Passing through the town, I stopped at Zi Filomena for lunch. Handed down from grandma to mother to son, Zi Filomena "has maintained its authentic traditions," according to its listing in the Michelin Guide. While Michelin also says people come for the meats and mushrooms, it was here I first tried the local wheat. The mom's *campanelle*, a tight, cone-shaped pasta, covered in a rich *ragu*, was substantive and firm. It was made with grain from the fields which we were about to harvest. Lunch in the belly, we crossed town and made our way onto a flattened hill and down a dirt road. With Caselle far above us across a valley, the houses petered out, and stone-walled plots, gardens, and fields blew by in a green and tan strobe. My stomach lifted and sank with each dip and rise. And then I arrived, to a meadow next to a rundown villa at the edge of a parcel of golden wheat stalks. Two figures, armed with sickles, stood just outside the border hedge under straw-brimmed hats.

Antonio was dark-haired, with a pointy, close-cropped beard and a fierce demeanor (not helped by a bandage on his throat). His no-nonsense energy radiated off of him. He led me into the hip-high grass and discussed how this farm had come to be; he spoke of it as if it were his child. He had been recovering ancient seeds since 2008, particularly focused on *russulidda* and *ianculidda*, varieties that were on the verge of disappearing.

Russulidda, a Sicilian ancient durum wheat, has health benefits (low gluten content, facilitation of digestion, high lignin content)[7] and a pleasing aroma.[8] Ianculidda is a soft wheat that used to be popular to make flour. Ianculidda grows over four feet tall, it is very disease resistant, and it adapts well to different soils. Local growers stopped growing these varieties in the 1970s for a number of reasons, including that the more modern wheats produce greater yields and are easier to harvest. Antonio sells the seeds (sometimes acquired via seed exchanges at the Slow Food festival in Turin) to local farms in coordination with the local Slow Food *Grano Di Caselle*, but he turned this field into a bedrock of the community. Here the eight localities of the commune come together once a year for a competition to see who can harvest the most wheat the fastest using ancient means. Grano Di Caselle says the week-long celebration is "not a reenactment but a real and authentic competition." Grano Di Caselle sees its work here as a reason for the community to come together for "meeting and joy and, above all, pride." It affirms traditions and roots, but Antonio says it is also a living social and innovation laboratory.

The Slow Food movement in Casselle, as elsewhere, focuses on producing healthy food through environmentally sound methods and providing fair working conditions and pay, while charging reasonable prices.

As we walked, Antonio told me that "the best way to preserve a seed is to sow it." This experimental field grows different varieties in different plots, and, in a way, the field almost acts as a "grain library." "It's an investment in memory and the future, the movement of roots and foliage, the wind, the sun, the rain." He showed me how to grip a collection of stalks and use the crescent-shaped blade to cut back towards one's legs—but not too hard, as the nick on my knee reminded me. The wheat stalk had to be golden brown and, importantly, I had to cut from the middle to low to the ground, knees bent, back aching. Antonio was frustrated as I sometimes pulled the wheat too hard and a root came out with the cut. But, over time, a rhythm grew. Once I cut the wheat properly, I held it in bunches with the seeds aligned. I then wrapped one of the stalks around the bunch, like a tourniquet, and the bundle was now a sheaf. I asked how many sheaves I needed for a pizza and Antonio held his hands wide. From there 'til the end,

I clutched, cut, and bundled. Soon it was only the three of us: the wheat, the scythe, and myself, hunched, shuffling, swinging, tying. Following in the footsteps of thousands of years.

The grains are enclosed by tough membranes called glumes, forming husks. Once harvested, the husks need to be removed by threshing or milling, to get at the grain. In the field, we threshed the dry wheat by banging wheat heads against the side of a basket to make the kernels fall off. Antonio had a shallow wicker basket—an ancient tool—to thresh into. We then had to winnow (or separate) the chaff from the wheat berry by blowing directly onto the chaff. The heavier berry fell into the basket, while the light covering hung in the air and floated away.

It felt nothing like the industrialized wheat farming I knew from visiting larger farms in America. This was artisanal farming as a way of life, integrated into the idea of slow food at every level of meaning, and helping to build a community that was not just about growing more and faster. Antonio was choosing to maintain a close, physical connection with his crops, harvesting old varieties by hand, rejecting the convenience of harvesting new varieties with a combine. Neuroscientist Kelly Lambert has tied modern depression to lack of "hands-on" work, "physical activities that involve our hands, particularly activities that produce tangible products that we can see, touch, and enjoy." With hands-on work, she writes, "you begin to feel more control over your environment and more connected to the world around you. This reduces stress and anxiety and, most important, builds resilience against the onset of depression." Working with my hands on the wheat gave me joy. Antonio spoke about cutting wheat as connecting himself with his peasant identity. To me, it was part of what I was looking for in setting out to connect to my food "from scratch."

It's easy to romanticize; it's highly unlikely that everyone in the world could be fed by artisanal hand-cut wheat. In South Africa, where I harvested spelt on a massive John Deere combine, we took in 1000 bushels in a couple of minutes and the machine cut, threshed, and winnowed them at the push of a gear. All the while I sat in the cab chatting and riding, disconnected from the process, learning nothing and feeling next to nothing except the air conditioning. Would the South African farm workers want to return to backbreaking, time-consuming harvesting by scythe? On the other hand, I knew what Antonio was doing was important; in preserving the old ways under modern conditions, he was finding meaning—he was keeping something from getting lost. And I felt a connection to my human identity different from in my daily life in LA. In this field, I lived in the moment; I felt humility and an attachment to all the people who came before, part of a large web. There was something liberating in literally walking each step of the harvest to completion. The next step was milling.

Antonio pointed me back into town to the associated local artisanal mill, Mulino a Pietra Monte Frumentario, a division of Terra di Resilienza. Terra de Resilienza is a cooperative focused on "social agriculture, experiential tourism, and all activities aimed at the recovery of traditional civil practices of rural areas and the development of social innovation" through "eco-sustainable agricultural practices and the enhancement of agro-food products." When I arrived, a large sack of dried wheat grain was waiting. The miller and I made four types of flour. Italian bread wheat flour is graded 00 to 2 based on the extraction rate—how much bran is taken out; flour with none of the bran removed is called *integrale*. Finely sifted white flour is 00, from the first stages of the milling process; an all-purpose flour, with all the bran (25 percent) removed, is 0; 2 is a coarser flour, with about 18 to 20 percent of the bran removed.

We poured the wheat grain into a stone mill where it was ground down. Then we passed it through a sifter. The flour rolled around in a slanted, cylindrical tube. The finest grains fell into one sack, slightly thicker in another and so on. Only 00 is used for pizza, which I threaded up in a paper sack and took with me for Emanuele and Da Michele.

* * *

Then we were off in search of tomatoes. Winding in and out of the mountain tunnels as we headed north, I got a snapshot flip-book of the little towns and the sea. Dark tunnel, bright sea, dark tunnel, Priano snug in its crevice, dark tunnel, lemon groves perched on a terraced hill. I opened my window to let the salt air in the car. Large yachts hugged the coastline as they skipped their way from Positano to Amalfi, maybe stopping for a dip between. The sea has an amazing pull here—most roads lead to it. But I took a right and, reluctantly, headed inland once again.

Tomatoes originated in the Andes as wild plants. The first tiny, cultivated tomatoes were yellow or orange.[9] Varieties of tomatoes made their way from South America to Central America and Mexico, where they were being cultivated by 700 BCE. The Aztecs, who were eating tomatoes around 700 CE, named them *xitomatl*,[10] from which "tomato" was ultimately derived. Tomato sauce was also developed in Mexico, with cooked-down tomatoes, onions, and peppers. Neither tomatoes nor tomato sauce seem to have been a particularly important food in the Americas prior to the Columbian Exchange.

The conquistadors brought tomatoes to Europe, where the first references to them were in the sixteenth century. Initially, they were grown just as an ornamental plant. They were regarded with suspicion and fear because they are related to deadly nightshade and to the mysterious, fascinating, and dangerous mandrake, and because their stems and leaves are toxic. But they were also considered to be an aphrodisiac. In the 1540s, the famed botanist Pietro Andrea Matthioli[11] was the first European to document the tomato[12], which he thought was poisonous. His diagrams showed it as yellow, which may be why tomatoes were known in Italy as "the apple of gold," or *pomo d'oro*,[13] which became today's *pomodoro*. (Another version of the naming story is that tomatoes were introduced to Italy from Morocco and were known as *pomo dei mori* or "apple of the Moors."[14]) By 1597, a variety of tomato was also being referred to as having "a shining red color." In France, tomatoes were known as *pommes d'amore*, which carried over in English to Britain and the United States as "love apples."

Because of the rich volcanic soil and the constant sun, which tomatoes love, tomatoes blossomed in Italy, but integration of tomatoes into the cuisine was slow, partly because the wealthy—though not the poor—ate off pewter plates; tomatoes leached the lead out of the pewter with poisonous effect. It took a while for the (surviving) wealthy to realize that the poor were not getting sick from them. The first Italian cookbook to include tomato sauce was Antonio Latini's *Lo Scalco alla Moderna* ("*The Modern Steward*") in the 1690s.[15] Tomatoes became increasingly significant in Italian recipes in the beginning of the eighteenth century, but it wasn't until the nineteenth century that many tomato dishes became fundamental to Italian cuisine as we know it.[16] Word of tomatoes as edibles spread slowly to northern Europe and the United States, and it wasn't until the later eighteenth and then nineteenth centuries that people there fully recognized tomatoes as safe to eat. Thomas Jefferson may have cultivated tomatoes as early as 1781 and is known to have been eating them by 1809. Reportedly, he caused a commotion by eating one in public to show it wasn't poisonous.

Tomatoes became even more popular once they began to be canned. Napoleon offered a large prize to anyone who could improve food preservation to better feed his army. The inventor Nicolas François Appert came up with sealing boiled foods in airtight jars and claimed the money. In Italy, Francesco Cirio used Appert's technique to begin canning tomatoes in 1856 and, by the beginning of the twentieth century, the Cirio company was producing large quantities of canned tomatoes.

There are now more than 15,000 species of tomatoes of various colors and shapes. One of the most famous varieties is the San Marzano, grown at the foot of Mt. Vesuvius in Naples. Italians take them so seriously that they are DOP-protected (*Pomodoro San Marzano dell'Agro Sarnese Nocerino D.O.P.*). Only growers within a defined area adhering to certain farming and canning techniques can sell tomatoes labeled San Marzano. The San Marzano is a plum tomato—sort of oval, and a little tear-drop-y. Drier and meatier, with fewer seeds than most tomatoes, it lends itself to making sauce and to canning. Because it's not watery when it's canned, it keeps its flavor. Due to its location near Naples, it became the tomato used for sauce on pizza. Emanuele told me it's good on a pizza because it's sweeter, with low acidity and a thick skin that is quick to peel.

The farm I was going to was filled with greenhouses with rows and rows of the prettiest, oval-shaped, red-colored San Marzanos. I collected a basketful and then headed down the road to a cannery. From the parking lot to the front door I spied a row of potted basil—some of which I proceeded to borrow for my sauce. The canner and I were making *pacchetelle di pomodoro*, typical of southern Italy; the tomatoes are cut in half and pasteurized in glass jars. When canning tomatoes, you must first add an acid to your jars to prevent the growth of *C. botulinum* bacteria, which causes botulism. Lemon juice can be used for this, but we didn't have to add it because we were going to eat the tomatoes the next day. In the cannery, we filled a jar up to the brim with quartered San Marzanos, mashing them a bit to fit, and topped them with basil and a small sprinkle of salt. After screwing the lid on, we submerged it in a steamer where it cooked for an hour. This hour was a lesson in patience.

One of the best and worst parts of sourcing your own foods is that the process of harvesting and then cooking slowly builds your craving. From the moment you pick or catch the meal, the clock on your hunger begins to tick…and the ticking only gets faster as you continue. The smells were tantalizing—the wet, earthy smell of the hothouse, the bright, tangy smell of the tomato, and the smell of the basil that leaves a memory on your hands for days, causing you to salivate every time you get a whiff. The slicing and crushing of the tomatoes in the jar releases a tart, almost fruity, scent, but also the visual taste of what's to come—crushed, sloppy flesh and juice. By the time the hour was up, only the super hot lid stopped me from grabbing the tomato sauce out with my hands. After finding a kitchen towel and unscrewing the lid, I just took in the steaming maelstrom as the smell wafted up to my face, getting my taste buds raring, and, tangentially, giving me a tomato facial. We each took a spoon and dipped it into this stew, blowing and sipping. By itself, without pasta or bread or cheese or pizza, this sauce—the sweet, fragrant flavor—was perfection. The joy of a simple dish with wonderful ingredients.

There was one more stop for me before returning to the cook. Buffalo mozzarella wasn't the only divergence from the

Da Michele iconic recipe, as I love anchovies. They were also an excuse to head down to the shore of Pisciotta and go out on a boat onto the Mediterranean, into the night with *menaica* nets. These are an ancient net used thousands of years ago by the Greeks and brought by them whenever they "settled" throughout the Mediterranean. They were likely the type of net used by the Galilee fishermen in the New Testament. Through a long night of fishing, Vittorio Rimbaldo, his brother, son, and I laid out nets which hung just under the calm sea. Vittorio says these nets are more sustainable because they don't drag the sea floor and also let smaller anchovies pass through.

Then, sopping wet, in chest-high waders, we plucked anchovies by hand, eating some sushi-style right there in the dark, sitting on the edge of the boat on the waves. Coming home refreshed and

Amalfi anchovies

Anchovy fishing in the Amalfi

buoyant, I was ready to meet a sunburnt Vittorio a few hours later to make *alici di menaica*. We gutted, decapitated, cleaned, and layered the anchovies between salt in a terracotta jar, then placed a half-inch thick wooden disc on top, just inside the jar mouth, and put a stone on it. Over time the rock and the wooden covering would squeeze the liquid out of the sardines, leaving a delicious, fermented oil/liquid (similar to patis from the Philippines) that could be used as a pungent dressing. It also leaves behind salted anchovies for Caesar salad and…pizza.

* * *

Back at Da Michele, I snuck in past the milling tourists waiting for the doors to open. I had an hour or so to make the pie. The restaurant was eerily quiet, with a ghostly feel hanging over the dining hall, empty chairs, and tables. Emanuele started me behind the counter and handed me an apron with the famous Da Michele insignia of the namesake's face across the front. We poured one cup of water into a metal bowl and mixed a couple handfuls and change of flour (three cups) and a liberal pinch of salt (half a teaspoon). We began kneading, slowly adding flour until the ball of dough was on the edge of tacky and shiny—he added a splash of olive oil to help with this. After kneading, Emanuele told me to watch him go through the process of making one of his pies so I could follow afterwards. He lowered one side of the soft-ball-sized dough (from Da Michele's batch—with yeast) into a pile of flour, used his palm to make a hollow, and then flopped it back and forth between his hands until it flattened out and got wider. Laying out a bit of flour, he took it and started pulling/pressing down and out with his fingertips. I followed suit, so far so good. He even gave me a "*Bravo!*"

Sadly, he didn't throw it in the air, but that was probably for the best as I could see that ending in disaster with my turn. Once the pizza was the size of a large platter, he applied two spoonfuls—a light shmear—of their sauce (from the same place we made ours) and placed five leaves of basil on top. He grabbed two handfuls of shredded cheese and layered them. As I mentioned, Da Michele doesn't use the more robust buffalo mozzarella, though Emanuele says it's fine for others to use. The *fior di latte* made from cow's milk has been the recipe since Da Michele's establishment, but also the cow cheese adds a lighter, sweeter flavor he enjoys. He then topped it with a drizzle of olive oil.

I spread my tomato sauce and made large slices of the mozzarella (about three ounces) that didn't cover the whole pie but were more like continents on the ocean of sauce. While my mozzarella balls looked lumpier than the experts' at Tenuta, they tasted just the same. Four rough-torn basil leaves followed. I placed my anchovies intermittently around the pie. Unknowingly, this is where things started to go south. I did not wash the salt off the fish before placing it. I drizzled the olive oil that I had made from scratch in South Africa.

Then the second misstep occurred. As I moved the pie onto the wooden pizza peel (the paddle), the edge caught on the counter and the center tore a little. It now looked like a large amoeba. Emanuele fused the hole but, stepping back to take a look, said we should start again. I shook him off because, for better or worse, this was my pizza, and I slid it into the oven. I will say, walking the pie over to that furnace and flicking the pizza off with a quick motion was something I'd dreamed of for years. I spun it once during the cook using the edge of the peel and, less than five minutes later, it was ready.

We took Emanuele's out and mine right after (my dismount onto the counter was very smooth). They both steamed next to the lip of the oven. My misshapen pie made me love it even more, in a way. That it wasn't so pretty, it felt more authentic, less studied. I cut a rectangle off and rolled it into a burrito as had been taught to me one night at a pizza spot just down Trastevere. Hot and cheesy, I used my apron as a net. Chewing, the too-salty flavor from the unwashed anchovies shocked me. Emanuele called out that the salt hadn't disintegrated. Had I ruined the whole pie?! I removed the anchovies and tried again. Not terrible. At the time I called it a double. Emanuele said the olive oil with the buffalo cheese was good. Then I tasted Emanuele's. Boom! Made mine taste more like a seeing-eye single. His was a home run. Just the right amount of sauce, of cheese, a dish evolved over hundreds of years.

And now I knew why Neapolitan pizzas are the best in the world—even better than New York's. It was the importance at each stage of doing things traditionally, correctly, and authentically. The pizza embodies the culture that goes into making it. At the same time, it is wrapped up in marketing. In France it's champagne and in Mexico it's tequila. In Naples it's "What kind of tomatoes are you using?" It's a pride in and a possessiveness of a unique product: *This is ours!*

But it's also because it is done well. The tires have been kicked. The folks that I met along the way were helping me skip the mistakes that had been made before. What I had felt as friction in the process was really a fear of my doing a disservice to their culture and way of life. As soon as I demonstrated that I respected what they were doing and that I wanted to learn the "right way" from them, a path opened up and I realized that the bumps were just the membership fees for the club. A club that reconnects us to nature, to our history, makes us use our hands, and gives us the knowledge learned over generations of how to feed ourselves delicious bread, cheese, tomato sauce, salted fish, and pizza from scratch.

Afterword

PEOPLE OFTEN ASK ME HOW I synthesize what I have learned in this exploration. What began as a desire to honor the work—creative and physical—that goes into creating food, as well as a chance to visit countries and restaurants around the world, has become much more. I've learned so much about cultures, cooking, and cuisine, about our economic, environmental, and climate crises, and about what's important to me in living my life.

Coming from many backgrounds and with varied styles, the chefs I met all cultivated close relationships with their suppliers. Some, such as Virgilio in Peru and Stefan in Malta, were local and deeply dedicated to exploring their homeland's ingredients and cuisine. Others, such as Antonia in Wyoming and Galen in Utah, came from away but were equally fascinated by their locale's ingredients and the cultures surrounding them.

I learned that you should crack eggs on a flat surface, not an edge (to keep the shells out of the bowl), and that a damp hand towel under a cutting board stops it from slipping. Mayonnaise spread on cooking meat and fish (and pretty much everything else) is a great way to boost flavor. Sharp knives are essential, especially if you aren't very good with cutting; they make things so much easier. These tips have made their way into my own kitchen. Cooking in a restaurant isn't only about being able to make a great meal, but also being able to replicate it each time—which is the hardest part. If people like a dish, they want to come back for that same dish. This also happens in my own kitchen with my family asking me not to alter recipes they have grown to love. And finally, to quote Gunnar, "If you pick the food yourself, you tend to prepare it with more care and have a much better story to tell."

As an omnivore, I started this adventure with the belief that if I were to eat meat, I had to be willing to confront that it meant that someone else was killing the animal that became my dinner. To avoid being a hypocrite, I had to be willing to do the killing myself and to think consciously about the conditions in which the animal lived and died; this led me to a deeper understanding of the devastating effects of factory farming on workers, communities, and animals other than human. It also led me to try to learn much more about the worlds of hunting, which were largely foreign to me.

I don't claim perfection, and I do still eat a fast-food burger every now and then, but I eat much more intentionally. Usually when I eat meat, it's from farms which provide humane conditions for the animals and pay the workers a living wage. This hits me in the wallet, which further encourages me to eat less meat. Karen and my meat consumption is way down, and we feed our son a nearly-vegetarian diet. Meat has become largely an appetizer or condiment.

I started this exploration because I realized that, whether at home or in restaurants, I was far removed from the sources of the food I was eating—food that often came wrapped in plastic or presented prettily on a plate. Even at family or friends' tables where someone said grace before the meal, I was largely oblivious to the actual work involved in actually getting it there. I'm no longer oblivious and am more conscious than ever of the conditions under which much of the food is grown and processed by "essential workers."

I came to understand much more deeply why scientists of multiple disciplines call this the Anthropocene Epoch, because the fate of the planet really is in our hands. Although 1950 is proposed as the official starting date of the epoch, the histories of Iceland's trees and New York Harbor's oysters tell us that people's profound impact on the environment long predates that.

The urgency is so immediately visible in the oceans that cover 71 percent of the earth's surface, as the fisherpeople I met around the world told me—whether the pollution and overfishing of the Mediterranean or the overfishing and coral destruction in the South China Sea, or the rise of sea levels around the world. That's why the stories of the marine protected areas in the Philippines and the total allowable catch in Iceland are exciting because they show that incipient disasters can be reversed. But creating effective MPAs in the Philippines (or around the world) and bringing them to a scale where they will make a systemic difference requires initiative and support from both governments and local people. And the top-down design of Iceland's ITQ without inclusion of those most affected has devastated villages while concentrating power and wealth to the detriment of social and political cohesion.

On land, of course, the crises are equally grave. Kenya has lost 70 percent of its wildlife since 1990. Land privatization and fragmentation has led, in the words of Dr. Ben Ole Koissaba of the Mara Civil Society Forum, to "massive loss of land, virtually rendering the affected people destitute."[1] He calls the root of the problem "widespread ignorance amongst the affected communities regarding their land rights."[2] Success of the conservancies, protection of the Sacred Forest, reforestation through agroforestry, and protection of the Maasai's land rights will all depend on genuine empowerment of those affected and commitment of the state. In South Africa, the work of Mama Christina and the Abalimi Bezekhaya is endangered by endemic governmental corruption, and meaningful land reform requires attacking bastions of wealth and power.

Malta will also need a unity of intent and action between the government and the people if it is to maintain an adequate water supply. A land with almost no freshwater sources, Malta has managed to cope with huge booms in population and tourism through desalination of seawater, but it faces lots of challenges if it is to avoid the collapses that have periodically marked its history. It will need clear leadership from the government and trust and buy-in from the people at large.

I was happy to encounter the Slow Food movement in different settings; I think of Antonio in Italy deliberately setting the clock back on agricultural "innovation" and prizing building a community around the food he is growing. I was excited to learn from Manuel in the Andes and Cynthia in Utah about the many varieties of potatoes that exist as alternatives to McDonald's monoculture. And my dad, who has diabetes, was happy to learn that if you cook potatoes (or rice) and then cool them overnight, they don't cause glucose spikes.

Finland is a story of how a country has transformed itself from a land of poverty to its "happiest country" status through intentionality and unity, applied to health care, education, food, and, recently, to changing conceptions of forests and reviving the lives of rivers. I think I was most struck by the thoughtfulness and humaneness by which Finns have confronted issues common to all countries. I want my son to go to school in Finland. Or alternatively, for California to become more like Finland!

Whether it is groups of gardeners in South Africa, Utah Diné Bikéyah reintroducing Four Corners potatoes in the US, or fisherfolk and scientists creating and protecting MPAs in the Philippines, I was introduced to people undertaking acts of necessity that are also acts of courage and persistence. I have no way of knowing whether we, as a species, can summon the will to enable everyone to live at the decent standard of living they deserve, much less whether we can grasp our limited time to save ourselves as a species and the many species that we are endangering. But I know that we have no alternative.

Recipes

The chefs have blessed us with recipes. Here they are in the formats they have sent. Please enjoy some of my favorite meals from this journey.

Kilawin

By Margarita Manzke (Wildflour, Manila)

Ingredients

400 g sushi-grade mackerel
400 g sushi-grade tuna
1 tsp patis
1 cup coconut vinegar
10 pcs calamansi
1 cup coconut cream
3 tbsp thinly sliced red onion
1 tbsp grated ginger
1 piece sili labuyo or thai chili, sliced
1 piece green sili or sili sigang, sliced
2 pieces kamias, thinly sliced
Salt to taste

Preparation

Marinate sliced or cubed fish in coconut vinegar, calamansi, and patis for 15 minutes. Discard remaining liquid. Mix ½ cup of coconut cream with the fresh fish. Add sliced red onion, grated ginger, chilis, kamias, salt, and ½ cup of coconut cream in a bowl. Mix together. Spoon and top on fish.

Four Corners Potato

By Chef Galen Zamarra (Yuta, Utah)

Ingredients

2 cups Four Corners potatoes
1 tsp baking soda
1 Tbsp vegetable oil
1 clove of garlic, chopped
1 shallot, minced
1 scallion, sliced thin
¼ tsp aji amarillo powder
Trout belly
½ tsp salt
½ tsp sugar
¼ tsp ground coriander
¼ tsp fennel pollen

Preparation

1. Dissolve the baking soda into 1 qt of water. Soak the potatoes in the water for 2 days. Strain and rinse the potatoes. Boil in salted water until tender, strain and reserve.
2. Sprinkle the salt, sugar, and spices on the trout belly. Let cure for 30 mins. Smoke at 160°F for 1 hr. Remove the skin from the trout. Slice the trout bacon into thin strips.
3. Heat a large sauté pan and add the vegetable oil. Add the potatoes and cook until lightly browned. Add the garlic, shallots, and scallion. Season with salt and aji amarillo. Add the trout bacon and cook for 1 min.

Halo Halo Clarified Milk Punch Cocktail

By Margarita Manzke (Wildflour, Manila)

Ingredients

16 calamansi (zested)
16 oz calamansi juice
1 pineapple
2 mangoes
1 lemongrass stalk (chopped)
30 g ginger (chopped)
2 cinnamon sticks
1 pandan leaf (chopped)
1 lb granulated sugar
36 oz Filipino coconut liquor
8 oz brewed lemongrass/mint tea
14 oz boiling water
30 oz full-fat coconut milk/cream

Preparation

1. Use a microplane or vegetable peeler to remove the zest from 16 calamansi. Add the zest to a large, airtight container.
2. Peel and core the pineapple and mangoes. Cut into large chunks and add them to the calamansi peels.
3. Coarsely grind the spices with a mortar and pestle. Add the spices and aromatics to the container, along with the sugar and 12 oz of calamansi juice. Muddle the mixture.
4. Pour in the brewed lemongrass/mint tea as well as the coconut liquor and stir to combine. Add boiling water and immediately cover so the liquid doesn't evaporate. Let sit overnight, then strain the mixture into a clean container.

5. Bring the coconut milk to a boil. Add the remaining 4 oz of calamansi juice. Then pour the strained punch mixture into the boiling coconut milk and calamansi juice. (You should taste at this point to adjust sugar and citrus levels for balance. The brighter it tastes, the better because it will soften as it clarifies.) The milk will curdle and the solids will coagulate. Refrigerate for 24 hours to settle. The coconut will form a raft at the bottom.

6. Strain the liquid a little at a time through a fine chinois lined with cheesecloth or serviette. You can clarify even more by pouring the strained liquid back through the cheesecloth with the strained coconut milk solids (the solids clarify the mixture so the more times you do it, the clearer it will come out.) Pour into a clean container, cover, and refrigerate overnight to give the remaining milk solids time to settle. Ladle the clarified punch into a clean container, taking care not to disturb the solids at the bottom.

Trout Piscator

By Chef Galen Zamarra (Yuta, Utah)

Ingredients

3 whole trout, approx. 12-inch sized fish
½ C heavy cream
½ lb wild nettles
½ C creme fraiche
1 tsp prepared horseradish
1 Tbsp chopped chives
1 green apple, julienned
1 bunch watercress
1 lemon
extra virgin olive oil, as needed
6 pearl onions
¼ C apple cider vinegar
¼ C sugar
1 C water
10 black peppercorns
1 bay leaf
12 red chili flakes

Preparation

1. Peel and slice thinly the pearl onions. Place in a mason jar. Bring to a boil the vinegar, sugar, water, and spices. Pour over the onions and let cool to room temp. Seal the jar and refrigerate for up to 1 month.
2. Filet the trout, keeping the skin on 4 of the filets. Remove all pin bones. Reserve the belly meat for the bacon. Remove the bottom 3 inches of tail meat and reserve any scraps of the trout filet to make the mousseline. Use 2 filet of trout for the mousseline without the skin, reserve the other 4 filet with the skin for later.

3. Bring a pot of salted water to a boil. Blanch the nettles and cook for 3 mins. Remove the nettles from the water with a slotted spoon and cool them rapidly in an ice bath. When cold, strain the nettles and remove any excess water.
4. In a food processor, mix the trout meat with salt until a smooth paste is formed. Add the blanched nettles and the heavy cream. Blend until smooth.
5. Lay the trout filet skin-side down on a board. Spread a 1-inch thick layer of the mousseline over the filet and place the other filet on top so that the skin is on the outside. wrap the fish in plastic film and tightly form a cylinder, tying off both ends. Poach the trout in simmering water for approximately 10 mins. Remove from the water and rest the fish at room temperature for 2 mins.
6. Slice the trout into 1-inch thick rounds and remove the plastic wrap. Mix the creme fraiche, horseradish, and chives in a bowl. Serve this as the sauce on the bottom of the plate. In another bowl, toss the watercress and julienned apples with a little fresh lemon juice and extra virgin olive oil. Place the salad on the creme fraiche and place the cooked trout medallions around the salad.

Brown Butter Crab, Artichoke Chawanmushi

Chef Matt Costello (Inn at Langley, Whidbey Island, WA)

Ingredients

2 large artichokes
2 lemons
Neutral oil (avocado, sunflower, grapeseed)
¼ lb lump Dungeness crabmeat, picked
40 g bonito flakes
1 piece kombu (6" long approx.) 30 g
6 large eggs
2 Tbsp dry milk
¼ lb butter

Preparation

Artichokes and Broth

1. Steam trimmed artichokes in large pot of cold, salted water. Add sliced lemons and enough olive oil to create a slick of oil completely covering the surface of the water. It will feel like a lot of olive oil. Bring to a simmer. When leaves pull off, remove from water and set aside to cool, stem up. Pulled leaves should still have resistance so as they cool they will not finish overcooked.
2. Reserve cooking water, skim off much of the oil, and strain through a fine mesh strainer.

Dashi

Measure 6 cups of the artichoke cooking liquid into a pot and add 2 cups fresh water and the kombu. Bring to a simmer and then add bonito flakes. Turn off heat and allow flakes and seaweed to settle for 5 minutes. Then strain artichoke dashi, discarding all solids. Season to taste. Should have a slightly bitter, slightly salty, fresh-fish taste. Set aside.

Chawanmushi

Place 3 cups of artichoke dashi in mixing bowl. Mix in 3 whole eggs and 3 egg whites (ratio is 1 whole and 1 white per cup). Taste and re-season. In a lidded, oven-proof, small bowl, ideally a chawanmushi bowl, ladle in the custard. Place in steamer with lid on and steam for 12 minutes, then turn off heat and allow to sit undisturbed for another 12. The remaining artichoke dashi does freeze OK.

Crab and Artichokes in Brown Butter

Trim artichokes and slice heart into chunks, approx. 1cm. Discard leaves or eat as you prep. Set aside. Toast milk solids in a dry pan. Should be slightly golden. Lower heat and add butter, then crab and artichoke heart to warm through. Do not cook crab or artichoke more, this is just for warming. Taste and season with salt and lemon juice.

To Serve

Spoon artichoke heart and crab mix on top of each chawanmushi. Be gentle, the custard is delicate. I like to garnish with lemon balm and scallion. Other light-flavored herbs of choice are up to you. Place lid back and serve with a small spoon while warm. The custard should separate as you eat, and the broth and solids are both delicious.

Da Michele Pizza Dough

Chef Michele Rubini (Da Michele, Los Angeles)

Ingredients

1 liter of water
65 g of sea salt
1 g of fresh yeast
1.7-1.8 kg of Caputo 00 flour (blue bag)

Preparation

1. Although there is something different between the recipes, in our pizza dough after you pour the water in a bowl and add the salt and mix them together until the salt is completely dissolved, you also add the yeast (which is weird because no one does that; everyone usually adds yeast while they are mixing the water and flour together). At this point mix everything together, then it is time for us to add the flour little by little for about 20 minutes until the mixture reaches its optimal point; it means that you have a ball that is soft and silky. So it's time for us to put the dough in an enclosed container and let it rise for 24 hours at room temperature (about 21 degrees Celsius). After the waiting time, we have to ball the dough (*staglio*) in small balls with a size of 330 grams for each ball and put them in an enclosed container and wait another 5-6 hours. Then it's time to make some pizzas.

2. The tomato we decided to use is a selection of the best Italian tomatoes including, of course, San Marzano tomatoes from the Vesuvius area, sweet and rich in minerals. Instead of the classic Parmigiano Reggiano as per grated cheese we use the Pecorino Romano DOP (protected designation of origin) to balance the absence of salt in the tomato (we are not adding anything to it) and then fresh basil, sunflower seed oil, and the best fior di latte cheese you can find around (from the small city of Agerola, it is well-known for its slow processing; the curds are left to rest for at least 14 hours before being stretched and then becoming definitely *fior di latte*).

Acorn Fritter

By Chef Galen Zamarra (Yuta, Utah)

Dry Ingredients

65 g acorn flour
60 g all-purpose flour
13 g baking powder
18 g sugar
3 g salt
1 g nutmeg, microplaned

Wet Ingredients

150 g milk
1 egg yolk
30 g butter, melted
1 egg white, stiff peaks

Preparation

1. Mix dry ingredients.
2. Mix wet ingredients, omitting stiff-peak egg whites.
3. Whisk wet ingredients into dry, being careful not to overmix. Fold in egg whites. Allow to rest for 10 minutes before use.

Nettle and Fennel Risotto, Octopus and Braised Fennel

Chef Stefan Hogan (Corinthia Palace, Malta)

Serves 4

Ingredients for Nettle and Fennel Risotto

800 g of nettles
200 g parsley, dill, and mint (mixed)
60 g of butter, salted
50 ml olive oil
2 liters vegetable stock
2 shallots, finely chopped
80 g soft sheep's cheese, blended
20 ml of whipping cream
360 g risotto rice, arborio (I personally prefer Acquerello)
100 ml of white wine
100 g dry pecorino sardo, grated
Salt
White pepper

Preparation

1. Start by blanching the herb and nettles in boiling salted water, transfer to an ice bath to cool down immediately as you want to retain the fresh, vibrant green color. Strain and squeeze out as much liquid as possible; ideally place in a colander in the refrigerator overnight with a weight on top to get as much liquid as possible out. Place the herbs and nettles in a food processor with some cold vegetable stock and blend to get a smooth puree. Transfer into a clean bowl.
2. In a small pan, cook the shallots in a tablespoon of olive oil until soft and translucent.

(continued)

3. To start the risotto in a pot, lightly toast the rice on a low flame in the dry pot, then add a tablespoon of olive oil and the shallots and cook for a few minutes. Deglaze with the white wine and cook until the wine has evaporated. Now start to gradually add the vegetable stock a ladle at a time; keep stirring to ensure an even cooking of all the rice kernels.

4. Once the rice is cooked but still al dente (bite into the rice kernel and it should have a bright white spot in the middle), turn the heat off and gradually add the soft sheep's cheese and the nettle/herb puree. Mix it thoroughly and check seasoning, adding salt and a soft pinch of white pepper to taste. Just before serving, finish with some butter and the grated pecorino. Allow to sit for a few minutes before serving onto warm plates.

5. Top with the grilled octopus, braised fennel, and fennel tops.

Ingredients for the Octopus

1 medium-sized octopus
2 garlic cloves
1 onion, sliced
1 carrot, sliced
2 bay leaves
1 lemon, cut in half
200 ml white wine
Few peppercorns
Salt

Preparation

1. To cook the octopus, place the garlic, onion, carrot, celery, bay leaves, cinnamon stick, and lemon haves in a large saucepan and add three liters of water.

2. Bring to the boil over a high heat and add 5 g of salt. With long kitchen tongs, dip the octopus 3 times in the liquid; this will curl the tentacles for presentation later in the dish. Then submerge and release them into the water.

3. Reduce the heat to low, cover the pan, and simmer the octopus for about 50 minutes, or until just tender (not too tender as we need to grill it just before serving). Remove from the heat and allow to cool in the water.

4. Cut the octopus tentacles and brush with some olive oil and harissa paste, char in a hot nonstick pan with a drizzle of olive oil, season, and plate onto the risotto.

Snails in Maltese Landscape

By Chef Stefan Hogan (Corinthia Palace, Malta)

Ingredients for Snails' Cooking Liquor

2 kg, snails, purged and washed
2 celery ribs, chopped
½ leek, chopped
1 onion, finely chopped
2 tomatoes, chopped
1 carrot, diced
6 garlic cloves, chopped
100 ml white wine
2 bay leaves
Some thyme, mint, marjoram, and parsley
A few peppercorns
2 litres chicken stock
50 ml olive oil
Lemon rind
Salt and pepper

Preparation

1. In a large cooking pot, heat the olive oil and add the celery, leek, onion, tomatoes, carrots, and garlic; sauté and season with salt and pepper. Add the tomato paste and cook for a further two minutes, deglaze with the white wine, and add the snails; add the chicken stock and the herbs, peppercorns, and lemon zest.
2. Simmer for an hour and allow to cool.
3. Strain the sauce and remove the snails from the shell with a toothpick. When you are ready to serve, warm the sauce and reduce, add the snails and toss, check seasoning before serving.

Ingredients for Edible Soil

100 g potato flour
100 g carob flour
150 g ground almonds
40 g wholemeal flour
40 g brown sugar
Salt
150 g butter, cold, cut into cubes
50 ml dark beer

Preparation

1. Mix the potato flour, carob flour, almonds, sugar, and whole-meal flour, and mix well. Season with the salt and add the beer. Mix thoroughly, add the butter, and gently rub it into the mixture. Do not overwork as it needs to retain a sand-like texture.
2. Transfer to a baking tray and cook in an oven set at 175 degrees Celsius. It will not take too long. Allow to cool and store in a plastic container until ready to use.

Ingredients for Confit Pumpkin

A few slices of pumpkin, cut into discs
Sprig of thyme
Sprig of rosemary
1 garlic clove
60 g butter
Splash of sherry vinegar

Preparation

In a nonstick pan warm some olive oil and place the pumpkin slices, season with salt and pepper, and cook until the presentation side is caramelized and golden. Add the herbs, garlic, and butter and continue cooking until the pumpkin is cooked but not soft. Season with salt and a splash of vinegar to get some nice acidity to the taste.

Ingredients for Onion Purée

2 kg white onions, sliced
1 bay leaf
Thyme sprig
100 ml fresh cream
200 ml water
30 g butter
100 ml olive oil
Salt and pepper

Preparation

1. For the onion purée, you will need to cook the onions low and slow to get a deep, sweet caramel flavor. Heat the oil and bay leaf in a heavy pot, add the sliced onions, thyme, and half the water and gently stew down over a low flame. Keep stirring to avoid onions sticking to the bottom and burning. You will need to cook the onions down for around one hour or until all the moisture has evaporated. Add the cream and butter and continue to stir until you get a smooth consistency with very little liquid.
2. Remove and discard the bay leaf from the onions and transfer to a food processor with the 300 ml of water, butter, salt, and pepper. Blend until very smooth.

Ingredients for Garnish

Baby yellow onion petals
Cauliflower, florets, dehydrated
Borage flowers
Capers
Wild rucola
Cauliflower
Salt

Preparation

Dress the plate with the carob soil, the warm snails, some onion puree, the roasted pumpkin and the wild herbs, flowers, sliced baby yellow onion, and raw cauliflower slices.

Boerewors Pap with Peri-Peri

By Marty Bleazard (South Africa)

I coaxed my South African director Martin (Marty) Bleazard to send me his secret family recipe for a meal based around pap. It's become a staple in the Moscow household for a few different reasons. I love the richness and level of heat. Karen likes that it combines dishes from a few Southern African food cultures into one stupendous dinner. And Harrison loves mixing the pap and stew into one glob of mush and then eating with his fingers. I have tried this as well, and he is on to something.

Ingredients

2 C cornmeal (pap)
500 g boerewors (South African sausage) or bratwurst or stewing meat (beef)
1 milk stout, 330 ml (or any dark beer like a Guinness)
1 onion
1 can—400 g—whole peeled tomatoes
1 can baked beans
2 Tbsp curry powder
1 Tsp smoked paprika
Salt to taste
2 garlic cloves (chopped)
Chili flakes
2 Tbsp beef stock powder or half a cube
Peri-Peri sauce.

Preparation

1. First comes the pap, the starch of the dish. Bring 3 cups of water to the boil in a large pot. Add 1 cup of cornmeal and put the lid on. Reduce the heat to medium and leave for 8 minutes (don't stir!). Then lift the lid and, using a strong wooden spoon, stir forcefully for a minute and more slowly for an additional 2 minutes to get rid of lumps. Slowly pour in another cup of cornmeal and stir forcefully to incorporate. Reduce heat to low and let it steam for 10 minutes.
2. Texture should be sticky but not dry (add water or milk if needed).
3. Next up is the sausage stew. In South Africa they use boere-wors (farmer's sausage) which is a very meaty, beef-based sausage with not much filler or other ingredients. If you can track one down, use it. If not, then a bratwurst will do just fine. To start, chop and fry an onion in a shallow puddle of oil on a medium heat. Add 1 T smoked paprika and 2 T curry powder. Cook until onions are sweating and curry smell is released. Brown 2 medium-sized boerewors in the pan. Cut them up when they are nice and brown. Then add 2 chopped garlic cloves, plus chili flakes to taste (I like it hot). One can of whole peeled tomatoes and a bottle of milk stout (Guinness will do) (leave a few sips for yourself). Add half a cube of beef stock. Stir. Leave to cook for 5 minutes. Come back in the kitchen for a sip of Guinness and to add a can of baked beans and allow to cook out for another 5 minutes or until thick gravy consistency is reached.
4. You wanna warm the pap up again. Microwaving for 4 minutes will do the trick. A pat of butter, a dash of salt, and add a hot sauce to taste. If you want to stay in the region I suggest Peri-Peri.
5. Dish up pap onto plate and very generously apply sauce. You need a lot for the pap! Pour the stew on top or on the side. Eat slowly to enjoy (and because it's hot).

Endnotes

Oysters: New York / Istria

1 Greg Kelly, "First Residents: The Lenape," Monmouth Beach Life.com, January 24, 2022, http://www.monmouthbeachlife.com/mb-history/lenape-indians-monmouth-county/.

2 Jenn Hall, "The Overlooked History of the Bayshore," Edible Jersey, July 6, 2017, https://ediblejersey.ediblecommunities.com/food-thought/overlooked-history-bayshore.

3 Thomas Hynes, "Aw Shucks: The Tragic History of New York City Oysters," Untapped New York, March 11, 2021, https://untappedcities.com/2021/02/03/history-new-york-city-oysters/.

4 Ibid.

5 Amelia Simmons, *The First American Cookbook: A Facsimile of "American Cookery," 1796*, Hardcover by Amelia Simmons – First Edition – from LibroWorld (SKU: Bib-9781626541962)," Biblio.com (A.R. Shephard & Co.), accessed February 17, 2022, https://www.biblio.com/book/first-american-cookbook-facsimile-american-cookery/d/1436184406.

6 Charles Mackay, *Life and Liberty in America: Or, Sketches from a Tour in the United States, 1857–1858*, Making of America Books, p. 22. https://quod.lib.umich.edu/m/moa/abj2063.0001.001/22?rgn=full+text;view=image.

7 Francis Lam, "How Thomas Downing Became the Black Oyster King of New York," The Splendid Table, March 14, 2018, https://www.splendidtable.org/story/2018/03/14/how-thomas-downing-became-black-oyster-king-new-york.

8 Amy Drew Thompson, "Oysters Farmed in Florida Are a Shucking Success among Tide-to-Table Crowd," *Orlando Sentinel*, September 16, 2019, https://www.orlandosentinel.com/food-restaurants/os-et-oysters-farmed-florida-20190916-l3tylj5hsvbojgtthh4psmcmnu-story.html.

9   Heidi L. Fuchs et al., "Hydrodynamic Sensing and Behavior by Oyster Larvae in Turbulence and Waves," The Company of Biologists (Oxford University Press, May 1, 2015), https://journals.biologists.com/jeb/article/218/9/1419/14590/ Hydrodynamic-sensing-and-behavior-by-oyster-larvae.

10 Michael Bartley, "The Growth and Decline of the Long Island Rail Road Freight Traffic In Suffolk County," Trainsarefun.com, accessed January 26, 2022, http://www.trainsarefun.com/lirr/lirr%20freight/The%20Growth%20and %20decline%20of%20the%20Long%20Island%20Rail%20Road%20 freight%20Traffic%20in%20Suffolk%20County.htm.

11 "2020 Status Assessment: European Flat Oyster and Ostrea Edulis Beds," OSPAR Commission (OSPAR), accessed February 13, 2022, https://oap.ospar. org/en/.

12 Nika Stagličić et al., "Distribution Patterns of Two Co-Existing Oyster Species in the Northern Adriatic Sea: The Native European Flat Oyster Ostrea Edulis and the Non-Native Pacific Oyster Magallana Gigas," Ecological Indicators (Elsevier, June 2020), https://www.sciencedirect.com/science/article/abs/pii/ S1470160X20301709.

13 Ivana and Janez Kranjc, "Will the Noble Pen Shell Go Extinct?," Mares, October 8, 2020, https://blog.mares.com/will-noble-pen-shell-go-extinct-10490.html.

14 Bob Granleese, "Are Oysters Vegan?," The Guardian (Guardian News and Media, September 27, 2019), https://www.theguardian.com/food/2019/sep/27/are-oysters-vegan-kitchen-aide.

15 Peter Singer, "Becoming a Vegetarian," in Cooking, Eating, Thinking: Transformative Philosophies of Food, ed. Deane W. Curtin and Lisa Maree Heldke (Bloomington: Indiana University Press, 1992).

Dune Spinach, Avocado: Cape Town / Johannesburg

1   Charles Human, "4Roomed Ekasi Is One of the Top 30 Restaurants in the World," Love Cape Town, October 9, 2019, https://www.capetown.travel/ 4roomed-ekasi-restaurant/.

2   "Flexing Mussels in Khayelitsha," From Scratch (FYI, December 2020).

3   Ibid.

4   William Sales, "Making South Africa Ungovernable ANC Strategy for the '80s," The Black Scholar, 15, no. 6 (1984): pp. 2-14, https://doi.org/10.1080/000642 46.1984.11760833.

5   Ingrid Sinclair, "Bad News for West Coast Rock Lobster: Skip the Kreef This Summer," Two Oceans Aquarium, December 22, 2016, https://www.aquarium. co.za/blog/entry/bad-news-for-west-coast-rock-lobster-skip-the-kreef-this-summer.

6   "Environment, Forestry and Fisheries Announces 2020/21 West Coast Rock Lobster Total Allowable Catch and Recreational Fishing Season," South African Government, October 23, 2020, https://www.gov.za/speeches/environment-forestry-and-fisheries-announces-202021-west-coast-rock-lobster-total-allowable.

7   Statistics South Africa, "The Extent of Food Security in South Africa," Statistics South Africa, May 16, 2019, http://www.statssa.gov.za/?p=12135.

8   UNICEF Fundraising Team, "What You Need to Know about Malnutrition & Feeding Children," UNICEF South Africa, October 20, 2020, https://www.unicef.org/southafrica/stories/what-you-need-know-about-malnutrition-feeding-children.

9   Robert Small, "Robert Small - Resource Mobilization Support - LinkedIn," https://www.linkedin.com/in/robert-small-social-farmer/?originalSubdomain=za, accessed January 31, 2022, https://za.linkedin.com/in/robert-small-social-farmer.

10   "Flexing Mussels in Khayelitsha," *From Scratch* (FYI, March 29, 2020).

11   Rafael Alunan III, "Like Rust, Corruption Is Corrosive," GMA News Online (GMA News Online, January 17, 2014), https://www.gmanetwork.com/news/opinion/content/344331/like-rust-corruption-is-corrosive/story/.

12   Nauro Campos and Ralitza Dimova, "Does Corruption Sand or Grease the Wheels of Economic Growth?," Vox, CEPR Policy Portal, December 24, 2010, https://voxeu.org/article/does-corruption-sand-or-grease-wheels-economic-growth.

13   William Gumede, "ANC Corruption Is a Major Cause of South Africa's Failure and the Polls Will Show It," *The Guardian* (Guardian News and Media, May 8, 2019), https://www.theguardian.com/commentisfree/2019/may/08/anc-corruption-south-africa-failure-polls.

14   "Wealth Inequality by Country 2022," World Population Review, accessed February 2, 2022, https://worldpopulationreview.com/country-rankings/wealth-inequality-by-country.

15   Francesco Berna et al., "Microstratigraphic Evidence of in Situ Fire in the Acheulean Strata of Wonderwerk Cave, Northern Cape Province, South Africa," PNAS (National Academy of Sciences, April 2, 2012), https://www.pnas.org/content/109/20/E1215.

16   Katherine J. Wu, "Humans Were Roasting Root Vegetables 170,000 Years Ago, Study Suggests," *Smithsonian Magazine* (Smithsonian Institution, January 7, 2020), https://www.smithsonianmag.com/smart-news/humans-were-roasting-root-vegetables-170000-years-ago-study-suggests-180973913/#:~:text=Humans%20Were%20Roasting%20Root%20Vegetables%20170%2C000%20Years%20Ago%2C%20Study%20Suggests,-The%20find%20may&text=The%20human%20hankering%20for%20roasted,years%20ago%2C%20new%20research%20suggests.

17 Africa Check, April 25, 2019, https://africacheck.org/fact-checks/factsheets/ frequently-asked-questions-about-land-ownership-and-demand-south-africa.

18 Mike Wilson, "Land Reform: South Africa's Ticking Time Bomb," Farm Progress, April 4, 2014, https://www.farmprogress.com/story-land-reform-south-africas-ticking-time-bomb-18-109953.

19 Ben Cousins, "Problematic Assumptions Raise Questions about South Africa's New Land Reform Plan," The Conversation, October 26, 2020, https:// theconversation.com/problematic-assumptions-raise-questions-about-south-africas-new-land-reform-plan-148665.

20 "Flexing Mussels in Khayelitsha," *From Scratch* (FYI, December 2020).

21 Christopher S. Henshilwood et al., "An Abstract Drawing from the 73,000-Year-Old Levels at Blombos Cave, South Africa," Nature News (Nature Publishing Group, September 12, 2018), https://www.nature.com/articles/ s41586-018-0514-3.

22 "San," Siyabona Africa, accessed February 2, 2022, www.krugerpark.co.za/africa_ bushmen.html#:~:text=The%20term%2C%20'bushman'%2C,freedom%20 from%20domination%20and%20colonization..

23 Ibid.

24 Jaco Prinsloo, "The Rise and Fall of South Africa's Super Plant," *Footprint Magazine* (Footprint Magazine, October 26, 2020), http://www.footprintmag.net/ the-rise-and-fall-of-spekboom-south-africas-super-plant/.

25 "TARA Galleries – South Africa," Trust For African Rock Art, accessed February 2, 2022, https://africanrockart.org/rock-art-gallery/south-africa/.

26 Christopher H. Low, "Different Histories of Buchu: Euro-American Appropriation of San and Khoekhoe Knowledge of Buchu Plants," Environment & Society Portal, August 2007, http://www.environmentandsociety.org/mml/ different-histories-buchu-euro-american-appropriation-san-and-khoekhoe-knowledge-buchu-plants, 333.

27 Tauhira Dean, "A Short History of SA's Miracle Herb: Buchu," Health24 (health24), August 26, 2015, https://www.news24.com/health24/natural/herbs/ buchu-the-famous-herb-20150826.

28 "Flexing Mussels in Khayelitsha," *From Scratch* (FYI, December 2020).

Beer, Octopus, Snails: Malta / Sardinia

1 Devon Godek and Andrew M. Freeman, "Physiology, Diving Reflex," StatPearls [Internet]. (U.S. National Library of Medicine, September 28, 2021), https:// www.ncbi.nlm.nih.gov/books/NBK538245/.

2 Kristina Abela, "Population Expected to Hit 668,000 by 2050," *Times of Malta*, June 3, 2021, https://timesofmalta.com/articles/view/population-expected-to-hit-668000-by-2050.876488.

3 Times of Malta, "700 Years Added to Malta's History," *Times of Malta*, March 16, 2018, https://timesofmalta.com/articles/view/700-years-added-to-maltas-history.673498.

4 Manuel Sapiano et al., "The Evolution of Water Culture in Malta: An Analysis of the Changing Perceptions towards Water throughout the Ages," accessed February 5, 2022, https://www.idaea.csic.es/meliaproject/sites/default/files/517612-MELIA-Evolution-of-water-culture-in-Malta.pdf, 100.

5 Times of Malta, "700 Years Added to Malta's History," *Times of Malta*.

6 Sapiano et al., "The Evolution of Water Culture in Malta: An Analysis of the Changing Perceptions towards Water throughout the Ages."

7 George Attard and Ernest A. Azzopardi (CIHEAM/EU DG Research, December 31, 2004).

8 "Breaking Stories & Updates," News Directory, accessed February 17, 2022, https://dir.md/wiki/Tribute_of_the_Maltese_Falcon?host=wikipedia.org.

9 Sapiano et al., "The Evolution of Water Culture in Malta: An Analysis of the Changing Perceptions towards Water throughout the Ages."

10 "The Maltese Corsairs and the Order of St. John of Jerusalem," *Catholic Historical Review* 46, no. 2 (July 1960).

11 "A Slavic Sword for a Maltese Corsair - Malta Maritime Museum," Google (Google), accessed February 5, 2022, https://artsandculture.google.com/exhibit/a-slavic-sword-for-a-maltese-corsair-malta-maritime-museum/rQKS4g7UX51bLA?hl=en.

12 "Water and Water Storage during the Knights of St. John," I Love Food, accessed February 5, 2022, https://www.ilovefood.com.mt/features/the-great-siege/water-and-water-storage-during-the-knights-of-st-john/.

13 Nora Boustany, "The Consummate Diplomat Wants Malta on the Map," *The Washington Post* (WP Company, July 13, 2001), https://www.washingtonpost.com/archive/politics/2001/07/13/the-consummate-diplomat-wants-malta-on-the-map/918c9a99-9e0f-48ba-9272-cc05d8a14c1c/.

14 "Malta," *Forbes* (*Forbes Magazine*), accessed February 17, 2022, https://www.forbes.com/places/malta/?sh=76a785f23908.

15 Malta Economy 2020, CIA World Factbook, January 27, 2020, https://theodora.com/wfbcurrent/malta/malta_economy.html.

16 P. Micalleff, G. Attard, and J. Mangion, "Water Resources Management in Malta: Cultural Heritage and Legal and Administrative Set-Up," accessed February 5, 2022, https://core.ac.uk/download/pdf/93183764.pdf.

17 Lindsey Hartfiel, Michelle Soupir, and Rameshwar S. Kanwar, "Malta's Water Scarcity Challenges: Past, Present, and Future Mitigation Strategies for Sustainable Water Supplies," Sustainability (MDPI, January 1, 1970), https://ideas.repec.org/a/gam/jsusta/v12y2020i23p9835-d450541.html.

18 Sapiano et al., "The Evolution of Water Culture in Malta."

19 "Fresh Water Resources Malta," ClimateChangePost, accessed February 5, 2022, https://www.climatechangepost.com/malta/fresh-water-resources/.

20 Hartfiel, Soupir, and Kanwar, "Malta's Water Scarcity Challenges."

21 Ibid.

22 Raphael Vassallo, "The Island That Turned Itself into a Desert," MaltaToday, August 10, 2017, https://www.maltatoday.com.mt/comment/blogs/79591/the_island_that_turned_itself_into_a_desert#.Yf3kQy1h3OQ.

23 Hartfiel, Soupir, and Kanwar, "Malta's Water Scarcity Challenges."

24 Kristina Abela, "Life Will Be Tough in Malta Unless We Make Changes," *Times of Malta*, August 9, 2021, https://timesofmalta.com/articles/view/life-will-be-tough-in-malta-unless-we-make-changes-climate-action.892435.

Wild Game: Texas / Wyoming

1 My Jewish Learning, "Jews and Guns," My Jewish Learning, October 8, 2021, https://www.myjewishlearning.com/article/hunting-in-judaism/.

2 Ibid.

3 "Let's Taco Bout Mexican Food," *From Scratch* (FYI, January 2020).

4 Nathan Rott, "Decline in Hunters Threatens How U.S. Pays for Conservation," NPR (NPR, March 20, 2018), https://www.npr.org/2018/03/20/593001800/decline-in-hunters-threatens-how-u-s-pays-for-conservation.

5 Christopher Fennell "The Plymouth Colony Archive Project," Plymouth Colony Legal Structure, December 14, 2007, http://www.histarch.illinois.edu/plymouth/ccflaw.html.

6 Lloyd C. Irland, "Magna Carter Covered Forest Rights, Too," Maine Woodland Owners (Maine Woodland Owners, May 19, 2016), https://www.mainewoodlandowners.org/articles/magna-carter-covered-forest-rights-too.

7 Philip Dray, *The Fair Chase: The Epic Story of Hunting in America* (New York: Basic Books, 2018).

8 Ibid., 229.

9 Ibid., 225.

10 Rott, "Decline in Hunters Threatens How U.S. Pays for Conservation."

11 Between The Waters, "The Culture and Tradition of Hunting in the South: Hunting in the New South, Class and Racial Divides, and Environmental Conservation (Part II)," Making History Together, September 3, 2016, https://makinghistorybtw.com/2016/09/03/the-culture-and-tradition-of-hunting-in-the-south-hunting-in-the-new-south-class-and-racial-divides-and-environmental-conservation-part-ii/.

12 Dray, *The Fair Chase*, 291.

13 "Why We Suck at Recruiting New Hunters, Why It Matters, and How You Can Fix It," Outdoor Life, October 15, 2019, https://www.outdoorlife.com/why-we-are-losing-hunters-and-how-to-fix-it/#:~:text=Hunters%20have%20historically%20been%20white,than%20half%20the%20U.S.%20population.

14 Eliza Brooke, "The History of Female Hunters," VICE, November 2, 2015, https://www.vice.com/en/article/z4jdya/the-history-of-female-hunter.

15 "US Fish And Wildlife Service National Hunting License Data Calculation Year 2019," accessed February 5, 2022, https://www.fws.gov/wsfrprograms/Subpages/LicenseInfo/Natl%20Hunting%20License%20Report%202020.pdf.

16 The Editors, "Everything You Need to Know about Hog Hunting," Field & Stream, January 13, 2020, https://www.fieldandstream.com/blogs/generation-wild/2008/06/hog-hunting-101/.

17 Johnny Carrol Sain, "Hogs Gone Wild," National Wildlife Federation, October 1, 2019, https://www.nwf.org/Magazines/National-Wildlife/2019/Oct-Nov/Animals/Feral-Hogs.

18 John Morthland, "A Plague of Pigs in Texas," *Smithsonian Magazine* (Smithsonian Institution, January 2011), https://www.smithsonianmag.com/science-nature/a-plague-of-pigs-in-texas-73769069/.

19 "Texas Insurance: Home, Auto and Life: Germania Insurance," Default, accessed February 5, 2022, https://germaniainsurance.com/home.

20 Morthland, "A Plague of Pigs in Texas."

21 Andrew Knowlton and Julia Kramer, "Dai Due," Bon Appetit, August 4, 2015, https://www.bonappetit.com/restaurants-travel/best-new-restaurants/article/dai-due#:~:text=This%20trailblazing%20Austin%20butcher%20sho.

22 "Deer Hunting," Texas Beyond History, accessed February 5, 2022, https://www.texasbeyondhistory.net/plateaus/prehistory/images/deer.html.

23 Texas Parks and Wildlife Department, "Big Game Harvest Survey Results 2005-06 THRU 2017-18," Texas Parks and Wildlife Department, July 26, 2018, https://tpwd.texas.gov/publications/pwdpubs/media/pwd_rp_w7000_0718b.pdf.

24 Aaron Smith, "The Wild Boar Business Is Booming in Texas," CNNMoney (Cable News Network), July 17, 2017, https://money.cnn.com/2017/07/14/smallbusiness/wild-boar-business-texas/index.html.

25 J.L. Anderson, *Capitalist Pigs: Pigs, Pork, and Power in America*, West Virginia University Press, 2019, https://www.scribd.com/document/553011338/Capitalist-Pigs-JL-Anderson.

26 "Transcript: Ezra Klein Interviews Mark Bittman," *The New York Times* (*The New York Times*, March 16, 2021), https://www.nytimes.com/2021/03/16/podcasts/ezra-klein-podcast-mark-bittman-transcript.html.

27 Nicholas Kristof, "Abusing Chickens We Eat," *The New York Times* (*The New York Times*, December 3, 2014), https://www.nytimes.com/2014/12/04/opinion/nicholas-kristof-abusing-chickens-we-eat.html.

28 Andrew Lisa, "Unpacking the History of America's Meat-Processing Industry," Newsweek, October 6, 2020, https://www.newsweek.com/unpacking-history-americas-meat-processing-industry-1530824.

29 Michael Pollan, *The Omnivore's Dilemma: The Secrets behind What You Eat* (New York: Penguin Publishing Group, n.d.).

30 "Let's Taco Bout Mexican Food," *From Scratch* (FYI, January 2020).

31 "Texas Hunter 500 Lb. Hide-a-Way Stand and Fill Deer Feeder," Texas Hunter Products, accessed February 4, 2022, https://www.texashunterproducts.com/texas-hunter-500-lb-hide-a-way-stand-and-fill-deer-feeder/.

32 "Let's Taco Bout Mexican Food," *From Scratch* (FYI, January 2020).

33 "The Joy of Pigs - About," PBS (Public Broadcasting Service, November 10, 1996), https://www.pbs.org/wnet/nature/the-joy-of-pigs-introduction/2123/.

34 Layla Khoury-Hanold, "50 States of Food Trucks," Food Network, accessed February 4, 2022, https://www.foodnetwork.com/restaurants/photos/best-food-truck-in-every-state.

35 Dray, *The Fair Chase*, 209.

36 Nick Bowlin, "Hunting and Fishing Provide Food Security in the Time of COVID-19," High Country News, April 29, 2020, https://www.hcn.org/articles/covid19-hunting-and-fishing-provide-food-security-in-the-time-of-covid-19.

37 Alex Brown, "The Pandemic Created New Hunters. States Need to Keep Them," The Pew Charitable Trusts, December 14, 2020, https://www.pewtrusts.org/en/research-and-analysis/blogs/stateline/2020/12/14/the-pandemic-created-new-hunters-states-need-to-keep-them.

38 "A Bow Hunt Wasn't Such a Good I-Deer," *From Scratch* (FYI, November 2021).

Round Scad, Patis: Philippines

1 23andMe.

2 Teodoro A. Llamazon and John P. Thorpe, "Review of Jose Villa Panganiban's Talahuluganang," 3(2) 130-139.

3 Glenn Aguilar, "The Philippine Indigenous Outrigger Boat: Scaling Up, Performance and Safety," Marine Technology Society Journal, Vol. 40, No. 3: 49, September 2006, https://www.researchgate.net/publication/233644288.

4   Mike Genoun, "Fish the Moon: Day or Night," Florida Sport Fishing, September 22, 2009, accessed February 6, 2022, http://floridasportfishing.com/fish-moon-day-night/.

5   Gregory B. Poling, "Illuminating the South China Sea's Dark Fishing Fleets," Stephenson Ocean Security Project, January 9, 2019, accessed February 6, 2022, https://ocean.csis.org/spotlights/illuminating-the-south-china-seas-dark-fishing-fleets/#:~:text=The%20South%20China%20Sea%20accounted,people%20and%20unofficially%20many%20more

6   Srijan Shukla, "What is Nine-Dash Line? The Basis of China's Claim to Sovereignty over South China Sea," *The Print*, July 28, 2020, accessed February 6, 2022, https://theprint.in/theprint-essential/what-is-nine-dash-line-the-basis-of-chinas-claim-to-sovereignty-over-south-china-sea/469403/

7   "What is Climate Change?," *National Integrated Climate Change Database and Information Exchange System*, accessed February 6, 2022, https://niccdies.climate.gov.ph/.

8   Amy Blitz, "Marine Fishing in the Philippines," *Cultural Survival Quarterly*, June 1987, accessed February 6, 2022, https://www.culturalsurvival.org/publications/cultural-survival-quarterly/marine-fishing-philippines.

9   Gregg Yan, personal communication, December 16, 2021.

10 Adam Greer, "The South China Sea is Really a Fishery Dispute," *The Diplomat*, July 20, 2016, accessed February 6, 2022, https://thediplomat.com/2016/07/the-south-china-sea-is-really-a-fishery-dispute/.

11 Gerry Marten, "Marine Sanctuary: Restoring a Coral-Reef Fishery and a Cherished Way of Life (Apo Island, Philippines)," *The EcoTipping Points Project | Turning Damaged Environmental Cycles into Healthy Ecological Systems,* June 2005, accessed February 6, 2022, https://ecotippingpoints.com/our-stories/indepth/marine-sanctuary-restoring-a-coral-reef-fishery-and-a-cherished-way-of-life-apo-island-philippines/.

12 Portia Nillos-Kleiven, "Replication of Apu Island's Example to Other Islands in the Philippines," EcoTipping Points, accessed February 6, 2022 https://ecotippingpoints.com/our-stories/indepth/philippines-apo-marine-sanctuary-coral-reef-fishery/

13 Sarah Gibbens, "Less than 3 Percent of the Ocean is 'Highly Protected,'" *National Geographic*, September 25, 2019, accessed February 6, 2022, https://www.nationalgeographic.com/environment/article/paper-parks-undermine-marine-protected-areas.

14 "Philippine Reef and Rainforest Conservation Foundation, Inc.," Philippine Reef and Rainforest Conservation Foundation, Inc., accessed February 6, 2022, http://www.prrcf.org/.

Endnotes

15 SeafoodSource Staff, "EC Warns PNG, Philippines over IUU Fishing," Seafood-Source Official Media, June 10, 2014, https://www.seafoodsource.com/news/environment-sustainability/ec-warns-png-philippines-over-iuu-fishing.

16 Personal communication, December 16, 2021.

17 "Last Line of Defence," Global Witness, September 13, 2021, accessed February 6, 2022, https://www.globalwitness.org/en/campaigns/environmental-activists/last-line-defence/.

18 Aguilar, Glenn. (2006). "The Philippine Indigenous Outrigger Boat," Marine Technology Society Journal 40(3): 69-78.

19 Francisco Blaha, "The Most Dangerous Job in the World," Francisco Blaha (Francisco Blaha, October 2, 2014), http://www.franciscoblaha.info/blog/2014/10/2/y5ged0791wwiu5sttjms4w65nnqy8u.

20 "How Do Salt and Sugar Prevent Microbial Spoilage?" Scientific American (Scientific American, February 21, 2006), https://www.scientificamerican.com/article/how-do-salt-and-sugar-pre/.

21 Omar Peñarubia, "Fish Salting 101: What You Need to Know," Food and Agriculture Organization of the United Nations, June 29, 2021, https://www.fao.org/flw-in-fish-value-chains/resources/articles/fish-salting-101-what-you-need-to-know/en/.

22 Personal communication, September 18, 2019.

23 Personal communication, April 2019.

24 Lisa Lim, "How Ketchup Was Invented in Southern China in 300BC, And How it Morphed from a Preserved Fish Sauce to Sweet Tomato Gloop," South China Morning Post, July 21, 2017, https://www.scmp.com/magazines/post-magazine/article/2103418/when-china-invented-ketchup-300bc-and-how-it-morphed.

25 Biblical Archaeology Society Staff, "The Garum Debate," Biblical Archaeology Society, January 25, 2012, https://www.biblicalarchaeology.org/daily/archaeology-today/biblical-archaeology-topics/the-garum-debate/.

26 Taras Grescoe, "Culinary Detectives Try to Recover the Formula for a Deliciously Fishy Roman Condiment," *Smithsonian Magazine* (Smithsonian Institution, November 2021), https://www.smithsonianmag.com/arts-culture/recoving-the-recipe-for-garum-180978846/.

27 Anna Lowenhaupt Tsing, *The Mushroom at the End of the World: On the Possibility of Life in Capitalist Ruins* (Princeton, NJ: Princeton University Press, 2015), p. 4.

Potatoes: Peru / Utah

1   Amanda Stephenson, "The Quechua: Guardians of the Potato," Cultural Survival, March 2012, https://www.culturalsurvival.org/publications/cultural-survival-quarterly/quechua-guardians-potato.

2   "The World's 50 Best Restaurants: The List and Awards," The World's 50 Best Restaurants, accessed February 5, 2022, https://www.theworlds50best.com/list/1-50.

3   Allie Lazar, "How Malena Martínez Is Changing the Future of Peruvian Cuisine," Eater (Eater, June 29, 2018), https://www.eater.com/2018/6/29/17509624/malena-martinez-mater-iniciativa-central-restaurant-peru-virgilio-martinez-interview.

4   Ibid.

5   William H. McNeill, "How the Potato Changed the World's History." *Social Research* 66, no. 1 (1999): 67–83. http://www.jstor.org/stable/40971302.

6   Turner, R. " After the famine: Plant pathology, Phytophthora infestans, and the late blight of potatoes, 1845-1960." *Historical Studies in The Physical and Biological Sciences*. 35. (2005) 341-370. 10.1525/hsps.2005.35.2.341.

7   Peter Buchert, "150 år sedan hungersnöden: Frosten och finanspolitiken fick finska folket på knä," Hufvudstadsbladet. pp. 12–14, September 9, 2017, https://www.hbl.fi/artikel/150-ar-sedan-hungersnoden-frosten-och-finanspolitiken-fick-finska-folket-pa-kna/.

8   Camper English, "The Potato, Explained," Alcademics, September 2, 2014, https://www.alcademics.com/2014/09/the-potato-explained.html.

9   Simon Romero, "A Space-Age Food Product Cultivated by the Incas," *The New York Times* (*The New York Times*, August 10, 2016), https://www.nytimes.com/2016/08/11/world/what-in-the-world/andes-incas-chuno.html.

10   Lydia Pyne, "Letter from the Four Corners," *Archaeology Magazine*, February 11, 2020, https://www.archaeology.org/issues/374-2003/letter-from/8449-four-corners-potato#art_page3.

11   Ibid.

12   Jessie Szalay and Jonathan Gordon, "Potato Nutrition Facts & Health Benefits," LiveScience (Purch, February 16, 2022), https://www.livescience.com/45838-potato-nutrition.html.

13   Ryan Raman, "7 Health and Nutrition Benefits of Potatoes," Healthline (Healthline Media, March 14, 2018), https://www.healthline.com/nutrition/benefits-of-potatoes.

14   Elyssa Goldberg, "This Restaurant Uses 50 Different Methods to Cook Potatoes," Bon Appetit, October 27, 2015, accessed January 26, 2022, https://www.bonappetit.com/people/chefs/article/virgilio-martinez-interview.

15 Grant Tinsley, "Cooling Some Foods after Cooking Increases Their Resistant Starch," Healthline (Healthline Media, September 1, 2017), https://www.healthline.com/nutrition/cooling-resistant-starch#TOC_TITLE_HDR_4.

16 "About Us," Hudson Valley Seed Company, accessed February 5, 2022, https://hudsonvalleyseed.com/pages/about-us.

17 "KAOLIN Edible Clay Chunks (Lump) Natural for Eating (Food)," UCLAYS, accessed February 5, 2022, https://uclays.com/shop/kaolin_edible_clay_chunks_lump_natural_for_eating_food.html.

18 "KAOLIN Edible Clay Chunks (Lump) Natural for Eating (Food)," UCLAYS.

Cod, Scallops, Salt: Iceland

1 "Season the Day in Iceland," From Scratch (FYI, January 2020).

2 Ibid.

3 Jared Diamond, Collapse: How Societies Choose to Fail or Survive (London: Penguin, 2013), 197-205.

4 Sigurdsson, Thorir. "Predicting the Collapse of a Fish Stock: The Case of the Atlanto-Scandian Herring." (2006).

5 "Solid Biofuels," biofuel.org.uk, accessed January 26, 2022, http://biofuel.org.uk/solid-biofuels.html.

6 "Season the Day in Iceland," From Scratch (FYI, January 2020).

7 Ibid.

8 Ibid.

9 "Flateyri Travel Guide," Guide to Iceland, accessed January 26, 2022, https://guidetoiceland.is/travel-iceland/drive/flateyri.

10 "Season the Day in Iceland," From Scratch (FYI, January 2020).

11 Vala Hafstað, "Swimming Across Fjord at Speed of Cow," Iceland Monitor (mbl.is, September 4, 2021), https://icelandmonitor.mbl.is/news/news/2021/09/04/swimming_across_fjord_at_speed_of_cow/

12 "Flateyri Travel Guide," Guide to Iceland.

13 OECD, "Sustaining Iceland's Fisheries through Tradeable Quotas," County Study, OECD environment policy paper No. 9, 2017. p. 9.

14 Rakel Gardarsdottir, Personal Conversation, January 5, 2022.

15 Andie Sophia Fontaine, "Iceland Says Yes to New Constitution," The Reykjavik Grapevine, October 22, 2012, https://grapevine.is/news/2012/10/22/iceland-says-yes-to-new-constitution/.

16 "Season the Day in Iceland," From Scratch (FYI, January 2020).

17 Orkustofnun, Icelandic Energy Authority, "Geothermal," Orkustofnun National Energy Authority, accessed January 14, 2022. https://nea.is/geothermal/.

18 "Iceland's Innovations to Reach Net-Zero – in Pictures," *The Guardian* (Guardian News and Media, December 30, 2020), https://www.theguardian.com/environment/gallery/2020/dec/30/icelands-innovations-to-reach-net-zero-in-pictures.

19 David Roberts, "Geothermal Energy Is Poised for a Big Breakout," Vox (Vox, October 21, 2020), https://www.vox.com/energy-and-environment/2020/10/21/21515461/renewable-energy-geothermal-egs-ags-supercritical.

20 Eli London, "Tracking down the Icelandic Sea Salt the World's Best Chefs Love," Yahoo! Finance (Yahoo!), accessed January 27, 2022, https://finance.yahoo.com/news/tracking-down-icelandic-sea-salt-153222749.html?guccounter=1&guce_referrer=aHR0cHM6Ly93d3cuZ29vZ2xlLmNvbS88&guce_referrer_sig=AQA-AACRGyCYqNUkjpTd66Dkbl0bpD07Vn6croo_2PJQoaX7rZDtl0V0Ez-V3ntW_iuSM6dcXAXJigzmptolsoXBxJyMhiBlZfwMwK37c7mnMsB4v-jV12ojH1iI4YK-nzJ

Goat, Barley, Honey: Kenya

1 Evelyn Araripe, "Ernst Götsch: The Creator of the Real Green Revolution," Believe Earth, February 15, 2018, https://believe.earth/en/ernst-gotsch-the-creator-of-the-real-green-revolution/.

2 George Obulutsa, "Kenyan Tourism Begins Recovery from Pandemic Slump as Locals Fuel Travel," Reuters (Thomson Reuters, January 19, 2022), https://www.reuters.com/world/africa/kenyan-tourism-begins-recovery-pandemic-slump-locals-fuel-travel-2022-01-19/.

3 "The Serengeti-Mara Squeeze – One of the World's Most Iconic Ecosystems under Pressure," ScienceDaily (ScienceDaily, March 28, 2019), https://www.sciencedaily.com/releases/2019/03/190328150743.htm.

4 "Kenya Wildlife Conservancies Association," KWCA, April 15, 2021, https://kwcakenya.com/.

5 Jitendra, "Kenya Is Losing about 100 Lions Each Year for the Past Decade," Down To Earth, December 31, 2017, accessed February 2, 2022, https://www.downtoearth.org.in/news/wildlife-biodiversity/kenya-is-losing-about-100-lions-each-year-for-the-past-decade-59359.

6 "Conservation International to Provide Lifeline for Maasai Mara Wildlife, Landowners Battered by Pandemic," Conservation International, November 19, 2020, accessed February 15, 2022, https://www.conservation.org/press-releases/2020/11/19/conservation-international-to-provide-lifeline-for-maasai-mara-wildlife-landowners-battered-by-pandemic.

7 "Http://Www.historyworld.net/Wrldhis/Plaintexthistories.asp?Historyid=ab57," History World, accessed February 16, 2022, http://www.historyworld.net/wrldhis/plaintexthistories.asp?historyid=ab57.

8 Koh Nomura et al., "Domestication Process of the Goat Revealed by an Analysis of the Nearly Complete Mitochondrial Protein-Encoding Genes," PLoS one (Public Library of Science, August 1, 2013), https://www.ncbi.nlm.nih.gov/pmc/articles/PMC3731342/.

9 Thomson Safaris, "Traditional Maasai Food: Blood and Milk," Thomson Safaris, January 16, 2014, https://thomsonsafaris.com/blog/traditional-maasai-diet-blood-milk/.

10 Amy Fleming, "The Geography of Taste: How Our Food Preferences Are Formed," *The Guardian* (Guardian News and Media, September 3, 2013), https://www.theguardian.com/lifeandstyle/wordofmouth/2013/sep/03/geography-taste-how-food-preferences-formed.

11 Katy Migiro, "Maasai Land Loss Raises Tensions in Kenya Ahead of Elections," Reuters (Thomson Reuters, June 20, 2017), https://www.reuters.com/article/us-kenya-land-election-idUSKBN19B2CP.

12 Frankline Kibuacha, "Mobile Penetration and Growth in Kenya," GeoPoll, January 13, 2021, https://www.geopoll.com/blog/mobile-penetration-kenya/.

13 Kelsey Piper, "What Kenya Can Teach Its Neighbors - and the US - about Improving the Lives of the 'Unbanked,'" Vox (Vox, September 11, 2020), https://www.vox.com/future-perfect/21420357/kenya-mobile-banking-unbanked-cellphone-money.

14 Joy Nyang'or, "An Analysis of the Growth of Motorcycle Use in Kenya," LinkedIn, November 29, 2018, https://www.linkedin.com/pulse/analysis-growth-motorcycle-use-kenya-joy-nyang-or/.

Porcini, Chanterelle: Finland / Whidbey Island, WA

1 Renee Johnson, "How Many Species of Fungi Are There?" (Bradbury Science Museum, January 10, 2018), https://www.lanl.gov/museum/news/newsletter/2018/01/fungi.php.

2 Nicolas P. Money, videotaped interview with author, September 18 2019.

3 "Finland Is Named the Happiest Country in the World – 4th Year in a Row," Finland Convention Bureau, March 22, 2021, accessed February 23, 2022, https://www.visitfinland.com/fcb/news/finland-named-the-happiest-country/.

4 Mike Colagrossi, "10 Reasons Why Finland's Education System Is the Best in the World," World Economic Forum, September 10, 2018, accessed February 23, 2022, https://www.weforum.org/agenda/2018/09/10-reasons-why-finlands-education-system-is-the-best-in-the-world/.

5 Salla Korpela, "Finland's Parliament: Pioneer of Gender Equality," thisisFINLAND, June 2019, accessed February 22, 2022, https://finland.fi/life-society/finlands-parliament-pioneer-of-gender-equality/.

6   Tsing, *The Mushroom at the End of the World: On the Possibility of Life in Capitalist Ruins,* 173.

7   Jan-Eric Ilmoni, "Why Did Finland Paid War Reparations for the Soviets Even Though the USSR Were the Ones Who Invaded Their Land?," Qoura, March 6, 2017, https://www.quora.com/Why-did-Finland-paid-war-reparations-for-the-Soviets-even-though-the-USSR-were-the-ones-who-invaded-their-land.

8   Heikki Hiilamo, Marko Merikukka, and Anita Haataja, "Long-Term Educational Outcomes of Child Care Arrangements in Finland," *SAGE Open* 8, no. 2 (2018): p. 215824401877482, https://doi.org/10.1177/2158244018774823.

9   Amy Halpern-Laff, "Transcript of the Episode 'Dodging Responsibility for Our Children: Reducing Learning to Test Scores,'" December 17, 2020, https://ethicalschools.org/2020/12/transcript-of-the-episode-dodging-responsibility-for-our-children-reducing-learning-to-test-scores/.

10 J Clausnitzer, "Finland: Pisa Student Performance 2000-2018," Statista, January 7, 2022, https://www.statista.com/statistics/986919/pisa-student-performance-by-field-and-score-finland/.

11 Amy Halpern-Laff, "Transcript of the Episode "Dodging Responsibility for Our Children."

12 Samuel E. Abrams, "Education and the Commercial Mindset," *Harvard University Press,* February 2016, https://doi.org/10.4159/9780674545786, 281-282.

13 "Fat to Fit: How Finland Did It," *The Guardian* (Guardian News and Media, January 15, 2005), https://www.theguardian.com/befit/story/0,15652,1385645,00.html.

14 Jaana Kiesiläinen, "Finland's 'Everyman's Rights' Offer the Most Open Access to Nature on Earth," Matador Network, November 5, 2019, https://matadornetwork.com/read/finlands-everymans-rights-open-access-nature-earth/.

15 Miliza Malmelin, "Nature > Everyman's Rights," Environment.fi, October 8, 2020, accessed February 5, 2022, https://www.ymparisto.fi/en-us/nature/everymans_rights.

16 Heino Lepp, "The Mycelium," Australian National Botanic Gardens, January 22, 2013, accessed February 5, 2022, https://anbg.gov.au/fungi/mycelium.html.

17 Hua Hsu, "The Secret Lives of Fungi," *The New Yorker,* May 11, 2020, https://www.newyorker.com/magazine/2020/05/18/the-secret-lives-of-fungi.

18 Tsing, *The Mushroom at the End of the World: On the Possibility of Life in Capitalist Ruins,* 167.

19 Hannes Mäntyranta, "Not Just Clearcutting – Finnish State Forests Are Harvested by Twelve Different Methods," Forest.fi, August 29, 2019, https://forest.fi/article/not-just-clearcutting-finnish-state-forests-are-harvested-by-twelve-different-methods/

20 Tsing, *The Mushroom at the End of the World,* 137-138.

21 Ferris Jabr, "The Social Life of Forests," *The New York Times* (*The New York Times,* December 3, 2020), https://www.nytimes.com/interactive/2020/12/02/magazine/tree-communication-mycorrhiza.html.

22 Jabr, "The Social Life of Forests."

23 Tsing, *The Mushroom at the End of the World*, 138-139.

Pizza: Amalfi Coast / NYC

1 Carol Helstosky, "Five Myths about Pizza," *The Washington Post* (WP Company, July 20, 2018), https://www.washingtonpost.com/outlook/five-myths/five-myths-about-pizza/2018/07/20/b879cd90-8b7c-11e8-a345-a1bf7847b375_story.html.

2 Alto Hartley, "The True Story of Pizza," Alto Hartley, September 15, 2021, https://altohartley.com/the-true-story-of-pizza/.

3 Gayle Turim, "Who Invented Pizza?" History.com (A&E Television Networks, July 27, 2012), https://www.history.com/news/a-slice-of-history-pizza-through-the-ages.

4 Shawn Pollack, "Why Italian Pizza Crust Tastes so Damn Good," Poco Pizza Blog, March 13, 2017, accessed February 1, 2022, https://www.pocopizza.com/blogs/news/why-italian-pizza-crust-tastes-so-damn-good.

5 Amy Grant, "What is Emmer Wheat: Information About Emmer Wheat Plants," Gardening Know How, December 28, 2020, accessed February 1, 2022, https://www.gardeningknowhow.com/edible/vegetables/wheatgrass/emmer-wheat-plants.htm.

6 Alister Doyle, "Africa Can Easily Grow Wheat to Ease Hunger, Price Shocks: Study," Reuters (Thomson Reuters, October 8, 2012), https://www.reuters.com/article/us-africa/africa-can-easily-grow-wheat-to-ease-hunger-price-shocks-study-idUSBRE89800520121009.

7 Maria Pilar Vinardell and Montserrat Mitjans, "Lignins and Their Derivatives with Beneficial Effects on Human Health," *International Journal of Molecular Sciences* (MDPI, June 7, 2017), https://www.ncbi.nlm.nih.gov/pmc/articles/PMC5486042/.

8 "Wine," Only Italian Products, accessed February 1, 2022, https://www.only-italianproducts.it/focus/ancient-wheats.html.

9 Heather Rhoades, "Tomato Varieties & Color: Learn About Different Tomato Colors," Gardening Know How, July 27, 2021, accessed February 1, 2022, https://www.gardeningknowhow.com/edible/vegetables/tomato/tomato-varieties-color-learn-about-different-tomato-colors.htm.

10 "The Discovery of Tomato Sauce," Italy Heritage, February 2002, accessed February 1, 2022, http://www.italyheritage.com/magazine/2002_02/0202_f.htm.

11 "Italian Tomatoes, a Red and Juicy Love Story," True Italian, June 10, 2021, https://trueitalian.top/2021/07/05/italian-tomatoes-a-red-and-juicy-love-story/#:~:text=The%20red%20fruits%20of%20this,the%20last%20stage%20of%20ripening.

12 Cat Gallagher, "Tomato," Food Origins, accessed February 2, 2022, https://tenochtitlan.omeka.net/exhibits/show/guacamole/tomato.

13 Texas AgriLife Extension Service, "The Tomato Had to Go Abroad to Make Good," Aggie Horticulture, accessed February 2, 2022, https://aggie-horticulture.tamu.edu/archives/parsons/publications/vegetabletravelers/tomato.html.

14 "Why Were Tomatoes Often Called 'Love Apples' and Considered Aphrodisiacs?" Papertrell, accessed February 2, 2022, https://www.papertrell.com/apps/preview/The-Handy-Biology-Answer-Book/Handy%20Answer%20book/Why-were-tomatoes-often-called-love-apples-and-considered-ap/001137031/content/SC/52cb00cd82fad14abfa5c2e0_Default.html.

15 Crystal King, "The World's First Tomato Sauce Recipe," Author Crystal King's Blog - Tasting Life Twice, September 21, 2020, https://blog.crystalking.com/the-first-tomato-sauce-recipe.

16 Alvin Choi, "History of the Tomato in Italy and China: Tracing the Role of Tomatoes in Italian and Chinese Cooking," Noodles on the Silk Road, July 3, 2018. https://scholarblogs.emory.edu/noodles/2018/07/03/history-of-the-tomato-in-italy-and-china-tracing-the-role-of-tomatoes-in-italian-and-chinese-cooking/.

Afterword

1 Ben Ole Koissaba, "Legitimization Crisis: Laws, Policies and Decrees as Tools for Maasai Land Appropriation," Farm Land Grab, November 26, 2014, accessed March 31, 2022, https://www.farmlandgrab.org/post/view/24274-legitimization-crisis-laws-policies-and-decrees-as-tools-for-maasai-land-appropriation.

2 Ibid.

Acknowledgments

As an actor and film producer writing a book about food production, cooking, history, biology, botany, and the environment, I am indebted to many.

Thank you to all the chefs who opened their kitchens to me, and who went beyond and introduced me to many of the food producers: Cristiano Andreini, Manuel Badilla, Matt Costello, Marina Gaši, Gunar Gislason, David Higgs, Stefan Hogan and Mark McBride, Dan Kluger, Emanuele Liguori, Marilú Madueño, Margarita Manzke and Ana De Ocampo, Virgilio Martínez, Véliz, Abigail Mbalo-Mokoena, Antonia Armenta Miller, Ariel Moscardi, Tvrtko Šakota, Jari Vesivalo, Emily Weinheimer, Galen Zamarra, and, finally, Ray Garcia, who gave us a chance when it was only a fanciful idea.

For help across the globe I want to thank the very talented producers and crew of *From Scratch*, the television show: Neild Agius, Wesley Ayliffe, Ryan Barrett, Shannon Cartwright, Matt Chavez, Frans van Der Merwe, Bruce Driscoll, Marcos Efron, Brian Eggleston, Luke Brandon Field, Jemma Ford, Emily Frisbie, Kenny Gallagher, Matt van Geothem, Danny Herrera, Clay Jeter, Nancy Ma, Melissa Mattson, Isabel Najjar, Diego Oliver, Alberto Orive, Jared Paisley, Hoai Pham, Joel Plotch, Marta Ramirez, Todd Remis, Gina Resnick, Kamilla Rifkin, Jorge Riotoc, Liam

Van Rooyen, Graeme Swanepoel, Suzann Toni, Derek Weiland, and Richie Wolff. It was not only their hard work that helped but their camaraderie and friendship.

While shooting, my executive producer Shannon Hunt, and my director, Marty Bleazard, provided invaluable insights into the stories I wanted to tell. Marty also supplied many of the photos that grace this book.

Thanks to Cynthia Wilson, Lisbeth Louderback, and Bruce Pavlik for sharing their expertise on the Four Corners potato. And to Manuel Choqque Bravo for his expertise on Peruvian potatoes.

Lynsey Gammon, Henry Hudson, Joe Ogdie, Barb Phillips, and Melissa Smolik graciously showed me around Wanship and the Saving Grace Farm, helping me source produce and forage for wild plants and greatly improving my fishing.

Hunting is a daunting topic. I never would have been able to write about it without the help of Jesse Griffiths.

I am grateful to Gene Leath, who, in addition to taking me on two memorable hunts, has answered numerous questions since. Thanks to Bob Barlow and John Matajov for showing me Story, Wyoming, as well as everyone at Spear-O-Wigwam and Canyon Ranch. Shawn Parker, executive director of Sheridan Travel & Tourism, was a lifesaver. He went out of his way so we could tell a good story.

Also, thanks to Amy Halpern-Laff, of Factory Farming Awareness Coalition, who talked about the devastating effects of factory farming and the ethical questions of killing creatures for food when alternatives exist.

For a hands-on lesson of how to harvest oysters, I want to thank Mike Osinski. Suzzana and Merc Osinski described what growing up oyster farming is like. Luka Katušić and Emil Sosić shared their expertise about the European flat oyster.

Acknowledgments

Looking at oyster vesicles with Emil in Istria

David Sacco spent hours explaining to me the complexities of water desalination and Malta's aquifer. Liam Gauci was an extraordinary guide through Maltese maritime and culinary history.

Renny Desira, Konrad Grixti, everyone at Lord Chambray Brewery, Vincent's Eco Estate, and Luke Cassar helped me understand the skill and fortitude it takes to produce food in Malta.

Thanks to everyone at Cultiva Garden as well as Tamalu Farm and Jess De Boer, Ed Cunningham, James Thiong'o, Sven Verwiel, and Fred Kipchumba. The rare mix of smarts and competence of Royal African Safari's executive team helped me immeasurably in foraging around Kenya. Much of what I learned there came directly from Indi Bilkhu, Alex Hunter, Uhuru Kiarii, Peter Silvester, and Nicky Williams. Thanks to William Sakeri, Simon Tira, and the rest of the Royal African crew, who invited me into their lives and were of tremendous assistance.

Without the permission and guidance of Laibons Parmuat Koikai and Oloali Osokai it would have been a hollow and shallow look at the Mara and forests. Our guides Nemorijo Kuroo and Alex Kuluo were a bastion of information of native plants and their uses.

I turned to the esteemed late Dr. Richard Leakey for help on my journey through Kenya. From the generous use of his plane to his help understanding such topics as evolution, climate science, and anthropology. I am deeply indebted to him and his wife Meave for all their help.

Thanks to Dr. Gerald Horne. Dr. Horne generously shared his knowledge of South African history. To Dian Pretorius for spending the afternoon with me, harvesting avocados and sharing memories of his father. I owe a debt to Sam Mokoena for guiding me around Khayelitsha and revealing his foraging spots, as well as to Goede Hoop Citrus and Carmién Teas.

I want to express my appreciation to Christina Kaba for all the amazing work she does for Khayelitsha and my gratitude for teaching me the ins-and-outs of running a community garden. Similarly, the work of James Sleigh and Camphill gave me hope in humanity during an often tough trip.

Ben (Benji) Rosen, you were a godsend throughout the Peru journeys, fixing and smoothing and interpreting all our hurdles away. Hope to see you and Ana again soon! I am grateful to Klever Marca who was an extraordinary guide in an extraordinary part of the world. I can't thank him enough for sharing his time and knowledge of the Sacred Valley and the Incan Empire.

Thank you, Conrado Falco and PromPeru for sponsoring the visit to Peru and sharing your personal thoughts with me. My debt to you and your country is enormous. Thank you, also, Carla Salina Avila and Sergio Aragon.

Thank you to Marco and all the other cheesemakers at Tenuta Vannulo farm, first for not kicking my ass, and second for taking me through the steps to make mozzarella. Vittorio Rimbaldo and the Rimbaldo family painstakingly guided me through the process of catching and salting anchovies. Antonio Pellegrino walked me back in time to show me how flour has been made for generations in Caselle.

Thank you to the crew of the Shammah and everyone at the Lorenzana food company for giving me a once-in-a-lifetime experience of making patis from scratch. Maria and "Grace" gave me Filipina perspectives of the state of the Philippines' environmentalism. Gregg Yan, a force and voice of hope for the future of the Philippine Sea, helped explain the complicated world of fish and MPAs.

Saimi Hoyer opened my eyes to the joy of mushrooms, and Nicolas P. Money and Travis Furlanic filled in the gaps.

John Peterson made my journey around Iceland super enjoyable. Thank you, Saltverk, for the hands-on tour and the smoked blue salt, and thanks, Simbi Hjalmarsson, for helping me descend below ten feet! Vídir Ingpórsson and the people of Flateyri opened their town to us. Environmentalist and filmmaker Rakel Gardarsdottir walked us through the history of overfishing in Iceland, the transition to the individual transferable quota, and the politics and economics of the quota system. Author Paul Greenberg shared his knowledge of the history and general state of the oceans, and author Mark Kurlansky of salt and cod.

Enormous thanks to Jason and Laura Dreyer, my long-time producing partners, who gave me the opportunity to create *From Scratch*. We had a vision and we made it happen! And they supported me even further as I wrote this book. I'm not sure if they know how much their support has meant.

This book might never have been attempted without my friend and lawyer, Marc Lane, who watched the show, saw something deeper there, and frequently nudged me into writing a book.

Thank you, Tim Brandhorst, my literary agent/attorney, for guiding us through the process of writing a book. He as much as anyone made this happen, from first culling through all the possible paths and then babysitting us through the first tentative steps all the way until we were running. You were always smart and probing and guided us with sage advice.

Thank you to Debra Englander, Heather King, and everyone at Permuted Press who took a flier on the idea that I could write a book. Your shot on an unproven writer and your belief made this a reality. Copyeditor Heather Steadham was as meticulous as she was thoughtful.

Thanks to the team at Book Highlight who have helped in so many ways.

There are many who read portions of the manuscript and helped in various ways, including Mike Camello, Jeffrey Chasen, Andy Cohen, Jon Denny, Nick Einenkel, Danielle Gardner, Gia Cavellini Guzman, LynNell Hancock, Catherine Kellner, Ken Mattson, Matt McCarty, John Pascarella, Jeff Pearlman, Kevin Powell, Ben Pruess, Joanna Pruess, Bruce Sterner, Teddy Wayne, and Noah Zimmerman.

Thanks to my brother, Lev Moscow, for encouraging me to reach out to guests he has had on acorrectionpodcast.com, his superb, political-economy podcast.

Thank you to my in-laws, Jorge and Anne Riotoc, and my wife's grandmother, Thelma Guevara, who at the height of the COVID pandemic, took us into their home to help us with childcare and, on top of that, kept us well-fed. I wouldn't have been able to write this book without them all. Thank you to my parents—Pat Sterner for her intuition, intelligence, and frankness. And Jon Moscow, brilliant writer, scholar, historian, and keeper of the endnotes.

Acknowledgments

And finally, I owe more than I can express to my wife, Karen Moscow. She read and edited every chapter of the book and fought to keep it interesting and accessible. It is to her this book is dedicated.

—*David Moscow*

I SHARE DAVID'S ACKNOWLEDGMENTS, and thank him for his kind comment about me. I've been tremendously pleased to have been able to work with him on this book. My dedication of this book is to my wife Pat for all the reasons David mentioned and many more.

—*Jon Moscow*

About the Authors

David Moscow is the creator, executive producer, and host of *From Scratch*. David made his feature film debut at age thirteen in *Big*, starring as the young Tom Hanks; years later, he starred with Christian Bale in *Newsies*. He has appeared in dozens of films, television shows, and theater productions over a thirty-five year career.

Most recently, David founded the production company UnLTD Pictures. He has executive produced more than twenty feature films, including *Under the Silver Lake, To Dust, Strawberry Mansion*, and *Wild Nights with Emily*. He also directed the thriller *Desolation*.

David also develops mixed-income sustainably green apartment buildings. He lives in Los Angeles with his wife and son.

Jon Moscow is David's father and creative partner, and is a writer on *From Scratch*. He is co-executive director of Ethics in Education Network and co-host of the *Ethical Schools* podcast (*ethicalschools.org*). He actively works to support asylum seekers with housing and links to social services. He has a BA in International Studies from Reed College and a master's degree from Bank Street College of Education. He and David's mother, Pat, live in Teaneck, NJ, with a Shih Tzu named Niki.

Index

Index